# دردشة

## بالعربي اللبناني

# Lebanese Arabic

# Dardashi

### 25 Immersive 'Podcast' Episodes with
### Transcripts, Vocabulary, and Questions

lingualism

ISBN: 978-1-962752-03-9

Edited by Charbel Ghaleb and Matthew Aldrich

website: www.lingualism.com
email: contact@lingualism.com

# Table of Contents

# *Introduction*

Welcome to **Lebanese Arabic Dardashi**! The word 'dardashi' (دَرْدَشِة) means 'chitchat' or 'casual conversation,' and that's exactly what this book is all about—light, everyday dialogues that will help you learn Lebanese Arabic in a fun, relaxed way. Each episode is designed like a mock podcast: while these recordings aren't published as real podcasts, they're structured in that same conversational, back-and-forth style you'd expect from a friendly talk show.

The dialogues in **Lebanese Arabic Dardashi** explore a variety of topics that mix culture and personal life, giving you a glimpse into Lebanon's rich heritage and everyday experiences. From learning about **Lebanese wine** and **famous artists**, to practical advice for **foreigners considering moving to Lebanon**, each episode offers a window into different aspects of life in Lebanon. Other topics include **hobbies**, **first jobs**, and even the unique experience of **shared taxis** in Beirut. The conversations are light-hearted and engaging, with no focus on heavy or political subjects, making this the perfect resource for enjoyable, stress-free learning.

This book has been designed with flexibility in mind to suit different learning styles and goals. Each episode includes:

**An English Introduction** to set the stage for the dialogue.

**Vocabulary Lists** to help you understand key words and phrases used in each conversation.

**Transcripts in Lebanese Arabic,** complete with diacritics, so you can see the words as they're spoken.

**English Translations** of the dialogue for you to check your comprehension.

**Comprehension and Discussion Questions** to engage you in deeper reflection, conversation, and language production.

Whether you prefer to focus on listening, reading, or speaking, the book offers multiple ways to approach the material. You can tailor your learning experience based on your preferences and pace, using the audio tracks, vocabulary, and transcripts to sharpen your skills in a way that works best for you.

A special thank you goes out to **Charbel** and his friends **Omar** and **Farah**, whose friendly voices and natural conversations bring the dialogues to life. They generously recorded all the audio for the episodes, making the learning experience as immersive as possible. A huge thanks especially to Charbel for editing the texts and helping write the questions.

# How to Use This Book

**Lebanese Arabic Dardashi** is designed to help you build your Lebanese Arabic listening, reading, speaking, and vocabulary skills through engaging dialogues and real-life conversation topics. The 25 episodes in this book follow Charbel as he chats with his friends Omar or Farah in natural, conversational Lebanese Arabic.

Each unit is packed with tools to help you dive deep into the language, so whether you're studying solo, with a teacher, or in a group, here's how to make the most of this book:

## 1. Start with the Introduction

Each unit begins with a brief introduction in English. This sets the scene for the dialogue, giving you an idea of what the conversation will be about. If you prefer to ease into the material, you can read the introduction first to get a sense of what to expect. On the other hand, if you like to challenge yourself, skip the intro and dive right into the audio. After your first listen, come back and read the introduction to check your understanding.

## 2. Listen to the Dialogue

 Every episode has a corresponding audio track, available for free download on our website at www.lingualism.com/audio. These dialogues are the heart of the book, showcasing the language as it's spoken in everyday conversations. Depending on your learning style, you can approach the audio in different ways:

**Intensive Listening:** Listen to the dialogue multiple times, focusing on how words and phrases sound. After each listen, try to pick out new words or phrases you didn't catch the first time.

**Listening with the Transcript:** Once you've listened a few times, move to the transcript. The Lebanese Arabic dialogue is written with diacritics to help you connect what you hear with what you see.

**Interactive Listening:** Pause the audio after each line or exchange and try to repeat what you hear. This helps with pronunciation and retention.

# 3. Study the Vocabulary

Before or after listening, spend some time with the vocabulary list. These keywords are taken directly from the episode, so learning them will help you better understand the dialogue when you listen. You can approach vocabulary learning in different ways:

**Before Listening:** Study the vocabulary first to familiarize yourself with key words and concepts.

**After Listening:** Listen first, and then study the vocabulary. Afterward, listen again to see if you can now hear and understand the words you've learned.

**Anki Flashcards:** The vocabulary lists are also available as **Anki flashcards** (sold separately), providing an efficient tool to help you memorize and retain the words more effectively.

# 4. Use the Transcript and Translation

Once you've listened to the dialogue and studied the vocabulary, it's time to work through the **transcript** in Lebanese Arabic and its **English translation**. This will solidify your understanding of both the meaning and structure of the language. You might choose to:

**Read Along with the Audio:** Follow along with the transcript as you listen to the dialogue, connecting the sounds of Lebanese Arabic with the written words.

**Compare the Translation:** After you've listened and read the transcript, go through the English translation to check your comprehension. This step helps you pick up nuances in the conversation and clarify anything you may have missed.

# 5. Answer the Comprehension Questions

Each unit includes **comprehension questions** in both Lebanese Arabic and English. These questions are designed to test your understanding of the dialogue. You can use them to:

**Self-Test:** Answer the questions out loud or write down your answers. Try to use full sentences, mimicking the style of the dialogue.

**Practice with a Teacher or Partner:** If you're learning with a teacher or study partner, use these questions to practice forming sentences and speaking more naturally. This will help you improve your language production and fluency in real-time conversations.

# 6. Engage with the Discussion Questions

After the comprehension questions, you'll find **discussion questions** to prompt more personal conversations. These are designed to help you talk about your own life, opinions, and experiences. Feel free to:

**Speak Freely:** Answer the questions out loud, practicing using new vocabulary and expressions.

**Write It Down:** If you prefer writing, use the questions as prompts for short essays or journal entries. This will help you practice both writing and reflecting in Lebanese Arabic.

## Suggested Learning Paths

Everyone learns differently, so here are some flexible ways to approach this book depending on your style and goals:

### For the Listening-Centered Learner:

If listening comprehension is your main focus, you might:

- Start by listening to the audio without reading anything.
- After several listens, go through the transcript to reinforce what you've heard.
- Answer the comprehension questions orally to practice speaking.
- Review the vocabulary only after you've fully engaged with the audio.

### For the Vocabulary-First Learner:

If you like to focus on building your word bank first:

- Study the vocabulary list before listening to the dialogue.
- Listen to the audio and try to spot the words you've studied.
- Go back and forth between the transcript and translation to expand your vocabulary.
- Use the discussion questions to apply the new words in personalized conversations.

### For the Reading-Focused Learner:

If you prefer reading over listening:

- Start with the transcript and translation to familiarize yourself with the dialogue.

- Study the vocabulary list.

- Listen to the audio while following along with the transcript.

- Use the comprehension and discussion questions as writing prompts.

### For the Speaking-Oriented Learner:

If your goal is to improve your speaking:

- After listening to the audio, repeat lines from the dialogue out loud, trying to match the speakers' pronunciation and rhythm.

- Answer the comprehension and discussion questions orally, focusing on full sentences and fluency.

- Practice shadowing the dialogue, speaking along with the audio as closely as possible.

## *Make It Your Own*

The beauty of **Lebanese Arabic Dardashi** is its flexibility. You can go through the episodes in order or focus on topics that interest you most. Take your time with each unit, and don't hesitate to revisit episodes to track your progress. Whether you're focusing on listening, reading, or speaking, this book gives you the tools to improve all aspects of your Lebanese Arabic. Enjoy the journey, and have fun with Charbel, Omar, and Farah!

# صِناعةُ النّبيد اللّبْناني
## The Lebanese Wine Industry

## In this episode...

Charbel and Omar take a look at the Lebanese wine industry. They discuss the centuries-old vineyards of the Bekaa Valley and renowned wineries like Château Ksara and Château Musar. You'll learn about the unique flavors of Lebanese wines and how the country's ideal climate and rich winemaking traditions have contributed to its growing international recognition. Additionally, they touch on the rise of wine tourism in Lebanon, making it a destination for wine enthusiasts from around the world.

## Vocabulary

| | |
|---|---|
| accommodation | إقامِة |
| ancient history | تاريخ عريق |
| soil | تُرْبِة |
| traditional | تِقْليدي |
| modern technology | تِكْنولوْجْيا حديثِة |
| roots | جُزور |
| quality | جودِة |
| tourism | سِياحة |
| village | ضَيْعة (ضِيَع) |
| grapes | عِنب |
| harvest (by hand), collecting | قْطاف |
| vineyard | كرِم (كْروم) |
| alcoholic beverage | مشْروب روحي |
| temple | معْبد (معابِد) |
| winery; press | معْصرة (معاصِر) |
| special, outstanding; unique, distinctive | مُميّز |
| discussion | مُناقشِة |
| view, landscape | منْظر (مناظِر) |
| wine | نْبيذ |
| flavor, taste | نكْهة |

## Transcript

**شَرْبِل:** هاي، كيفْكُن اليوْم؟ تمام؟ اليوْم رح نِسْتكْشِف مَوْضوع مُمْتِع، special. بدْنا نِحْكي عن النِّبيد اللِّبْناني. أنا شرْبِل ومعي صديقي عُمر. كيفك اليوْم يا عُمر؟

**Charbel:** Hi, how are you all today? Doing well? Today we're going to explore an interesting topic, something special: we're going to talk about Lebanese wine. I'm Charbel, and with me is my friend Omar. How are you today, Omar?

**عُمر:** والله يا شرْبِل، أنا هلّأ صِرِت مْنيح لأنّو مَوْضوع النِّبيد اللِّبْناني كْتير كْتير بيهِمُّني ومع إنّو هُوِّ أقلّ شِهْرة مِن مثلاً العرق وغير مشْروبات روحية بِلِبْنان بسّ فِعْلاً فِعْلاً مَوْضوع بيسْتحِقّ المُناقشِة.

**Omar:** Honestly, Charbel, I'm feeling great now because the topic of Lebanese wine really interests me a lot. Even though it's less famous than, for example, arak and other spirits in Lebanon, it's definitely a topic worth discussing.

**شَرْبِل:** ليْك أكيد، لِبْنان عِنْدو تاريخ عريق وغني بِصِناعِةْ النِّبيد. وعِنّا كْتير معاصِر مِنْتِشْرة بِكِلّ أنْحاء البلد وبِالبِقاع خُصوصاً يَلّي مشْهور بِكْرومو، بِمساحْتو، وبِصِناعِةْ النِّبيد.

**Charbel:** For sure, Lebanon has a long and rich history in wine production. We have many wineries spread across the country, especially in the Bekaa Valley, which is famous for its vineyards, its vastness, and its wine production.

**عُمر:** إنْتَ بْتعْرِف يا شرْبِل إنّو البِقاع مثلاً مَوْقِع مثالي لِصِناعِةْ النِّبيد الطّقْس هوْنيك مُمْتاز، بِالصّيْف، الشّمِس، الهَوى، التّرْبِة اللي عِنْدُن ياها مثالية لتعْطيك أجْوَد وأحْسن أنْواع العِنب.

**Omar:** You know, Charbel, the Bekaa Valley is an ideal location for wine production—the weather there is excellent, with the summer sun, the air, and the soil they have being perfect for producing the best and highest quality grapes.

**شَرْبِل:** واو! عنْجدّ! ومعْبد... إنْتَ بْتعْرِف إنّو بْعلْبك فيا معْبد باخوس هُوِّ مْخصّص هيْدا الإله للنِّبيد الرّوْماني. بيدِلّ قدّيْش كانِت المِنْطْقة مْهِمّة تاريخِيّاً لِصِناعِةْ النِّبيد، ومِن الرّائِع جِدّاً إنّو نْشوف جُذور هالتّقاليد العميقة.

**Charbel:** Wow! Really! And the temple... You know that Baalbek has a temple dedicated to Bacchus, the Roman god of wine. This shows how important the region was historically for wine production, and it's amazing to see the deep roots of these traditions.

**عُمَر:** يَلّي عم تْقولو شرْبِل كْتير مظْبوط. وهَيْدا بيوَضِّح إنّو الرّابِط التّاريخي مَوْجود مِن زمان وإنّو صِناعةْ النّبيد بِلِبْنان مِنّو شي جْديد وهُوَّ فِعْلاً جِزْء لا يَتَجزّأ مِن ثقافِتْنا مِن زمن طَويل. المُعاصِر اللِّبْنانية اليوْم بْتِنْتِج نْبيد مُمْتاز بِالْجودة، بِالطّعْمِة، وصراحة بِمعايير دُوَلية بِاعْتِراف الجّميع، مِش حتّى بسّ اللِّبْنانية بسّ يَلّي بْيَعْمْلوا نْبيد مِن كلّ أنْحاء العالم.

**Omar:** What you're saying, Charbel, is absolutely right. This highlights that the historical connection has existed for a long time and that wine production in Lebanon isn't something new; it's truly an integral part of our culture from way back. Today, Lebanese wineries produce excellent wine in terms of quality and taste, and honestly, to international standards recognized by everyone, not just the Lebanese but also wine producers from all over the world.

**شرْبِل:** صحّ، مِنْصدِّر النّبيد لعِدّة دُوَل والنّبيد اللِّبْناني عم بيصير أكْتر وأكْتر مشْهور عالمِياً. المُعاصِر عِنّا مِتِل شاتّو كْسارة، شاتّو كِفْريّا، شاتّو موزار أسْماء معْروفِة وكْتير مِنُّن يَعْني بْيِرْفعوا الرّاس.

**Charbel:** Exactly. We export wine to many countries, and Lebanese wine is becoming more and more famous globally. Our wineries, like Château Ksara, Château Kefraya, and Château Musar, are well-known names, and many of them make us proud.

**عُمَر:** صحّ، وبْتعْرِف شرْبِل إنّو النّبيد اللِّبْناني بْتِقْدر تْميّزو دغْري لأنّو عِنْدو نكْهة فريدِة وجَوْدِة عالْيِة بِتْميّزو عن غيْر نْبيد بغيْر مناطِق بِالْعالم. والسِّرّ إنّو هُوَّ جمع بيْن طُرُق تْقْليدية بِصِناعةْ النّبيذ وتكْنوْلوْجية... تكْنوْلوْجْيا حديثِة ساعدِت إنّو تِرْفع مُسْتوى هَيْدا النّبيد وتميّزو عن على الأقلّ الدُّوَل المِنْطْقة.

**Omar:** True, and you know, Charbel, you can recognize Lebanese wine right away because it has a unique flavor and high quality that sets it apart from wine produced in other regions around the world. The secret is that it combines traditional winemaking methods with modern technology, which has helped elevate this wine and set it apart, at least in the region.

**شَربِل:** أكيد الكُروم بِلبنان بتِستفيد مِن تنوُّع التِّربة وهَيدا بيَعطي النُّبيد خصائِص مُميَّزة حتّى يَعني إنّ كان نبيد أحمَر قَوي أوْ نُبيد أبْيض وهيْك بيِنشرب بالصّيْف. في كْتير إشيا تْقدِّرا بالنُّبيد اللُّبْناني!

Charbel: Indeed, the vineyards in Lebanon benefit from the diverse soil, which gives the wine unique characteristics, whether it's a strong red wine or a white wine that's perfect for summer. There's so much to appreciate about Lebanese wine!

**عُمر:** صحّ! وعَ فِكرة شرّبِل، مِش بسّ تِتزوّق النُّبيد اللُّبْناني هُوّ تجرُبة بحدّ ذاتو، بسّ إنّك تْروح وتْزور معامِل النُّبيد والمْعاصِر والكافات هُوّ شي مُمتع جدّا. صراحة أنا زِرت عدد كْبير مِن هالْمعاصِر بِبَيْروت... بِلبْنان وعَ طول بيقدُّموا جَوْلات تِتْعرّف فيا عن طريقةِ تِصنيعِ النُّبيد وين بيِنْحطّ، قدّي بيْتْخمّر، شو الأنْواع وهيْك بْتاخُد فِكرة عامّة عن الطّريقة وهَيْدا شيء جِداً جِداً تجْرِبِة مُميَّزة.

Omar: Right! And by the way, Charbel, not only is tasting Lebanese wine an experience in itself but visiting the wineries and cellars is also very enjoyable. Honestly, I've visited a lot of these wineries in Beirut... in Lebanon, and they always offer tours where you can learn about the wine-making process, where it's stored, how long it ferments, and what types there are. It gives you a general idea of the process, and it's truly a unique experience.

**شرّبِل:** بْوافْقك الرّأي يا عُمر. عنْجدّ سياحةِ النُّبيد عم تِكبر بِلبْنان وهِيِّ تجْرِبة كْتير حِلْوة لتْروح وتِستْكشِف الضّيَع وتِستْمتِع بالْمناظِر الحِلْوة وأكيد إذا اللي بدّو بْحبّ يْدوق النُّبيد المُميّز عنّا.

Charbel: I agree with you, Omar. Honestly, wine tourism is growing in Lebanon, and it's a great experience to explore the villages, enjoy the beautiful scenery, and of course, for those who want to, taste the unique wine we have.

**عُمر:** على فِكْرة شرّبِل! سْمِعِت إنّو في كْتير مِن معاصِر النُّبيد بِلبْنان صاروا حتّى عم بِقدّموا إيقامةِ. يَعني فيك تْروح تْقضّي عِنْدُن ويِك أند بْتعْمُل تجْرِبة مثالية وخاصّةً للأشْخاص اللي بيحِبّوا النُّبيد، بْياخدوك على كْروم العِنب وخاصّةً بمَواسِم القْطاف بِتْساعد الشّباب والصّبايا يَلّي بيقطُفوا العِنب بْتاخْدُون على المْعاصِر، وهيْك صراحة

بِتْكون تجرِبِة كْتير حِلْوِة ومِتْكامْلِة. خاصّةً إنّو أَغْلَبِية المْعاصِر بِلِبْنان هِيِّ مَوْجودِة بِمناطِق طبيعِيّة جِدّاً حِلْوِة جِدّاً مُميّزِة وفِعْلاً تجْرِبِة بِتْكون غير عن كِلّ التجارِب.

**Omar:** By the way, Charbel! I've heard that many of the wineries in Lebanon are even offering accommodations now. So, you can go spend time there and have a perfect experience, especially for those who love wine. They take you to the vineyards, especially during the harvest season, where young men and women help pick the grapes, then they take you to the wineries. Honestly, it's a wonderful and complete experience, especially since most of the wineries in Lebanon are located in very beautiful and unique natural areas, making the experience truly different from all others.

**شرْبِل:** عنْجَدّ، ميرْسي لأَلك يا عُمر على هَيْدا الحديث المُمْتع على النّبيد اللُّبْناني. وشُكْراً للِّي كِلّ عم بْيِسْمعْنا وبِتْأمّل إنّو تْكونوا كْتير نْبسطّوا وأخدْتوا فِكْرة عن النّبيد عنّا، وتْعرّفْتوا أَكْتر على صِناعِةْ النّبيد اللُّبْناني هيْك لَنّو فِكْرة صْغيرِة.

**Charbel:** Really, thank you, Omar, for this enjoyable talk about Lebanese wine. And thanks to everyone who is listening. I hope you had fun and got an idea about our wine and learned more about Lebanese wine production, even if just a small insight.

**عُمر:** ميرْسي شرْبِل لأَلك ومِتِل ما بِنْقول بِاللُّبْناني كاسْكُن ودايْمِة.

**Omar:** Thank you, Charbel. And as we say in Lebanese, 'cheers and always full.'

**شرْبِل:** بْصِحّتْكُن كمان أَوْ cheers أَوْ اللي بدّك ياه! نشالله تْضلّوا بْخير وأكيد سْتمْتعْتوا بِهَيْدا التّسْجيل أَوْ الـaudio.

**Charbel:** Cheers to you too, or whatever you prefer to say! I hope you all stay well and enjoyed this recording, or audio.

## Comprehension Questions

١. وِيْن مِنْتِشْرين المْعاصِر بِلِبْنان، وخاصّةً ويْن؟

٢. ليْش البْقاع مَوْقع مِثالي لِصِناعةْ النُّبيد؟

٣. شو هُوِّ معْبد باخوس وشو علاقْتو بِصِناعةْ النُّبيد؟

٤. كيْف بْتِجْمع المْعاصِر اللّبْنانية بيْن الطُّرُق التِّقْليدية والتِّكْنوْلوْجْيا الحديثِة؟

٥. شو بيميِّز النُّبيد اللّبْناني عن غيْر نْبيد بالْعالم؟

٦. شو الأنْواع المشْهورة مِن المْعاصِر اللّبْنانية؟

٧. ليْش سِياحِةْ النُّبيد عم تِكْبر بِلِبْنان؟

٨. كيْف بِتْكون التّجْرِبة بِزْيارِةْ معاصِر النُّبيذ بِلِبْنان؟ شو الأشْياء اللي بِتْشوفا وبِتْجرُّبا هوْنيك؟

1. Where are wineries spread across Lebanon, and especially where?
2. Why is the Bekaa Valley an ideal location for winemaking?
3. What is the Bacchus Temple, and what is its connection to winemaking?
4. How do Lebanese wineries combine traditional methods with modern technology?
5. What distinguishes Lebanese wine from other wines in the world?
6. What are the famous Lebanese wineries?
7. Why is wine tourism growing in Lebanon?
8. What is the experience like when visiting wineries in Lebanon? What do you see and experience there?

## Discussion Questions

١. بْتْحِبّ النُّبِيد؟ شو النّوْع المُفضّل عِنْدك؟

٢. كيف صِناعةْ النُّبِيد بِبلدك؟ عِنْدْكُن مناطِق مشْهورة بِزِراعةْ العِنب؟

٣. شو رأيَك بِدمْج الطُّرُق التّقْليدية مع التّكْنُوْلوْجْيا الحديثةِ بِصِناعةْ النُّبِيد؟

٤. زِرِت معاصِر نِبِيد مِن قبِل؟ خبِّرْنا عن تجْرِبْتك.

٥. شو هُوّ مشْروبك الرّوحي المُفضّل وليْش؟

٦. كيف بِتْأثّر الظُّروف الجوّية والترِّبة على جودةْ النُّبِيد بِبلدك؟

٧. عِنْدْكُن شي مهْرجانات أوْ فعّالِيّات مِتْعلّقة بالنُّبِيد؟ شاركْنا تجْرِبتك.

٨. إذا زِرِت لِبْنان، بِتْحِبّ تْروح جَوْلةٍ سياحية بالْمعاصِر؟ ليْش أوْ ليْش لا؟

1. Do you like wine? What is your favorite type?
2. How is the wine industry in your country? Do you have regions famous for growing grapes?
3. What do you think about combining traditional methods with modern technology in winemaking?
4. Have you ever visited wineries before? Tell us about your experience.
5. What is your favorite alcoholic beverage and why?
6. How do weather conditions and soil quality affect the quality of wine in your country?
7. Do you have festivals or events related to wine? Share your experience.
8. If you visit Lebanon, would you like to go on a wine tour? Why or why not?

# نصايِح للأجانِب اللي عم يْفكُّروا بالإنْتِقال للبْنان

## Tips for Foreigners Considering Moving to Lebanon

### In this episode...

Charbel and Farah share practical advice for foreigners thinking about moving to Lebanon. They cover key topics like adapting to the local culture, learning some Arabic, finding housing, and navigating transportation. You'll also hear about Lebanon's economic challenges, healthcare options, and its vibrant cultural scene. Whether you're planning a move or just curious, this episode provides useful insights for settling into life in Lebanon.

## Vocabulary

| | |
|---|---|
| rent | أَجار |
| local economy | إقْتِصاد محلّي |
| moving, relocation | إنْتِقال |
| Arabic | العربية |
| traditional houses | بْيوت تقْليدية |
| economic fluctuations | تقلُّبات إقْتِصادية |
| culture | ثَقافة |
| trust | ثِقة |
| currency exchange rate | سِعْر العِمْلة |
| housing | سكن |
| shared taxi | سيرْفيس |
| new apartments | شِقق جْديدة |
| health insurance | ضمان صُحّي |
| customs and traditions | عادات وتقاليد |
| local language | لُغة محلّية |
| expat(riate) | مِغْتِرِب |
| advice, tip | نصيحة (نصايِح) |
| lifestyle | نمط الحَياةْ |
| public transportation | وَسائِل نقِل عامّ |
| economic situation | وَضْع إقْتِصادي |

# Transcript

**شَرْبِل:** هاي، كيفْكُن؟ تمام؟ اليوْم مَوْضوعْنا لح يْكون كْتير مْهِمّ عدد كْبير مِن يَلّي عم بِيْسمعونا. هِيِّ نصايح للْأجانِب اللي عم بيفكّروا بالإنْتِقال لِلِبْنان. أنا شرْبِل ومعي اليوْم رْفيقْتي فرح. كيفِك يا فرح؟

**Charbel:** Hi, how are you all? Good? Today's topic is going to be very important for many of those who are listening to us. It's tips for foreigners who are thinking about moving to Lebanon. I'm Charbel, and with me today is my friend Farah. How are you, Farah?

**فرح:** أهْلا شرْبِل، أنا مْنيحة. هَيْدا المَوْضوع مْهِمّ كْتير. لِبْنان بلد كْتير حِلو وعِنْدو كْتير لَيْقدّمو. بسّ مِتِل أيّ إنْتِقال بْيِجي مع تحدِّيّات وفُرَص.

**Farah:** Hi Charbel, I'm good. This is a very important topic. Lebanon is a beautiful country and has a lot to offer. But like any move, it comes with challenges and opportunities.

**شَرْبِل:** أكيد، الإنْتِقال لبلد جْديد بيكون كْتير هيْك صعِب وبذات الوَقِت هيْك مِتْحمِسِة لإلو. أوّل نصيحة بْحِبّ أعْطيا لأيّ حدا عم يْفكّر يِنْتِقِل لِلِبْنان هِيِّ إنّو يَعْمُل research أوْ بحْث جْديد يِتْعلّم أكْتر عن الثّقافة، نمط الحَياة والوَضِع الإقْتِصادي والسِّياسِة الحالي.

**Charbel:** Definitely. Moving to a new country can be both difficult and exciting at the same time. The first piece of advice I'd like to give anyone thinking of moving to Lebanon is to do thorough research, learn more about the culture, the lifestyle, and the current economic and political situation.

**فرح:** صحّ إنّو تِفْهم التّفاصيل والثّقافِة مْهِمّ كْتير. لِبْنان معْروف بْكرم ضِيافْتو وشعْبو المْحِبّ. بسّ لازِم كمان تْكون واعي للْعادات والتّقاليد الإجْتِماعية. إنّو تِبْني علاقات ويْكون في ثِقة هُوِّ المِفْتاح.

**Farah:** Right, understanding the details and the culture is very important. Lebanon is known for its hospitality and friendly people. But you also need to be aware of the social customs and traditions. Building relationships and trust is key.

**شَرْبِل:** مِيِّة بالْمِيِّة. هَيْدي نُقْطة كْتير صحيحة عم تِحْكي عنّا. جانِب مْهِمّ تاني هُوّ إنّو تعلُّم شْوَيّ اللّغة المحلّية. يَعْني حتّى لأنّو كْتير مِن النّاس بلِبْنان بْيِحْكوا English

وFrench، إنْكليزي وفرنْسي، العربية هِيِّ اللّغّة الأساسية. إنّو تعْرِف بعْض العِبارات الأساسية كْتير بِتْساعِد إنّو تِنْتِقِل بِالْحَياة اليَوْمية وإنّو تِتْواصل مع النّاس بلِبْنان.

**Charbel:** Absolutely. That's a very true point you're making. Another important aspect is learning a bit of the local language. Even though many people in Lebanon speak English and French, Arabic is the main language. Knowing some basic phrases will really help you get by in daily life and communicate with people in Lebanon.

**فرح:** أكيد هَيْدا الشّي بيبيِّن إحْترامك للثّقافة وبيخلّي تجارْبك أسْهل بكْتير. وكمان فكّر بِالْجَوانِب العملية مِتِل السّكن والتّنقُّل. بِبَيْروت مثلاً فيا مجْموعة كْتير مِتْنوّعة إنّك تِخْتار السّكن، في شِقق جْديدة، بْيوت تِقْليدية. كْتير مْهِمّ تْحُطّ حالك بِالصّورة بِخْصوص الأجارات والمناطِق اللي بِتْناسْبك.

**Farah:** For sure. This shows respect for the culture and makes your experiences much easier. Also, think about practical aspects like housing and transportation. In Beirut, for example, there's a wide range of housing options, from new apartments to traditional houses. It's very important to understand the rent prices and the neighborhoods that suit you.

**شرْبِل:** أيْه والتّنقُّل مُمْكِن يكون بْيِخْتِلِف شْوَيّ عَ اللي مِتْعَوّدين عْلْيه. لأنّو في وَسائِل نقِل عامّ مِتْوَفْرة بسّ كْتير مِن النّاس بْيِعْتِمْدوا على التّاكْسيّات المُشْترِكة يَعْني، إذا بدّكُن تاكْسيّات الجماعية اللي هية بلِبْنان مِنْقلا السّيرْفيس أوْ السّيّارات الخاصّة. وعِنّا applications مِتِل Uber،Bolt كمان بْيِسْتعمْلُوا تاكْسيّات وعِنّا نقْليات عامّة مِتِل الباصات. لازِم حتّى يَعِرْفوا إنّو العجْقة كْتيرة خاصّةً بقلْب بَيْروت.

**Charbel:** Right, and transportation might be a bit different from what you're used to. While public transportation is available, many people rely on shared taxis, or collective taxis, which we call "service" taxis, or private cars. We also have apps like Bolt and Uber for taxis and public buses. It's also important to know that traffic can be heavy, especially in central Beirut.

**فرح:** وبِالنّسْبة للصّحّة، كْتير مْهِمّ تِفْهم النّظام الصّحّي بلِبْنان. في عِنْدو مزيج مِن الرِّعايَة الصُّحّية العامّة والخاصّة. المِسْتشْفايات الخاصّة بِتْقدّم رِعايَة مْهِمّة بسّ مُمْكِن تْكون غالْية. أحْسن إنّو يْكون عِنْدك تأْمين صِحّي بيغطّيك بلِبْنان.

**Farah:** Regarding healthcare, it's very important to understand the healthcare system in Lebanon. There's a mix of public and private healthcare. Private hospitals offer excellent care but can be expensive. It's best to have health insurance that covers you in Lebanon.

**شَرْبِل:** ولازِمِ ما نِنْسى الجانِب المالي. الإقْتِصاد اللِّبْناني كْتير واجَه تحدِّيّات كْبيرِة بِالفَتْرِة الأخيرة. ومِن الضَّروري يْكون الواحد يْكون مِسْتَعِدّ للتَّقَلُّبات المُحْتَمِلة لأنّو لِبْنان عِنّا مِنّو stable، عَ طول في عِنّا قِصَص جْديدِة بِتْحرُّك الإقْتِصاد اللِّبْناني. فا ضروري الواحد يْكون على إطِّلاع بِتحرُّك الإقْتِصادي بِلِبْنان وحتّى يَعْرِف شْوَيّ مفهوم عن العُمْلِة خاصّةً مع هلّأ الـ inflation اللي عم بِتْصير وكيف عم يْكون سِعْر العُمْلِة مُقابِل الدّوْلار. فا عَ طول لازِمِ الواحد يْكون عِنْدو فِكْرة عن العُمْلِة اللِّبْنانية وقَدّيْ بِتْسْوى وكمان يْجرِّب يْوَفِّر خدمات مصْرِفية أكْتر.

**Charbel:** And we shouldn't forget the financial aspect. The Lebanese economy has faced significant challenges recently. It's crucial to be prepared for potential fluctuations because Lebanon isn't stable; there are always new events that affect the economy. So, it's important to stay informed about the economic situation in Lebanon and have some understanding of the currency, especially with the current inflation and how the exchange rate with the dollar is fluctuating. It's always important to have an idea of the value of the Lebanese pound and try to secure more banking services.

**فرح:** صحّ والشّي الإجابي بِلِبْنان عِنْدو مشْهد ثقافي غني وفي كْتير مَواقِع تاريخية تِسْتكْشِفا ومهْرجانات تِحْضرا، أسْواق تْزورا، مطاعِمِ تِسْتمْتِع فِيا ومحلّات سهر وغَيْرا كْتير.

**Farah:** That's right, and the positive thing about Lebanon is that it has a rich cultural scene with many historical sites to explore, festivals to attend, markets to visit, restaurants to enjoy, nightlife spots, and much more.

**شَرْبِل:** أكيد وواحْدِة مِن أفْضل الإشيا إنّو واحد يْجرِّبا ويْعيشا بِلِبْنان هِيِّ التّنوُّع بِهالتّجارِب كِلّا وهالثّقافات كِلّا وحتّى معْروف عِنّا بِلِبْنان إنّو في واحد يِطْلع يَعْمُل تزَلُّج عَ الجّبل بِذات الوَقِت إنّو في يْكون في عالم عم بْتِتْسبّح عَ البحِر.

**Charbel:** Absolutely, and one of the best things to experience in Lebanon is the diversity of all these experiences and cultures. Lebanon is also known for being a place where you can go skiing in the mountains and, at the same time, have people swimming in the sea.

**فرح:** ولازِم ما نِنْسى أهميةْ المُجْتمّع إذا إنْتَ انْضميْت لمجْموعات محلّية أوْ حتّى مُجْتمّعات المغْترِبين، هَيْدا الشّي كْتير مُفيد بيخلّيك هيْك تْحِسّ بالإنْتماء.

Farah: And we shouldn't forget the importance of community. If you join local groups or even expatriate communities, it can be very beneficial and help you feel more connected.

**شرْبِل:** هَيْدا الشّي مظْبوط وإنّو تِبْني هيْك شبكِة مِن الأصْدِقاء والرِّفْقا وتعمْلي معارِف بيساعْدِك إنّو تْحِسّي أكْتر إنّك إنْتي عنْجدّ بِيْتِك وبْيَعْطيكي هيْك إحْساس بالإنْتماء للبلد وبيوفِّرْلِك نصايح كْتير مُفيدِة إنّو كيف تْعيشي بلِبْنان. وبْيِبْقى إنّو واحد كمان يطّلِّع عَ الأخْبار والأحْداث المحلّية كمان بيتْساعْدِك أكْتر لتْفوتي وتِنْدِمْجي مع المُجْتمّع بِالْبلد.

Charbel: That's true, and building a network of friends and acquaintances helps you feel more at home and gives you a sense of belonging in the country. It also provides you with a lot of useful advice on how to live in Lebanon. And it's always good to keep up with the local news and events; it helps you integrate better into the society in the country.

**فرح:** صحّ، وأخيراً أنا دايْماً بْقول يْكون الواحد صبور لأنّو الإنْتِقال لبلد جْديد دايْماً بيكون فيو قُصص جْديدِة تِتْعلّما وهيْك بْتِحْتِضن الإخْتِلافات وواحد هيْك ياخُد وقْتو ليتِأقْلم. لِبْنان بلد مِلْيان بِالتّناقُضات وهَيْدا جِزء مِن سِحْرو.

Farah: Exactly, and finally, I always say to be patient because moving to a new country always comes with new things to learn, so embrace the differences and take your time to adapt. Lebanon is a country full of contradictions, and that's part of its charm.

**شرْبِل:** فرح، thank you كْتير على هالنصايح الحِلْوِة وانْشالله تْكون عم بِتْفيد اللي عم يِسْمعونا. ميرْسي لمْشاركْتِك وميرْسي للمُسْتمِعين اللي سِمعونا اليوْم. انْشالله تْكونوا سْتفدْتوا مِن هالنِّقاش الصِّغير هيْك أخدْتوا فكْرة عَ الإنْتِقال لِلِبْنان وانْشالله نِلْتِقي مرّة الجاية بمَوْضوع جْديد وخبرْيات جْديدِة مِن حَياتْنا بلِبْنان. لَوقْتا ضلّوا بْخيْر وأكيد سْتْمِتْعوا بِالرِّحْلِة.

**Charbel:** Farah, thank you so much for these great tips, and hopefully, they'll be useful to those listening to us. Thank you for joining us, and thanks to all our listeners today. We hope you benefited from this small discussion and got an idea about moving to Lebanon. We hope to meet again next time with a new topic and new stories from our life in Lebanon. Until then, stay well and, of course, enjoy the journey.

**فرح:** شُكْراً إلك يا شرْبِل وشُكْراً لكِلّ اللي سِمْعونا.

**Farah:** Thank you, Charbel, and thanks to everyone who listened.

## Comprehension Questions

١.  شو هُوّ مَوْضوع الحلْقة اللي حِكْيوا عنّو شرْبِل وفرح؟

٢.  ليْش مْهِمّ يَعْمُل الشّخِص بحْث قبِل ما يِنْتِقِل للبْنان؟

٣.  شو هِيّ النّصيحة اللي قدّمِتا فرح بِخْصوص تعلُّم اللغّة؟

٤.  كيف بْتِخْتِلِف خيارات السَّكن بِبَيْروت؟

٥.  شو هِيّ وَسائِل النّقِل المتُاحة بِبَيْروت؟

٦.  ليْش مْهِمّ يْكون عِنْدك تأُمين صُحّي بِلِبْنان؟

٧.  كيف بيوَضِّح شرْبِل أهميةْ فهْم الوَضِع الإقْتِصادي اللِّبْناني؟

٨.  شو هِيّ الأنْشِطة الثّقافية اللي مُمْكِن تِسْتمْتع فيا بِلِبْنان؟

1.  What is the topic of the episode that Charbel and Farah discussed?
2.  Why is it important for someone to do research before moving to Lebanon?
3.  What advice did Farah give about learning the language?
4.  How do housing options in Beirut differ?
5.  What transportation options are available in Beirut?
6.  Why is it important to have health insurance in Lebanon?
7.  How does Charbel emphasize the importance of understanding the Lebanese economic situation?
8.  What cultural activities can you enjoy in Lebanon?

## Discussion Questions

١. إذا فكّرِت تنْتِقِل لبلد جْديد، شو هِيِّ الأُمور اللي بِتْحِبّ تعْرِفا قبِل الإنْتِقال؟

٢. كيف بِتْحضِّر حالك لتحدِّيّات الإنْتِقال لبلد جْديد؟

٣. شو هِيِّ أهميةْ تعلُّم اللُّغة المحلّية بسّ تِنْتِقِل لبلد جْديد؟

٤. كيف بِتْشوف دوْر المُجْتمّع بمُساعدةْ المِغْترْبين للإنْدِماج؟

٥. شو هِيِّ التحدِّيّات اللي مُمْكِن تْواجِها بلِبْنان بخْصوص السّكن والتّنقُّل؟

٦. كيف بِتْقَيِّم أهميةْ الرِّعايَة الصُّحّية بلد جْديد؟

٧. شو هِيِّ الأنْشِطة الثّقافية اللي بِتْحِبّ تِسْتكْشِفا بِبلد جْديد؟

٨. كيف بِتْشوف تأْثير الوَضِع الإقْتِصادي على حَياتك كمِغْترِب؟

1. If you thought about moving to a new country, what things would you like to know before moving?
2. How do you prepare yourself for the challenges of moving to a new country?
3. What is the importance of learning the local language when moving to a new country?
4. How do you see the role of the community in helping expatriates integrate?
5. What challenges might you face in Lebanon regarding housing and transportation?
6. How do you assess the importance of healthcare in a new country?
7. What cultural activities do you like to explore in a new country?
8. How do you see the impact of the economic situation on your life as an expatriate?

# الموسيقى والفِنّانين اللّبْنانيّين المشْهورين

## Music and Famous Lebanese Artists

### In this episode...

Charbel and Omar discuss the vibrant world of Lebanese music and its legendary artists. From the iconic voice of Fairouz and the musical masterpieces of the Rahbani brothers to the powerful performances of Wadi' al-Safi and the revolutionary works of Ziad Rahbani, they explore the timeless music that has shaped Lebanon's cultural identity. They also reflect on the new generation of stars like Nancy Ajram and Wael Kfoury, whose talents continue to carry Lebanese music to global audiences. Tune in for a nostalgic journey through Lebanon's rich musical heritage.

## Vocabulary

| | |
|---|---|
| performance | أَداء |
| legend | أُسْطورة |
| song | أُغْنية (أَغاني) |
| icon | أَيْقونة |
| creativity | إبْداع |
| feeling | إحْساس |
| heritage | تُراث |
| concert, event | حفْلة |
| tenderness | حنان |
| ambassador | سفير |
| voice | صوْت |
| vigor | عنْفُوان |
| art | فنّ |
| artist, singer | فِنّان |
| to compose | لحّن (يْلحِّن) |
| excited | مِتْحمّس |
| play, musical | مسْرحية |
| famous | مشْهور |
| music | موسيقى |
| nostalgia | نوْسْتالْجْيا |

# Transcript

**شَرْبِل:** هاي جميعاً، اليوْم مَوْضوعْنا قريب عَ قَلْبي وعَ قْلوب كِلِّ اللي عم يِسْمَعْنا: الموسيقى والفِنّانين اللّبنانيّين المشْهورين. أنا شرْبِل ومعي رْفيقي عُمر، كيفَك عُمر؟

Charbel: Hello, everyone! Today our topic is close to my heart and the hearts of all our listeners. We're talking about Lebanese music and famous Lebanese artists. I'm Charbel, and with me is my friend Omar. How are you, Omar?

**عُمر:** يا ميجنا و يا ميجنا! آه سوْري شرْبِل سوْري أنا تْحمّسْت كْتير. أنا مْنيح إنْتَ كيف؟ كْتير مِتْحمّس لِنِحْكي عن مَوْضوع الموسيقى اللّبنانية ونتْذكر هيْك أهمّ الموسيقيّين والفِنّانين يَلّي قطعوا بْتاريخْنا.

Omar: Ya Meijana, Ya Meijana! Oh, sorry, Charbel, I got a bit too excited. I'm good; how are you? I'm really excited to talk about Lebanese music and reminisce about the most important musicians and artists who have made their mark on our history.

**شَرْبِل:** أكيد أكيد، الموسيقى اللّبنانية غنية كْتير ومِتْنوّعة. وعِنّا كْتير فِنّانين أُسْطوريّين تركوا بصْمة دايْمة مِش بسّ بِلِبْنان بسّ بِكِلّ العالم العربي. خبّرْنا يا عُمر هيْك شْوَيّ، مين إذا بدّك الفِنّان اللّبناني اللي بِتْحِسّوا هيْك أوْ إذا بدّك مُفضّل عنْدك؟

Charbel: Absolutely, Lebanese music is very rich and diverse, and we have many legendary artists who have left a lasting impact, not only in Lebanon but throughout the Arab world. Tell us a bit, Omar, who is your favorite Lebanese artist, or who do you feel is the most significant?

**عُمر:** والله يا شرْبِل هَيْدا سُؤال صعْب! لأنّو عنْجدّ بلا مُبالغة عِنّا كْتير فِنّانين عُظما بِلِبْنان، بسّ إذا ولابُدّ لازِم إخْتار ما بِتْردّد وقول السِّتّ فَيْروز. هَيْدا الصّوْت السّاحِر والأغاني يَلّي بْتِخْلَق بْقلْبك نوْسْتالْجْيا وبِترْجْعك لِذكْرَيات قديمة، موسيقِتا خالْدة بْتِلْمُس القْلوب كِلّ اللي بْيِسْمعوا ومِشان هيْك بْلَقّبوا بِلِبْنان بِسفيرتْنا إلى النُّجوم.

Omar: Wow, Charbel, that's a tough question! Honestly, without exaggeration, we have so many great artists in Lebanon. But if I had to choose, I wouldn't hesitate to say Fairuz. Her magical voice and songs create nostalgia and take you back to old memories. Her music is timeless, touching the hearts of everyone who listens, which is why she's known in Lebanon as our ambassador to the stars.

**شَرْبِل:** عَنْجَدّ فَيْروز بَسّ نِحْكي عَنّا، عَنْجَدّ هِيِّ أَيْقونِة، أَيْقونِةْ الفَنّ، أَيْقونِةْ الموسيقى اللّبْنانية. أغانيا الصّباحية جِزء أساسي مِن كْتير بْيوت بِلِبْنان. أغانيا ما بيفارْقوا المطاعِم ما بيفارْقوا السّيّارات، بْتِذكَّر كِنت أوْعى على صَوْتا على الرّاديو خْصوصاً بِالأعْياد الإحْساس هيْك بِالحَنان بِالدِّفء ما بْيِنْوَصَف. يَعْني مِتِل هلّأ عم خَبِّرُك وعم بِتْخايَل هالأغاني كِلّا يَعْني شي لا يوصف.

**Charbel:** Truly, when we talk about Fairuz, we're talking about an icon—an icon of art, an icon of Lebanese music. Her morning songs are an essential part of many homes in Lebanon. Her songs are always playing in restaurants and cars. I remember waking up to her voice on the radio, especially during the holidays. The feeling of warmth and comfort is indescribable. Just talking about it now, I'm imagining all those songs—it's something beyond words.

**عُمَر:** على سيرةْ السّتّ فَيْروز عَ بالي هيْك خبِّرُك خَبْرِية شْوَيّ بِتْضحِّك. في أحد الصّحفيّين بِمْقابلة معا سألا: "عادةً كِلّ اللّبْنانية الصُّبْح بْيِسمعوا السّتّ فَيْروز. إنْتي شو بْتِسمعي الصُّبْح؟" صفنِت هيْك سكتِت وقالتْلو: "بِسْمع صَوْتي مِن بْلاكين العالم."

**Omar:** Speaking of Fairuz, let me share a funny story. In an interview, a journalist asked her, "Usually, all Lebanese people listen to Fairuz in the morning. What do you listen to in the morning?" She paused, thought for a moment, and replied, "I listen to my voice from the balconies of the people."

**شَرْبِل:** عَنْجَدّ حِلو حِلو ليْك بَسّ نِحْكي عن فَيْروز بدّنا نِحْكي عن الرّحابْني أكيد يَعْني ما فينا نِنْسى الموسيقى تبعُن، عِنْدك فِكْرة شْوَيّ هيْك تْخبِّرْنا عن الأخَوانالرّحْباني مِتِل عاصي ومنْصور.

**Charbel:** That's great! And when we talk about Fairuz, we also have to talk about the Rahbani brothers, no doubt. We can't forget their music. Do you have any idea who they are? Can you tell us a bit about the Rahbani brothers, Assi and Mansour?

**عُمَر:** أكيد أكيد، الأخَوان الرّحْباني عاصي ومنْصور كان إلُن فضل كْبير على الرّيبِرتْوار اللّبْناني وعلى أغاني يَعْني أغْلبية الأغاني اللي غنّتا فَيْروز هِنّي لحّنُوا، وخلقوا مسرحيّات موسيقية جميلة جدّاً مِتِل مَيْس الرّيم، مِتِل بتْرا مِتِل يَعْني سِلسِلة طَويلة مِن المسرحيّات يَلّي عَنْجَدّ غنّيت مِتِل ما بيقولوا الثّقافة اللّبْنانية.

**Omar:** Absolutely, the Rahbani brothers, Assi and Mansour, had a huge influence on the Lebanese repertoire. Most of the songs Fairuz sang were composed by them. They also created beautiful musical plays like *Mais el-Rim*, *Petra*, and a long list of other plays that have really enriched Lebanese culture.

**شرْبِل:** شاركوا كْتير عدد كْبير مِن الفَنّانين اللي هِنّي كمان أُسْطورة. وقبل ما نِحْكي عن مَوْضوع الفَنّانين بدْنا إحْكي شْوَيّ عن فَيْروز كمان إنّو هِيّ كانت معْروفة بِشخْصِيّتا اللي بيبيّن إنّو وِجّا كْتير جدّي على المسْرح، بسّ هِيّ فِعْلاً اللي كِلّ بيِحْكي عنّا هِيّ إنْسان سوبِرّ مهْضوم وسوبِرّ قريب للْقلب وحِلو واحد يِقْعُد يِحْكي معو. وبتِمنّى أنا كان مِتِل إنّو حِلِمٍ، مِتِل كِلّ هاللِبْنانية إنّو يِقعْدوا يِتْعرّفوا شخْصِياً على السّيِّدة فَيْروز. لنْكَمِّل شْوَيّ هيْك عن المسْرحيّات اللي كانوا يَعمِلُوا الرّحْبِني هِيّ كانِت بِتْضِمّ عدد كْبير مِن الفَنّانين مِتِل ما قِلْنا وضِمِنُن كان وَديع الصّافي اللي هُوَّ الله يِرْحمو كان يُعْتبر كمان أَيْقونة للِبْنان بِصَوْتو القَوي وصَوْتو الحِلو.

**Charbel:** They worked with many artists who also became legends. Before we talk about the artists, I want to mention that Fairuz was known for her serious demeanor on stage, but everyone who talks about her says she's actually a very charming and down-to-earth person. It's a dream for many Lebanese people, including myself, to meet her in person. Let's continue with the plays the Rahbanis used to produce, which included many artists like we mentioned earlier, including Wadih El Safi, who was also considered an icon of Lebanon with his strong and beautiful voice.

**عُمر:** مظْبوط. وَديع الصّافي هُوَّ مِن أرْوَع الأصْوات والخامات الصَّوْتية يَلّي قطعِت على تاريخ الفنّي بلِبْنان. بْحِبّ هيْك ذكُرك بِأغاني مِتِل لِبْنان يا قِطْعةٍ سما. قدّيْش كانِت هيْك مِلْيانة عُنْفُوان وفخِر وحُبّ للْبلد. مِن كم سِنة هيْك لَوَرا حْضُرْتِلّو حفْلة وكانِت تجْرِبِة رائْعة. بِتْحِسّ إنّو صَوْتو على المسْرح لَوْ كان عُمْرو شْوَيّ مِتْقدّم كان بعْدو بيْنْبُضّ بالقوّة وهيْك خامات طبقية وصَوْتية عظيمة جِدّاً.

**Omar:** That's true. Wadih El Safi had one of the most powerful and unique voices in Lebanese music history. Let me remind you of songs like *Lebanon, Oh Piece of Heaven*. They were full of vigor, pride, and love for the country. A few years back, I attended one of his concerts, and it was an amazing experience. Even though he was a bit older, his voice on stage still resonated with power and had such a rich tone.

**شَرْبِل:** لَيْك عُمَر بَسّ نِحْكي عَ هالْفَنّ وهالْموسيقى بالذّات مْنِحْكي عن تُراث، لأنّو كِلّو بْيِرْتِبِط بلِبْنان يَعْني. خاصَّةً كانِت هالأغاني نَحْنا رْبينا عْلَيَا كِلَّا تْلات رْباعا بْتِحْكي عن لِبْنان بْتِحْكي عن هالْبَلَد الحِلو بْتِحْكي عن هالْحِلْمِ اللّي ما بعْرف أيْمْتِلح يِتْحَقّق. كمان لَيْك هلّأً، lately إذا بدّك، كمان قارِن شْوَيّ بالْموسيقى عم يْكون في كْتير هيْك ثَوْرة موسيقية بلِبْنان بَيْن تجدُّد وبَيْن أغاني جْديدة. وبْذكُر مِن آخِر هالجّيل الحِلو وهُوّ الله يِرْحمو الرّاحِل مِلْحِم بركات اللّي كان عِنْدو طاقة وبْيِنْذكر بْطاقْتو الكْبيرةِ عَ هالْمَسْرح.

Charbel: Omar, when we talk about art and music, we're really talking about heritage because it's all tied to Lebanon. Many of these songs we grew up with are about Lebanon, about this beautiful country, about this dream that we're still waiting to come true. Recently, there's been somewhat of a musical revolution in Lebanon, with a mix of innovation and new songs. I remember one of the latest greats, the late Melhem Barakat, who had an incredible energy and is remembered for his powerful performances on stage.

**عُمَر:** أيْه مظْبوط. مِلْحِم بركات المُلَقّب بالْموسيقار كان هيْك عَ طول خارِج عن القَواعِد والمعْروف يَعْني إذا بدّك. وكان شخص يِقْدُر يَعْمِل أداء كْتير حِلو عَ المَسْرح بهضامْتو وبِصَوْتو وبأغاني وكان الجُّمْهور كْتير يِتْفاعل معو. وقبِل ما هيْك إذا بدّك نْنِتِقِل لجيل جْديد مِن الفنّانين بْحِبّ هيْك إتْذكّر كمان الصّبّوحة. صبّوحة شخص كمان ترك بصْمة بعالم الفَنّ بلِبْنان وكانوا مِن الأشْخاص يَلّي هيْك مِتِل ما بيقولوا فنّان شامِل يَعْني إسْتِعْراضي بأزْياء وبِشَكْلا وبيروحا يَلّي كانِت عَ طول مُتْجدِّدةِ، يَعْني عنْجدّ هيْك شرْبِل رجّعْتِني لإيّام كْتير حِلْوة.

Omar: Yes, that's right. Melhem Barakat, known as "The Musician," was always breaking the rules, so to speak. He was someone who could give amazing performances on stage with his charm, voice, and songs, and the audience would always respond enthusiastically. Before we move on to the new generation of artists, I'd also like to mention Sabah. Sabah was another artist who left a mark on Lebanese art. She was known as a versatile performer, with her glamorous costumes, style, and always fresh spirit. You've really taken me back to some great memories, Charbel.

**شرْبِل:** عنْجدّ عُمَر، صباح كانِت مِش بَسّ صَوْتا حِلو كان هِيّ إنْسان جميل مِن برّا ومِن جُوّا. ومِش بَسّ كموسيقى، مثّلِت كْتير بفْلومي ومسْرحيّات، مثّلِت لِبْنان بِكِلّ فخِر وعِزّ

كمان الله يِرْحَمُن هالْفنّانين. ليْك عُمر lately هالْ... عنّا كْتير فنّانين طالْعين جْداد بسّ بيكبْرُوا الْقلْب مِتِل نانْسي عجْرم، إليسًّا، وائل كْفوري، مرْوان خوري يَعْني وعم بيكون الْفنّ تبعُن رائع. وقبل ما نِنْتِقِل لإلُن شْوَيِّ نِحْكي عنُّن ما بدّنا نِنْسى زياد الرّحْباني اللي هُوِّ فِكِر كْبير بالْفنّ بالْمسْرح وهُوِّ إبْنا لفَيْروز.

**Charbel:** Honestly, Omar, Sabah wasn't just a beautiful voice—she was a beautiful person inside and out. And she didn't just sing; she acted in many films and plays, proudly representing Lebanon. May they all rest in peace. Recently, we have many emerging artists who are really impressive, like Nancy Ajram, Elissa, Wael Kfoury, Marwan Khoury, and their art is wonderful. But before we move on to talk about them, we can't forget Ziad Rahbani, who is a great thinker in music and theater and is Fairuz's son.

**عُمر:** مظْبوط. زياد مِن الأشْخاص اللي إذا بدّك كتب مسْرحِيّات ولحّن أغاني بعْدا للْيوْم كأنّو عم تِسْمعا وعم تِحْكي عن الواقع الحالي اللي نحْنا مَوْجودين فيه. وهَيْدا بيدلّ عن إبْداع فنّي كْتير كْبير لشخِص يِقْدُر يِخْلق قِصص تْضلّ عايْشِة معْنا بْحياتْنا اليوْمية.

**Omar:** That's true. Ziad is someone who has written plays and composed songs that still resonate today as if they're talking about the current reality we're living in. This speaks to his great artistic talent, creating stories that stay with us in our daily lives.

**شرْبِل:** مِيِّة بالْمِيِّة إذا بدّنا نْضلّ نِحْكي عن الْفنّ والموسيقى والفنّانين بِلْبْنان يا عُمر ما مْنِخْلص، عنْجدّ نِحْنا عنّا ثقافِة كْبيرة وغنية وإذا بدّك مِنْخرِّج موسيقى حِلْوة لهالْمِنْطقة.

**Charbel:** Absolutely, Omar. If we keep talking about art, music, and artists in Lebanon, we'll never finish. We truly have a rich and vast culture, producing beautiful music for the region.

**عُمر:** صحيح يَلّي عم تْقولو شرْبِل، مظْبوط. وهَيْدا الشّي عم نْشوفو اليوْم لأنّو في كْتير طلب على الفنّانين والفنّانات اللّبْنانية بالْمهْرجانات العربية وكِلّ الحفلاتالأعْراس وحفلات الرّسْمية يَلّي عم بِتْصير بالْعالم العربي. وهَيْدا الشّي بيكبِّر الْقلِب وعم بْينِقْلوا الأغْنية اللّبْنانية لأنْحاء العالم.

**Omar:** You're right, Charbel. And we see that today because there's a high demand for Lebanese artists at Arab festivals, weddings, and official events throughout the Arab world. This makes us proud, as they're spreading Lebanese music to different parts of the world.

**شَرْبِل:** مِيّة بالْمِيّة عُمر. عُمر thank you so much عَ هالْحديث الحِلو وهالذِّكْرَيات الحِلْوة. عنْجدّ رجّعِتْنا لنوسْتالْجْيا حِلْوة. ميرْسِي للْمُسْتمعين وبِتْمنّى اللي ما بْيَعْرِف فَيْروز أوْ الأَشْخاص اللي حْكينا عنُّن يْكون عمر نْعرَّفُن عْلَيُن، انْشالله مْنِلْتِقي بمَوْضوع جْديد مرّة تانْية وخبْرية جْديدِة مِن لِبْنان.

**Charbel:** Exactly, Omar. Omar, thank you so much for this wonderful conversation and the great memories. You really brought back some sweet nostalgia. Thanks to our listeners as well—I hope we introduced you to Fairuz and the other artists we talked about if you weren't familiar with them. We'll meet again with a new topic and another story from Lebanon.

**عُمر:** شُكْراً إلك شرْبِل وشُكْراً لكِلّ اللي سْتمعوا لإلْنا. عَ طول خلّوا صوْت الموسيقى عالْية بِحَياتْكُن ونْبُسْطوا.

**Omar:** Thank you, Charbel, and thank you to everyone who listened. Always keep the music playing loud in your lives and enjoy it!

## Comprehension Questions

1. مين هُوّ الفِنّان اللِّبْناني المُفَضّل عِنْد عُمر، وليْش بْيِخْتار هَيْدا الفِنّان؟

2. شو أهميّةْ موسيقى فَيْروز بْثقافةْ لِبْنان حسب شرْبِل؟

3. كيف ردّت فَيْروز لمّا سألُوا شو بْتِسْمع الصُّبْح، وشو بيدِلّ هَيْدا الشّي عنّا؟

4. مين كانوا الأخَوان الرّحْباني، وشو كان دَوْرُن بْتِشْكيل الموسيقى والمسْرح اللِّبْناني؟

5. أيْمتى حُضِر عُمر حفْلة مُباشْرة لَوَديع الصّافي، وكيف كانِت تجرِبْتو؟

6. وينْ شرْبِل وعُمر بيشوفوا إرْتِباط الموسيقى اللِّبْنانية بالتُّراث، وليْش بْيِعْتِقْدوا هالإرْتِباط مُهِمّ؟

7. ليْش بْيِعْتِقِد شرْبِل إنّو الفِنّانين اللِّبْنانيِّين الجْداد عم بيكمِّلوا بْتُطْوير السّاحة الموسيقية اللِّبْنانية؟

8. كيف بْيوصَف عُمر إرْث صباح، وشو كان تأْثيرا على الفنّ والثّقافةِ بْلِبْنان؟

1. Who is Omar's favorite Lebanese artist, and why does he choose them as his favorite?
2. What is the significance of Fairuz's music in Lebanese culture according to Charbel?
3. How did Fairuz respond when asked what she listens to in the morning, and what does this reveal about her?
4. Who were the Rahbani brothers, and what role did they play in shaping Lebanese music and theater?
5. When did Omar attend a live performance by Wadih El Safi, and what was his experience like?
6. Where do Charbel and Omar think Lebanese music connects with heritage, and why do they believe this connection is important?
7. Why does Charbel believe that modern Lebanese artists are continuing to grow the Lebanese music scene?
8. How does Omar describe the legacy of Sabah, and what impact did she have on Lebanese art and culture?

## Discussion Questions

١. مين هُوِّ الفَنّان اللِّبْناني المُفَضَّل عِنْدك، وشو اللي بيخلّي موسيقْتو تِلْمِسك على الصَّعيد الشَّخْصي؟

٢. كيف بِتْفكِّر إنّو الموسيقى بِبلدك بِتْأثِّر على الهَوية الثَّقافية تبعو؟

٣. شو الدَّوْر اللي برأيَك بِتِلعِبْو الموسيقى بِتِعْزيز الفخِر والوِحْدِة الوَطنية بِبلدك؟

٤. ليْش بِتْفكِّر إنّو موسيقى فيْروز إلا هالتَّأْثير الدّايِم، مِش بسّ بِلِبْنان بسّ بِكِلّ العالم العربي؟

٥. ويْن بِتْشوف تَأْثير الفنّانين الجْداد مِن بلدك عَ السّاحة الموسيقية العالمية، وكيف بيمثْلوا ثقافةْ بلدك؟

٦. لمّا بْتِسمع موسيقى تِقْليدية مِن بلدك، كيف بتْحِسّ إنّا بِتْوَصِّلك بِترُاث بلدك؟

٧. شو برأيَك مُسْتقْبل الموسيقى بِبلدك، ومين النُّجوم الصّاعْدين اللي لازِم نِنْتِبِهْلُن؟

٨. شو نوْع الموسيقى اللي بِتْحِبّ تِسِمْعا أكْتر شي؟ وكيف بِتْشوف إنّا بِتْأثِّر على حَياتك اليَوْمية أَوْ مزاجك؟

1. Who is your favorite Lebanese artist, and what makes their music resonate with you on a personal level?
2. How do you think the music of your country influences its cultural identity?
3. What role do you believe music plays in promoting national pride and unity in your country?
4. Why do you think Fairuz's music has such a lasting impact, both in Lebanon and across the Arab world?
5. Where do you see the influence of modern artists from your country in the global music scene, and how do they represent your country's culture?
6. When you listen to traditional music from your country, how does it make you feel connected to your heritage?
7. What do you think is the future of music in your country, and who are the rising stars that we should be paying attention to?
8. What type of music do you enjoy listening to the most? And how do you feel it influences your daily life or mood?

# شو تعْمِل بِالصّيْفية بِلِبْنان
## What to Do in the Summer in Lebanon

### In this episode...

Charbel and Farah share exciting ideas for making the most of summer in Lebanon. From enjoying the stunning beaches of Batroun and paragliding over Jounieh, to hiking around hidden gems like Chouwen Lake, they cover a variety of activities. They also highlight Lebanon's vibrant nightlife, summer festivals, and popular tourist spots like Byblos and Baalbek. Whether you're into adventure, culture, or simply relaxing by the sea, this episode is packed with great tips for an unforgettable Lebanese summer.

## Vocabulary

| | |
|---|---|
| ruins, historical sites | أثار |
| cedars, cedar trees | أرِز |
| tourist spots | أماكِن سِياحية |
| sea | بحِر |
| lake | بُحَيْرة |
| sunbathing | تِشْميس |
| temperature | حرارة |
| concert | حفْلة |
| night out | سهْرة |
| beach | شاطِئ (شْواطِئ) |
| hot | شوْب |
| summer | صَيْفية |
| weather | طقِس |
| cave | كهْف |
| restaurant | مطْعم (مطاع) |
| cave, grotto | مُغارة |
| adventure | مُغامرة |
| natural scenery | مناظِر طبيعية |
| festival | مهْرجان |
| hiking | هايْكينْغ |

## Transcript

**شَرْبِل:** مَرحبا جميعاً! اليوْم رح نِحْكي عن شي هيْك كِلُنا مُنْطرو: أكيد الصَّيْفية بِلِبنان. معْكُن شرْبِل ومعي اليوْم صديقْتي فرح. كيفِك يا فرح اليوْم؟

Charbel: Hello, everyone! Today we're going to talk about something that all of us look forward to: of course, the summer in Lebanon. I'm Charbel, and with me today is my friend Farah. How are you today, Farah?

**فرح:** أهْلا شرْبِل، أنا مْنيحة. مْحمّسِة كْتير نِحْكي عن خِطط الصَّيْف. لِبْنان فيو كْتير أشْيا حِلْوِة!

Farah: Hi, Charbel! I'm good. I'm really excited to talk about summer plans. Lebanon has so many beautiful things!

**شَرْبِل:** مِيّة بالْمِيّة، الطَّقس كْتير حلو كْتير بيساعِد. بالصَّيْفية بيوصل... بْتوصل الحرارة بيْن ٣٣ لـ٣٥ درْجِة، مِئَويِة أكيد عم نِحْكي. وما في مِتِل ما تْقضّي الصَّيْفية هوْن. يَعْني عنْجدّ فرح بِنْصح الكلّ. خبّرينا شْوَيّ إنتي شو بْتعِمْلي عادةً بالصَّيْفية بِلِبْنان؟

Charbel: Absolutely! The weather is amazing and really helps. In the summer, the temperature reaches between 33 to 35 degrees–we're talking Celsius, of course. There's nothing like spending summer here. Honestly, Farah, I recommend it to everyone. Tell us, what do you usually do during the summer in Lebanon?

**فرح:** بْحِبّ روح عَ البحر كْتير بالصَّيْفية. عنّا شْواطِئ بِلِبْنان كْتير حِلْوِة على السّاحِل. مِن المناطِق المُفضّلِة لإلي هِيِّ البترون. المايّ كْتير حِلْوة كْتير صافْية، البحر كْتير نْضيف، كْتير حِلو الواحد يِقْدر يِسْبح فيه. وأكيد بدّنا نِتْشمّس لأنّو بلا التّشْميس بالصَّيْفية وبِلِبْنان ما بيِمْشي الحال. وإنْتَ يا شرْبِل شو أكْتر شي بِتْحِبّ تعِمْلو؟

Farah: I love going to the beach a lot in the summer. We have some really beautiful beaches in Lebanon along the coast. One of my favorite areas is Batroun. The water is so nice and clear, and the sea is very clean—it's great to swim in it. And of course, we have to sunbathe because, without sunbathing, summer in Lebanon just doesn't feel right. What about you, Charbel, what do you love to do the most?

**شَرْبِل:** الصّراحة في كْتير قِصص، يَعْني بْتِحْتاري شو بدِّك تعِمْلي بِلِبْنان. أنا كمان بْحِبّ روح على البحِر أكيد. بسّ زْيادِة عن هيْك بْحِبّ إسْتكْشِف وأطّلِع على المناظِر الطبيعية

اللي عِنّا ياها بِلِبْنان. رحتي مرّة على بُحَيْرَةِ الشُّوّان؟ هيِّ يَعْني إذا بدِّك هيْك جَوْهرة مِخْفية. لازِم تِمْشي كْتير هيْك مِتِل هايكينْغ، بسّ المنظر بْيِسْتاهل! والبُحَيْرة بِتْجنِّن وعنْجدّ إذا بدِّك تعمْلي بيكْنيك وحتّى فيكي تِتْسبّحي سوبّر حِلو.

Charbel: Honestly, there are so many things to do that it's hard to choose. I also love going to the beach, of course. But in addition to that, I love exploring and hiking in the beautiful natural landscapes that we have in Lebanon. Have you ever been to Lake Chouwen? It's like a hidden gem. You have to hike a lot, but the view is totally worth it! The lake is gorgeous, and if you want, you can even have a picnic or swim there. It's really lovely.

فرح: سِمْعِت عنّا لهالْبُحَيْرة وحابّة زورا. هيِّ على اللِّيسْت تبعي وشكْلا مُغامرة كْتير حِلْوة رح تْكون. وبِالنِّسْبة للأنْشِطة، جرّبِت الـparagliding؟

Farah: I've heard about that lake and would love to visit it. It's definitely on my list, and it looks like a great adventure. Speaking of activities, have you ever tried paragliding?

شرْبِل: minimum! أكيد جرّبْتا. كْتير شي حِلو! هيْك إنّو تْطيري فوْق الخليج تبع جونْية تجْرِبة عنْجدّ ما بْتِتْكرّر وبِنْصح الكلّ يْجرّبا. شُعور هيْك بِالْحُرّية، المنْظر مِن فوْق بْياخُد العقِل والأدْرينالين يَعْني ما بْيِتْصدّق. إنْتي جرّبْتيا شي؟

Charbel: Of course, I've tried it! It's such a cool experience. Flying over the bay of Jounieh is something you don't get to do every day, and I totally recommend it. The feeling of freedom, the breathtaking view from above, and the adrenaline rush are just incredible. Have you tried it?

فرح: لا بعِد ما جرّبْتا بسّ كمان هَيْدي on the list. أكيد رح جرّبا. في كْتير أشْيا تانْية بْحِبّ أعْمِلا بِلِبْنان. بْحِبّ السّهر، بْحِبّ روح إسْهر كْتير! عنّا night clubs وbars كْتير حِلْوين. بْيَعمْلوا فيْن shows وبيضلّوا العالم سهْرانين لوجّ الضّوّ. إنْتَ شو المحلّ هيْك المفضّل عِنْدك بِتْحِبّ تْروح تِسْهر فيه؟

Farah: Not yet, but it's definitely on my list too. There are many other things I love doing in Lebanon as well. I enjoy going out at night, I love to party! We have some really great nightclubs and bars. They have shows, and people stay out until dawn. What's your favorite place to go out?

**شِرْبِل:** صراحة أنا بْحِبّ روح إسْهَر بسّ في محلّات هيْك أرْوَق شْوَيّ. بْحِبّ روح إسْهَر بِمار مْخايِل بِبيْروت مثلاً، أوْ جِمّيْزة. في pubs وهيْك بْتاخدي drink بْتِشربي بْتِتعرّفي بْتْشوفي عالم كْتير يَعْني كْتير قِصص هيْك، كْتير محلّات حِلْوة. وعِنْدا مثلاً إنْتي و عم تِسْهري إنْتي وعم تاخدي drink فيكي تاكْلي قِصص طَيْبة أوْ تاخدي سْناك. وبِالْحديث عن الأكِل يَعْني شو أكْتر طبق هيْك بِتْحبّيه وخاصّةً هيْك بِالصّيْف؟

**Charbel:** Honestly, I enjoy going out, but I prefer slightly quieter places. I like going out in Mar Mikhael in Beirut or Gemmayzeh. There are pubs where you can have a drink, meet people, and just enjoy a nice atmosphere. You can even grab a snack while having a drink. Speaking of food, what's your favorite dish, especially in the summer?

**فرح:** هَيْدا سُؤال صعْب. كْتير بْحِبّ الأكِل بِالصّيْفية وخْصوصةً الأكِل البحْري.مِتل السّمك المِشْوي عَ البحِر وطبْعاً ما نِنْسى الـsalads اللي بِتْكون fresh والمازة البارْدِة. وإنْتَ؟

**Farah:** That's a tough question. I love summer food, especially seafood. Grilled fish by the sea, and of course, we can't forget fresh salads and cold mezze. What about you?

**شِرْبِل:** أنا معْكي بِهَيْدا الشّي. يَعْني أكِل الـseafood أوْ أكِل البحْري ومع تبّولة هَيْدا الشّي مِن المُفضّل عِنْدي وخاصّةً بِالصّيْفية. ما بِدّنا كْتير نحْكي عن الأكِل لأنّو ما مْنِخْلص هيْك مِنخصّصْلو إذا بدّك مَوْضوع لحالو. بسّ عَ بالي أحْكي شْوَيّ عن كمان شو بيصير بِالصّيْفية بِلِبْنان، المهْرجانات الصّيْفية اللي بِتِلّي المناطِق بِلِبْنان. شي مرّة حْضِرْتي شي مهْرجان مُؤخّراً؟

**Charbel:** I totally agree with you. Seafood with tabbouleh is one of my favorites, especially in the summer. We could talk about food for hours, so we should probably dedicate a whole topic to that! But I also want to talk a bit about the summer festivals in Lebanon. Have you been to any festivals recently?

**فرح:** أكيد. هَيْديك السّنة رِحِت على مهْرجان بجْبيْل بيْبلوس، مهْرجان بيْبلوس الدُّوَلي. كان شي كْتير حِلو ورائِع! موسيقى حِلْوة، مكان كْتير حِلو، عَ البحِر الجّوّ كان رائِع. وإنْتَ شي مرّة حاضِر شي مهْرجان أوْ حفلات؟

**Farah:** Yes, last year I went to the Byblos International Festival. It was such a wonderful experience! Great music, an amazing location by the sea, and the atmosphere was perfect. Have you been to any festivals or concerts?

**شَرْبِل:** صراحة أنا رايح مِن زمان على مهرجان بْعَلْبك الدُّوَلي. هيْك مُشاهدِة أَوْ بْتِحْضِري هَيْدي الحفْلِة بين أثار بْعَلْبك تجْرِبِة هيْك بْتاخُد العقِل بِتْصيري غير محلّ.

**Charbel:** A long time ago, I went to the Baalbek International Festival. Watching a concert between the ancient ruins of Baalbek is an experience like no other.

**فرح:** شكْلو كان المهْرجان رائِع. لبْنان دايماً بْيِجْذُب كْتير مُغنّيِين وفِرق مشْهورة. حِلو نْشوف فِنّانين عالمِيّين عم يِجوا على لِبْنان ويْغنّوا بِبلدْنا. وزيادِة عن هيْك بِالْمهْرجانات، عِنْدك إنْتَ شي أماكِن سياحية مُفضّلِة بِتْحِبّ تْزورا؟

**Farah:** It sounds like it was a fantastic festival. Lebanon always attracts a lot of famous singers and bands. It's great to see international artists coming to Lebanon and performing here. Besides the festivals, do you have any favorite tourist spots you like to visit?

**شَرْبِل:** ليْكي صراحة lately البتْرون عم بِتْكون booming بِلِبْنان، بسّ ما بدْنا نِنْسى بيْبْلوس (جْبيْل)، أكيد واحْدِة مِن المُفضّلِة عِنْدي. التّاريخ، السّوْق القديم، المينا، combination رَوْعة. وفي عِنْدك بْعَلْبك كمان لازِم تِنْشاف بأثارا الرّومانية القديمة، هيْك شي ما بْيِنْوَصف. وإنْتي شو رأْيِك؟

**Charbel:** Recently, Batroun has been booming in Lebanon, but we also can't forget Byblos (Jebeil). It's definitely one of my favorites. The history, the old souk, the port—it's a beautiful combination. And you have Baalbek as well, which must be seen with its ancient Roman ruins; something like that can't be described. What do you think?

**فرح:** أكيد. كْتير بْحِبّ زور مْغارة جْعيتا، كيف هالكّهْف مْحافظ بعْدو على شكْلو الرّائِع. بِتْحِسّ كأنّك فتِت على عالم تاني. وكمان هيْك شي رِحْلِة للأرْز دايماً بالصّيْفية خْصوصاً وبِهالطقِس الشّوْب، بيكون كْتير طقِس شوْب، بْتطْلع هيْك بِتْبَورِد بالأرز.

**Farah:** Definitely! I love visiting Jeita Grotto, that incredible cave that still maintains its stunning beauty. It feels like entering another world. And I always enjoy a trip to the Cedars in the summer, especially when it's so hot down here—you go up there, and it's much cooler.

**شَرْبِل:** أكيد. وليْكِي ما... عَ طول ما بدُّنا نِنْسى الأكِل الطَّيِّب اللي فيكي تِسْتِمْتِعي فيه بهالْبَلد وإنْتي وعم تِبرِمي وتْشوفي الأماكِن الحِلْوة مِن بحرٍ، مِن جبل، مِن الـactiviteis اللي بْتِنْعمل. عنْجدّ لِبْنان بلد كْتير حِلو وخاصّةً بالصّيْف كْتير بيسلّي.

Charbel: Absolutely. And we can't forget all the delicious food you can enjoy while exploring these beautiful places—whether it's the beach, the mountains, or all the activities you can do. Lebanon is truly amazing, especially in the summer when it's so lively.

**فرح:** صحّ. ميّة بالْميّة. شُكْراً لمُشارَكْتِك وتجْرِبْتِك يا شرْبِل، وشُكْراً لكلّ المُسْتمعين. وأكيد مُنْتمنّى إنّكُن تْكونوا سْتفدْتوا مِن حديثْنا وحْصِلْتوا على أفْكار حِلْوة لصَيْفيِتْكُن بلِبْنان.

Farah: Definitely. 100%. Thanks for sharing your experiences, Charbel, and thanks to all our listeners. We hope you got some great ideas for your summer in Lebanon!

**شَرْبِل:** ميرْسي لإلِك فرح وعنْجدّ هيْك شوّقْتينا وشوّقْتي اللي عم يِسْمعْنا عنْجدّ يِجي يْزورْنا بلِبْنان. يَلّا انْشالله مُنْلْتِقي بالْمرّة اللي جاية بمَوْضوع جْديد ولَوَقْتا نُبْسطوا وسْتِمْتعوا بالصّيْفية وسْتفيدوا مِن كلّ شي بلِبْنان.

Charbel: Thanks to you, Farah, and honestly, you've made me and everyone listening excited to visit Lebanon. Hopefully, we'll meet again next time with a new topic. Until then, enjoy your summer and make the most of everything Lebanon has to offer!

## Comprehension Questions

١. شو هُوّ مَوْضوع الحلْقة اللي حِكْيوا عنّو شرْبِل وفرح؟

٢. شو هِيِّ الأنْشِطة اللي بِتْحِبّ فرح تعْمِلا بالصّيْفية بِلِبْنان؟

٣. وِيْن بْحِبّ شرْبِل يْروح لَيِسْتكْشِف المناظِر الطّبيعية؟

٤. شو هِيِّ الأنْشِطة الرِّياضية اللي حِكْيوا عنّا شرْبِل وفرح؟

٥. شو هِيِّ الأنْشِطة اللّيْلية اللي بِتْحِبّ فرح تعْمِلا بالصّيْفية؟

٦. شو هُوّ المكان المُفضّل عِنْد شرْبِل للسّهر؟

٧. شو هِيِّ الأكْلات اللي بيحِبّوا شرْبِل وفرح يِسْتمِتعوا فِيا بالصّيْفية؟

٨. شو هِيِّ المهْرجانات الصّيْفية اللي حُضْرِتا فرح وشرْبِل؟

1. What is the topic of the episode that Charbel and Farah discussed?
2. What activities does Farah like to do in the summer in Lebanon?
3. Where does Charbel like to go to explore natural landscapes?
4. What sports activities did Charbel and Farah mention?
5. What nightlife activities does Farah enjoy in the summer?
6. What is Charbel's favorite place to go out at night?
7. What are the summer foods that Charbel and Farah enjoy?
8. What summer festivals have Farah and Charbel attended?

## Discussion Questions

١. شو هِيّ الأنْشِطة اللي بِتْحِبّ تعْمِلا بالصَّيْفية بِبلدك؟

٢. كيف بِتْقضّي يوْم مِثالي بالصَّيْفية؟

٣. شو هِيّ محلّاتك المُفضّلة للإسْتِجْمام بالصَّيْفية؟

٤. كيف بِتْشوف تأْثير المهْرجانات الصَّيْفية على السِّياحة؟

٥. شو هِيّ الأكْلات المُفضّلة عِنْدك بالصَّيْفية؟

٦. عِنْدك ذِكْرَيات خاصّةً عن الأنْشِطة الصَّيْفية مع الأصْدِقاء أوْ العَيْلةِ؟

٧. كيف بِتْشجّع الأجانِب يْزوروا بلدك بالصَّيْفية؟

٨. شو هِيّ الأنْشِطة الرِّياضية اللي بِتْحِبّ تْجرِّبا بالصَّيْفية وليْش؟

1. What activities do you like to do in the summer in your country?
2. How do you spend an ideal summer day?
3. What are your favorite places to relax in the summer?
4. How do you see the impact of summer festivals on tourism?
5. What are your favorite summer foods?
6. Do you have special memories of summer activities with friends or family?
7. How do you encourage foreigners to visit your country in the summer?
8. What sports activities would you like to try in the summer and why?

# ذِكْرَيات حِلْوة ومُضْحِكة مِن المدْرسة

## Sweet and Funny School Memories

### In this episode...

Charbel and Omar take a fun trip down memory lane as they share amusing and heartwarming school memories. From forgotten lines during school plays to mischievous science experiments gone wrong, they recall the moments that made their school days so memorable. They also reminisce about field trips, schoolyard games, and the friendships they built along the way. Join them for a lighthearted conversation full of laughter and nostalgia about the unforgettable experiences of growing up in Lebanon.

## Vocabulary

| | |
|---|---|
| to remember | تْذكّر (يِتْذكّر) |
| memory | ذِكْرى (ذِكْرَيات) |
| school trip | رِحْلِة مدْرسية |
| sports | رِياضة |
| courtyard, playground | ساحة |
| guy, young man; (plural) young people, youth | شابّ (شباب) |
| friend | صاحِب (أصْحاب) |
| class, classroom | صفّ |
| to laugh | ضحِك (يِضْحك) |
| arts | فُنون |
| you know, look, hey | ليْك |
| unknown | مجْهول |
| school | مدْرِسة |
| principal | مُدير |
| play, theater performance | مسْرحية |
| teacher | مْعلِّم |
| playground, sports field | ملْعب |
| embarrassing moment | مَوْقف مُحْرِج |
| script; text | نصّ |
| homework | واجِب |

## Transcript

**شربِل:** مرْحبا يا جماعة! اليوْم مَوْضوعْنا هيْك شْوَيّ حِلو. رح نِحْكي عن ذِكْرَيات المدْرسِة اللي كِنّا هيْك نِتْذكّرا ونِضْحك وكْتير نِتْبْسم. أنا شرْبِل ومعي اليوْم رْفيقي عُمر. كيفك يا عُمر؟

**Charbel:** Hello, everyone! Today, our topic is a bit light-hearted. We're going to talk about school memories that we remember and laugh at, things that make us smile. I'm Charbel, and with me today is my friend Omar. How are you, Omar?

**عُمر:** هاي شرْبِل. الحمْدِلله. كيفك إنْتَ؟

**Omar:** Hi Charbel. Thank God, I'm good. How about you?

**شربِل:** تمام تمام. ليْك عُمر هيْك بسّ نِحْكي عن المدْرسِة مْنِتْذكّر كْتير قُصص. المدْرسِة عنْجدّ كانِت مِلْيانِة ذِكْرَيات وفي كْتير قِصص حِلْوِة، في كْتير قِصص بِتْضحّك. بْتِتْذكّر يا عُمر أوّل مرّة كان ...أوْ أوّل يوْم إلك بالمدْرسِة شي؟

**Charbel:** I'm great, great. You know, Omar, when we talk about school, we remember a lot of stories. School was really full of memories, with many funny and sweet stories. Do you remember your first day at school, Omar?

**عُمر:** أوف يا شرْبِل أكيد بِتْذكّر! كِنت كْتير مِتْوَتّر ومتْحمّس بِذات الوَقِت. كان بِقلْبي في خوْف مِن المجْهول. بسّ بِسرْعة صار عِنّدي كْتير أصْحاب. بْتِذكّر مرّة نْسيت الواجِب تبعولي بالْبيْت وكان الْمْعلِّم عِنّا كْتير قاسي وصارِم. ضلّيْت خايِف كِلّ الحِصّة إنّو يْقاصِصْني. بسّ والله بالنِّهايِة عطاني فِرْصة تانْية.

**Omar:** Oh, Charbel, of course I remember! I was so nervous and excited at the same time. My heart was full of fear of the unknown. But quickly, I made a lot of friends. I remember one time I forgot my homework at home, and our teacher was really, really strict. I was scared the whole class that he would punish me. But in the end, he gave me a second chance.

**شربِل:** عنْجدّ يَعْني هالقُصص بِتْصير معْنا كِلّنا. خبِّرْنا شْوَيّ يا عُمر وَقْتا كِنت عم تْحضِّر لَيوْم المسْرحية بالْمْدْرسِة ونْسيت النّصّ تبعك.

**Charbel:** Honestly, we all go through those kinds of experiences. Tell us a little about that time you were preparing for the school play and forgot your lines.

**عُمر:** أيْه والله يا شرْبِل كان مَوْقف كْتير مُحْرِج. بْتِتْذَكَّر وَقْتا كِنت عم بِلْعب دوْر جَيْشي ونْسيت كِلّ الكلام، بطّل يجي شي على راسي. رْفيقي اللي كان عم بْيِلْعب دوْر الضّابِط جرّب يْساعِدْني بسّ طْلِعْنا عم نِضْحك أنا ويّاه قِدّام الكلّ. بسّ والله بِالنّهايِة الجُمْهور كِلّو صار يِضْحك معْنا.

Omar: Oh man, Charbel, that was such an embarrassing moment. I was playing the role of a soldier and forgot all my lines. Nothing was coming to mind. My friend, who was playing the officer, tried to help me, but we both ended up laughing in front of everyone. But in the end, the whole audience started laughing with us.

**شرْبِل:** وليْك في مِن اللّحْظات اللي بْتِضلّ بِالذّاكِرة. عِنْدي تجْرِبة بِالصّفّ وواحد مِن الشّباب مِن رِفْقاتْنا قرّر نْجرّب يَعْمُل شي ع طريقْتو يخْلُط مَوادّ بِطريقة غلط يَعْني. وفجْأة صار في دخّان بِالصّفّ وصِرْنا كِلّنا نِضْحك والإسْتاذ جنّ وخِرِف وفكّر معْقول يْصير شي بِالصّفّ. بسّ بِالآخِر تعلّمْنا إنّو لازِم ع طول نِلْتزِم بِالتّعْليمات وخاصّةً بهيْك حِصص.

Charbel: And you know, some moments just stay in your memory. I remember once during a science experiment, one of our classmates decided to mix some materials in his own way, but he did it wrong. Suddenly, there was smoke in the classroom, and we all started laughing while the teacher freaked out, thinking something serious might happen. But in the end, we learned that we should always follow the instructions, especially in such classes.

**عُمر:** مِيّة بِالمِيّة، وَقِت نْهارِتا الله ستر وما صار في حريقا. بسّ كانِت ع طول هيْك تجارِب العُلوم دايْماً كانِت مِلْيانة مُغامرات. ليْش ما بعْدك بْتِتْذكّر كيف كِنّا نِنْتِظر فِرْصة لنِهْرُب مِن الدّرْس ونِضْهر مِن الصّفّ لنِلْعب باسْكيت بِالسّاحة بِالمِلْعب؟ كِنّا نِسْتِغِلّ أيّ فِرْصة صْغيرة لنْروح ونِلْعب.

Omar: Absolutely, that day we were lucky nothing caught fire. But those science experiments were always full of adventures. Do you still remember how we used to look for any opportunity to sneak out of class and play basketball in the courtyard? We would seize any small chance to go and play.

**شَرْبِل:** أَيْه بْتِتْذَكَّر مَرّة كُنّا عَم نِلْعَب بَاسْكِيت وَالطَّابة ضَرَبِت بِوِجّ المُدِير بِالْغَلَط، وكُنّا خَايْفِين كْتِير إنّو يْقَاصِصْنا بَسّ بَدَل مَا يْعَصِّب تْضَحِّك وقَال إنّو كَان بْيِلْعَب كْتِير هُوِّ مْنِيح بَاسْكِيت وَقِت كَان صَبِي... وَقِت كَان شَابّ يَعْني يِلْعَب مَعْنا وَقْتا.

Charbel: Yeah, I remember once we were playing basketball, and the ball accidentally hit the principal in the face. We were so scared he would punish us, but instead of getting angry, he laughed and said he used to play basketball well when he was a young man, and he ended up playing with us that day.

**عُمَر:** أَيْه مَظْبوط. وعَ فِكْرة هَيْك هَلّأ بَسّ فَتَحْت المَوْضوع عَم بِتْذَكَّر كْتِير قُصَص صَارِت مَعْنا بِالمَدْرَسة كَانِت هَيْك عَنْجَدّ بِتْضَحِّك وأَوْقَات حِلْوة. يَعْني أَكْتَر شِي هَلّأ عَم بِتْذَكَّر كَمَان رِحْلَات المَدْرَسِية. إذَا بْتِتْذَكَّر، مَرّة رِحْنا عَلى مْغَارةٍ جْعِيتا وكَان في عَصْفور فَات بِقَلْب البَاص. وَقْتا صَارُوا كِلّ الطُّلّاب يْصَرْخوا ويِرْكُضوا ويْصِيروا يْجَرّبوا يِلْقَطوا، والمْعَلّمة ضَاعِت مَا عِرْفِت شو عِمْلِت. وبِالآخِر بْتِتْذَكَّر الشّوْفور؟ قِدِر يْطَلِّع العَصْفور وصِرْنا كِلّنا نْزِقّ ونِضْحَك.

Omar: That's right. And now that you've brought it up, I'm remembering so many stories from school that were really funny and full of good times. The thing I'm remembering most now is the school trips. If you remember, once we went to Jeita Grotto, and a bird flew into the bus. All the students started screaming and running around, trying to catch it, and the teacher was lost, not knowing what to do. In the end, I remember the driver managed to get the bird out, and we all clapped and laughed.

**شَرْبِل:** عَنْجَدّ هَوْل الرِّحْلات كَانِت كْتِير حِلْوة ومِلْيانة قِصَص ومُغَامَرات. بْتِتْذَكَّر لَمّا أَخَدونا عَلى البَحِر وكُلّنا قَرّرْنا هَيْك نِسْبَح حَتّى الإِسْتَاذ كَان عَم بِيرَاقِبْنا مِن بْعِيد، وكَان كْتِير خَايِف عْلَيْنا بَسّ بِذَات الوَقِت كَان مَبْسوط إنّو عَم يْشوفْنا عَم نِنْبُسَط صَرَاحة.

Charbel: Those trips were really fun and full of stories and adventures. You'll remember when they took us to the beach, and we all decided to swim. Even the teacher was watching us from afar, very worried about us, but at the same time, he was happy to see us enjoying ourselves.

**عُمَر:** أَيْه مَظْبوط، بَسّ هَلّأ عَم فَكِّر مَا بِحْسِدو عَ هَالْمَوْقِف، إنّو كَانِت مَسْؤُولِية وكَان عَم يْرَاقِب كِلّ هَالتَّلَامِيذ. وَالله يا شَرْبِل المَدْرَسة بِلِبْنان عَنْجَدّ مِلْيانة لَحْظَات حِلْوة وبِتْضَحِّك. كِلّ يوْم كَان في شِي جْدِيد نِتْعَلّمو ونِتْسَلّى فِيه، مِن حُصَص الرِّيَاضة

لحتّى دْروس الفُنون والموسيقى والمسرح. بْتذكّر مرّة رسمْنا على وْجوهْ بعْض كنّا بصفّ الفُنون والمِعلّمة ضِحْكِت وعيّطِت للمُدير وصاروا... يَعْني كانِت لحْظات عنجدّ ما بْتِنْتسا.

**Omar:** Yeah, that's true. But now that I think about it, I don't envy him for that responsibility—watching over all those students. Honestly, Charbel, school in Lebanon is really full of sweet and funny moments. Every day, there was something new to learn and enjoy, from PE classes to art, music, and theater lessons. I remember one time we were painting each other's faces in art class, and the teacher laughed and called the principal. Those were moments that really can't be forgotten.

**شرْبِل:** عُمر صحّ، المدْرسة مِش بسّ متِل ما قِلْنا هيْك محلّ للدِّراسة هيِّ إذا بدّك بْتعيش حَياة... يَعْني تِتعرّف وبْتعْمِل أصْحاب. وكلّ أصْحاب هلّأ اللي إنْتَ صُحْبي معُن هِنّي أصْحابك اللي كانوا معك بالْمدْرسة الأغْلبية يَعْني. وهيِّ هيْك محلّ لتْكون ذكْرِيّات حِلْوة ويْضلّوا بذاكِرْتك. عُمر بدّي قِلّك thank you عَ هالمُشاركة الحِلْوة وميرْسي عَ هالذِكْرَيات الخبرّتْنا عنّا. وميرْسي لكلّ المُسْتمِعين ومْنِتمنّا تْكونوا هيْك نْبسطّوا معْنا وضْحِكْتوا معنا بهالذِّكْرَيات. انْشالله مْنِلْتقي بمرّة جاية بمَوْضوع جْديد وخبرِيّات جْديدة مِن حَياتْنا بلِبْنان. لوَقْتا نْتِبْهوا عَ حالْكُن ونْبُسطوا.

**Charbel:** Omar, you're right. School isn't just a place for studying—it's a place where you live life. You make friends, and most of the friends you have now are those who were with you in school. It's a place for creating sweet memories that stay with you forever. Omar, I want to thank you for this wonderful conversation and for sharing these memories with us. And thanks to all our listeners; we hope you had fun and laughed with us while remembering these stories. We hope to meet again next time with a new topic and new stories from our life in Lebanon. Until then, take care and have fun.

**عُمر:** شرْبِل ميرْسي إلك ، وميرْسي لكِلّ المُسْتمِعين. مِنْشوفْكُن المرّة الجاية!

**Omar:** Thanks to you, Charbel, and thanks to all our listeners. See you all next time!

## Comprehension Questions

١. لَيْش كان عُمر مِتْوَتّر بِأوّل يوْم إلو بِالْمدْرسِة؟

٢. شو صار مع عُمر لمّا نِسي النّصّ تبعو بِيوْم المسْرحية بِالْمدْرسِة؟

٣. كيف شرْبِل ورِفْقاتو تْصرّفوا لمّا دخّن الصّفّ وَقِت درْس العُلوم؟

٤. شو صار لمّا كانوا شرْبِل ورِفْقاتو عم يِلْعبوا باسْكيت بِالسّاحة؟

٥. لَيْش المُدير ضِحِك بدل ما يْعصّب لمّا ضربتو الطّابِة؟

٦. شو صار خِلال الرِّحْلِة المدْرسية لِمغارةْ جْعيتا؟

٧. كيف كانِت ردّة فِعل الإسْتاذ لمّا قرّروا الطُّلّاب يِسْبحوا بِالْبحِر وَقِت الرِّحْلِة؟

٨. شو اللي صار بِصفّ الفُنون اللي خلّى المِعلْمِة تِضْحك وتْعَيِّط للْمُدير؟

1. Why was Omar nervous on his first day of school?
2. What happened to Omar when he forgot his lines on the day of the school play?
3. How did Charbel and his friends react when smoke filled the classroom during science class?
4. What happened when Charbel and his friends were playing basketball in the playground?
5. Why did the principal laugh instead of getting angry when the ball hit him?
6. What happened during the school trip to Jeita Grotto?
7. How did the teacher react when the students decided to swim during the trip to the beach?
8. What happened in the art class that made the teacher laugh and call the principal?

## Discussion Questions

١. شو هِيِّ أكْتر ذِكْرى مُضْحِكة أَوْ مُحْرِجة بْتِتْذكّرا مِن إيّام المدْرسة؟

٢. كيف كانِت تجْرِبْتك بِأوّل يوْم إلَك بالْمدْرسة؟ كِنت مِتْوَتِّر أَوْ مِتْحمِّس؟

٣. شو كانِت المادّة المُفضّلة عِنْدك بالْمدْرسة؟ ليْش؟

٤. كيف كانِت رِحْلات المدْرسة بِبلدك؟ عِنْدك ذِكْرى مْميِّزة مِنّا؟

٥. كيف كِنت تِتْصرّف لمّا تِنْسى الواجِب أَوْ تِكْسُر قَواعِد المدْرسة؟

٦. شو كانِت رِدّةْ فِعْلك لمّا كان يْصير شي مُضْحِك أَوْ مُحْرِج بصفّك؟

٧. كيف كان أُسْلوب مْعلّمينك بالتّعامُل مع المَواقِف الغريبة أَوْ المُضْحِكة بالصّفّ؟

٨. كيف بْتِعْتِقِد إنّو رح تْكون ذِكْرَيات الأطْفال بالْمدارِس اليوْم مُقارنةً بِذِكْرَياتك؟

1. What is the funniest or most embarrassing memory you remember from your school days?
2. How was your experience on your first day of school? Were you nervous or excited?
3. What was your favorite subject in school? Why?
4. How were the school trips in your country? Do you have a special memory from one of them?
5. How did you handle it when you forgot your homework or broke school rules?
6. How did you react when something funny or embarrassing happened in your class?
7. How did your teachers deal with strange or funny situations in the classroom?
8. How do you think children's school memories today will compare to your own memories?

# الهِوايات ووَسائل التَّرْفيهْ

## Hobbies and Entertainment

### In this episode...

Charbel and Farah discuss popular hobbies and leisure activities in Lebanon. From sports like Pilates and hiking in nature to enjoying local food festivals and music events, they explore how people unwind and stay active. They also touch on other beloved pastimes like reading, biking, and even fishing. Whether it's exploring the beautiful outdoors or enjoying a quiet coffee with friends, this episode offers great ideas on how to make the most of your free time in Lebanon. Tune in for some fun suggestions and inspiration for your next hobby!

## Vocabulary

| | |
|---|---|
| musical instrument | آلِة موسيقية |
| nature walks, hiking | المشي بِالطّبيعة |
| cycling | رُكوب البيسيكْلات |
| novel | رِوايِة |
| to make relax | ريّح (يْريح) |
| travel | سفر |
| food market | سوق الأكِل |
| waterfall | شِلّال |
| class | صفّ (صْفوف) |
| fishing | صيْد |
| hospitality | ضِيافِة |
| backgammon | طاوْلِة |
| nature | طبيعة |
| really | عنْجدّ |
| oud (a traditional stringed instrument) | عود |
| café | كافيْه |
| physical fitness | لِياقة بدنية |
| absolutely | مِيّة بِالْمِيّة |
| hobby | هِواية |
| means of entertainment | وَسائِل التّرْفيه |

## Transcript

**شرْبِل:** مَرْحبا يا جَماعة! اليوْم رح نِحْكي عن الهِوايات ووَسائِل التّرْفيهْ اللي بيحِبّا النّاس بِلِبْنان. أنا شرْبِل، ومعي رْفيقْتي فرح. كيفِك يا فرح؟

Charbel: Hello, everyone! Today we're going to talk about hobbies and entertainment that people in Lebanon enjoy. I'm Charbel, and with me is my friend Farah. How are you, Farah?

**فرح:** أهْلا شرْبِل! أنا مْنيحة، كيفك إنْتَ؟

Farah: Hi, Charbel! I'm good, how are you?

**شرْبِل:** أنا تمام الحمْدِلله. بِلِبْنان في كْتير هِوَيات ووَسائِل تِرْفيه بيحِبّ يَعِمْلُوَا النّاس. شو الهِوايات اللي بِتْحِبّي تعِمْليا يا فرح إنّتي؟

Charbel: I'm doing well, thank God. In Lebanon, there are a lot of hobbies and entertainment activities that people love to do. What hobbies do you enjoy, Farah?

**فرح:** شرْبِل أنا كْتير بْحِبّ الرّياضة خاصّةً إنّي إتْسجّل بـ gym. مثلاً أعْمُل صْفوف مِتِل الـpilates، مِتِل الـspinning. يَعْني الـpilates هيِّ عِبارة عن مِتِل stretching للْجِسِم، كْتير بِترْيِّح. وصفّ الـspinning هُوّ بيكون بيسيكْلات مْثبّت بالأرْض وبِتصير مع الموسيقى تِقْوى حركات الإجْران. فا هَيْدا الشّي كمان بسّ تْخلّص هالصّف بِتْحِسّ حالك هيْك إنْسان جْديد. فا هَيْدا الشّي كْتير مْهِمّ، وكْتير بْحِبّ المشي بالطّبيعة. وإنْتَ يا شرْبِل؟ شو هِوَاياتك؟

Farah: Charbel, I really love sports, especially signing up for a gym. For example, I take classes like Pilates and spinning. Pilates is like stretching for the body; it's really relaxing. And the spinning class involves cycling on stationary bikes and you pedal to the rhythm of the music, which strengthens the leg movements. After finishing the class, you feel like a new person. It's really important, and I also love walking in nature. What about you, Charbel? What are your hobbies?

**شرْبِل:** أنا بْحِبّ كْتير أقْرا خاصّةً روايات وكمان بْحِبّ السّفر وإكْتِشِف أماكِن جْديدة. بسّ أكيد ما في شي بيريِّح مِتِل هيْك قعْدِة مع الأصْحاب بِشي كافيهْ أوْ عم نِشْرب فِنْجان قهْوِة أوْ هيْك عم نِتْحدّث.

**Charbel:** I really love reading, especially novels, and I also love traveling and discovering new places. But nothing is as relaxing as hanging out with friends at a café, having a cup of coffee, or just chatting.

**فرح:** أكيد القهوة جزء كْتير مْهِمّ مِن ثقافتْنا بِلِبْنان. النّاس بيحِبّوا يِجْتِمْعوا بِالْقهاوي، يِحْكوا، يِتْسلّوا، يِلْعبوا طاوْلة. كمان عِنّا حُبّ كْتير لِلْموسيقى. بِتْلاقي كْتير ناس بْيِعِزْفوا على آلات موسيقى مِتل العود أَوْ بيحِبّوا حتّى يْغنّوا بِالْكاراوْكي.

**Farah:** Absolutely, coffee is a big part of our culture in Lebanon. People love gathering in coffee shops to talk, have fun, and play backgammon. We also have a great love for music. You'll find many people who play musical instruments like the oud, or even enjoy singing karaoke.

**شرْبِل:** مظْبوط والمهْرجانات الموسيقية بِلِبْنان مْتلّاية الدِّني، كْتير مشْهورة. في مهْرجانات بِالصّيْف بْتجْمع ناس مِن كِلّ أنْحاء البلد لَيِسْتمْتْعوا بِالْموسيقى والأجْواء الحِلْوة. وكمان ما نِنْسى الـevents اللي بْتِنْعمل كِرْمال الأكِل مِتل سوق الأكِل يَلّي هِيِّ بْيِقْطع على كذا مِنْطْقة بِلِبْنان. شي مرّة رِحْتي على واحْدِة مِن هالـevents؟

**Charbel:** That's right, and music festivals in Lebanon are everywhere and very popular. There are summer festivals that bring together people from all over the country to enjoy the music and the great atmosphere. And let's not forget the food events like the 'Food Market,' which takes place in various areas across Lebanon. Have you ever been to one of these events?

**فرح:** أكيد أنا بِنْطرو مُناطرة لسوق الأكِل كِلّ سِنة. وأكيد بْروح مِن مِنْطْقة لمِنْطْقة لأنّو بْتِخْتِلِف أنْواع الطّبْخ بِلِبْنان، وهَيْدا عنْجدّ شي كْتير حِلو. يَعْني بِتْصير تْشوفوا مِن كِلّ المناطِق بِلِبْنان بيروحوا على هالْمِنْطقة تَيْجرّبوا شي جْديد. والشّعْب اللّبْناني كْتير بيحِبّ هَيْدي الشّغْلات، يْجرّب شي جْديد، يَعْمُل experience جْديدة. وكْتير عنْجدّ حِلو سوق الأكِل بِلِبْنان.

**Farah:** Of course! I look forward to the food market every year. I go from one region to another because the types of cooking differ across Lebanon, and that's really wonderful. You see people from all over Lebanon coming to these events to try something new. Lebanese people love trying new things and having new experiences. The food market in Lebanon is really amazing.

**شَرْبِل:** عَنْجَدّ مِيّة بِالْمِيّة! ومِش بَسّ إنّو عم مْنِحْكي عن الأكل الطّبْخ جزْء كْبير مِن ثقافِتْنا. يَعْني كِلّ مِنْطْقة بِلِبْنان عِنْدا أكْلتا الخاصّة المْميّزة. ومِتِل ما قِلْتي بِيحِبّوا يْجرّبوا ويِبْتِكِروا قُصص جْديدة. وكمان في هواية مِنْتِشْرة هِيّ المشي بِالطّبيعة والـ hiking يَعْني معْروفة بِلِبْنان. لِبْنان مِلْيان بْمناطِق حِلْوة لْتِمْشي فِيا وتِسْتِكْشْفي الطّبيعة.

Charbel: Absolutely, 100%! And not only are we talking about food, but cooking is also a big part of our culture. Every region in Lebanon has its own special, unique dishes. And as you said, people love to try and create new things. Another popular hobby is hiking, which is well-known in Lebanon. Lebanon is full of beautiful areas where you can walk and explore nature.

**فرح:** صحّ. المشي بِالطّبيعة بِيريّح الأعْصاب وبْيَعْطيك هيْك mood حلو. بْتِسْتَمْتِع بِهالْمناظِر الطّبيعية. بْتِذكّر مرّة رِحْنا على شلالات جِزّين كانت عَنْجدّ مِشْوار كْتير حِلو. وكِلّنا نْبسطْنا بِالْهَوى الحِلو بِالْهَوى النّقي يَعْني برّات بَيْروت والمناظِر عنْجدّ الكْتير حِلْوة.

Farah: Right. Walking in nature is so relaxing for the nerves and puts you in a good mood. You get to enjoy these natural landscapes. I remember once we went to the Jezzine waterfalls, and it was truly a wonderful trip. And we all enjoyed the nice weather, the fresh air, I mean outside of Beirut, and the views were truly very beautiful.

**شَرْبِل:** عَنْجدّ بْتْخيّل المِشْوار كان بعقّد. وكمان في قِصص مِن الهوايات اللي عم تِنْتِشِر وكْتير بْحِبّزا بِلِبْنان هِيّ رُكوب البيسيكْلات. في كْتير ناس بيحِبّوا يِبْرموا بِالطّبيعة والمناطِق بالضّيع يَعْني مِن خْلال البيسيكْلات. وحتّى بِبَيْروت هَيْدا شي بْيَعْطيكي هيْك حُرّية وبْتِعْمْلي حركة وكمان لِياقة بدنية.

Charbel: I can imagine the trip was amazing. Another hobby that's becoming popular and that I really like in Lebanon is cycling. A lot of people enjoy biking through nature and the villages. Even in Beirut, it gives you a sense of freedom and helps you stay active and fit.

**فرح:** وما نِنْسى كمان في هوايِةْ الصَّيْد. كْتير مِن النّاس بِلِبْنان بيحِبّوا يْروحوا على البَحِر ويْتْصيّدوا، شي بيريِّح الأعْصاب ويْبَعْطيك هيْك فُرْصة إنّك تِهْرُب مِن ضَجّةْ بَيْروت يَعْني المدينِة. إنْتَ جرّبِت الصَّيْد مِن قبل؟

**Farah:** And let's not forget fishing. Many people in Lebanon love going to the sea to fish; it's a great way to relax and escape the noise of the city. Have you ever tried fishing?

**شرْبِل:** أيْه جرّبْتو كذا مرّة هيْك تجْرُبِة مُمْتِعة وعنْجَدّ هيْك بِتريِّح الأعْصاب. بسّ صراحة أنا أكْتر شي بْحِبّ قَضّي وَقْتي بِالقْرايِة يَعْني وحتّى شوف movies. هَيْدي هيِّ هيْك طريقْتي لإسْترْخي.

**Charbel:** Yes, I've tried it a few times, and it was a really enjoyable and relaxing experience. But honestly, I prefer spending my time reading and watching movies. That's my way of unwinding.

**فرح:** حِلو! كِلّ واحد عِنْدو طريقة يِسْتَمْتِع فِيا بِوَقْتو. والهوايات بِتْخَلّينا نِكْتِشِف أشْيا جْديدِة مِن شخْصيّتْنا ونِتْعلّم مهارات جْديدِة. شو آخِر كْتاب قْريتو؟

**Farah:** That's nice! Everyone has their own way to enjoy their time. Hobbies help us discover new things about ourselves and learn new skills. What was the last book you read?

**شرْبِل:** آخِر كْتاب صراحة قْريتو كان رواية تاريخية عن الحضارة الفينيقية. كان كْتاب مُمْتِع ومِلْيان معْلومات هيْك مُثيرة. وفرح أنا سْمِعِت عنّك إنّك بِتْحِبّي تِحْضُري movies كمان. خبّرينا شْوَيّ عن آخِر movie حْضُرْتي.

**Charbel:** The last book I read was a historical novel about Phoenician civilization. It was an interesting book, full of fascinating information. And Farah, I've heard that you also love watching movies. Tell us a bit about the last movie you watched.

**فرح:** صراحة أنا بْحِبّ أحْضُر movies لِبْنانية. بِتْخلّيني إسْتَمْتِع. يَعْني بْصير نبِّش عْلَيْن هِنّي مِنُّن كْتار بسّ بْحِبّ نبِّش عْلَيْن تِإحْضُرُن. مثلاً آخِر movie حْضُرْتو هُوّ لِبْناني أكيد. ولْمُمثِّل كْتير مشْهور إسْمو وسام صبّاغ إسْمو Welcome to Lebanon. وعنْجَدّ هيْك بيفرْجي واقِعْنا بِلِبْنان، بيفرْجي الأهِل بِلِبْنان الشَّعْب كيف بِيِسْتَقْبِل العالم مِن برّا والضّيافِة. يَعْني عنْجَدّ أنا بْنِصح كِلّ حدا يِحْضُروا.

**Farah:** Honestly, I love watching Lebanese movies. They give me a lot of enjoyment. I search for them, even though there aren't many, but I love finding and watching them. The last movie I watched was Lebanese, of course, and starred a very famous actor named Wissam Sabbagh. The movie is called "Welcome to Lebanon," and it really shows the reality of life in Lebanon, how the people welcome those from abroad, and our hospitality. I honestly recommend everyone to watch it.

**شرْبِل:** أكيد وليْكي الأفْلام والـmovies بْتاخِدْنا هيْك لعالم تاني وبِتْخلّينا نْعيش مُغامرات مِخْتِلْفة. طيِّب شو رأْيك نْشارك شْويّ هيْك اللي عم يِسْمعونا بِشْويّةْ نصايح لَيْنقّوا هِواياتُن.

**Charbel:** Absolutely, movies take us to another world and let us experience different adventures. So, what do you say we share some advice with our listeners on how to choose their hobbies?

**فرح:** أكيد النّصيحة الأولى اللي أنا عنْجدّ بْنصحا لكِلّ حدا إنّو عنْجدّ جرّبوا شي جْديد وما تْخافوا مِن الفشل. كِلّ تجْرِبة جْديدة بِتْعلّمك شي جْديد. والنّصيحة التّانْية هِيّ إنّو تِخْتاروا الهِوايِة اللي عنْجدّ إنْتو بِتْحِبُّوا وبْتِسْتِمْتعوا فِيا. مِش لأنّو الغيْر بيحِبّا أوْ بْيَعْمِلا.

**Farah:** Sure! The first piece of advice I would give is to try something new and not be afraid of failure. Every new experience teaches you something new. The second piece of advice is to choose a hobby that you genuinely love and enjoy, not just because others like it or do it.

**شرْبِل:** مِيّة بالْمِيّة وأنا بَعْطيْن نصيحة هيْك صْغيرِةْ إنّو يْخصِّصوا وَقِت لِلْهِواية. لأنّو الهِوايات صراحة بِتْساعِد هيْك تعمِلْي تَوازُن بيْن الحَياةْ بيْن الشِّغِل والشّخْصِية وأكيد بِتْريّحِك. فرح بِدّي قلّك thank you على هالْحديث الحِلو وميرْسِي لكِلّ اللي عم يِسْمعنا. انْشالله نِلْتِقي مرّة الجاية كمان جْديد وخبْرية جْديدِة مِن حَياتْنا مِن لِبْنان. لَوَقْتا خلّوا بالْكُن مِن حالْكُن ونْبُسْطوا وسْتِمْتعوا بِحَياتْكُن.

**Charbel:** 100% agreed. I'd also add a small tip to make time for your hobby. Hobbies help create a balance between work and personal life, and they definitely help you relax. Farah, thank you for this great conversation, and thanks to everyone who's listening. Hopefully, we'll meet again next time with a new topic and a new story from our lives in Lebanon. Until then, take care of yourselves and enjoy your lives.

**فرح:** شُكْراً إلك يا شرْبِل، وشُكْراً لكِلّ المُسْتمِعين.

**Farah:** Thank you, Charbel, and thanks to all the listeners.

## Comprehension Questions

١. شو هِيِّ الهِوايات اللي بِتْحِبّ تعْمِلا فرح وكيف وَصفِت تجْرِبتا معا؟

٢. شو هِيِّ الهِوايات المُفضّلة عِنْد شرْبِل وكيف بِتْساعْدو يِرْتاح؟

٣. كيف بْتعْتِبِر القهْوة جِزْء مْهِمّ مِن الثّقافة اللّبْنانية حسب فرح؟

٤. شو هِيِّ الأنْشِطة الموسيقية والمهْرجانات الشّعْبية اللي ذكرا شرْبِل وفرح؟

٥. شو أهمِيةْ الأسْواقْ مِتِل "سوق الأكل" بِثقافةْ لِبْنان؟

٦. كيف وَصفوا شرْبِل وفرح تجْرِبةْ الـ hiking والإسْتِمْتاع بالطّبيعة بِلِبْنان؟

٧. شو هِيِّ الهِوايةِ الجْديدةِ اللي عم تِنْتِشِر بِلِبْنان وذكرا شرْبِل؟

٨. كيف بْشوفوا شرْبِل وفرح قيمةْ تجْرِبةْ هِواياتْ جْديدة وتخْصيص وَقِت إلا؟

1. What hobbies does Farah enjoy, and how does she describe her experience with them?
2. What are Charbel's favorite hobbies, and how do they help him relax?
3. How is coffee a significant part of Lebanese culture, according to Farah?
4. What are some of the popular musical activities and festivals mentioned by Charbel and Farah?
5. What is the importance of food markets like "Souk el Akel" in Lebanese culture?
6. How do Charbel and Farah describe the experience of hiking and enjoying nature in Lebanon?
7. What new hobby is becoming popular in Lebanon that Charbel mentions?
8. How do Charbel and Farah see the value of trying new hobbies and dedicating time to them?

## Discussion Questions

1. شو هِيِّ الهِوايات اللي بِتْحِبّ تَعْمِلا وكيف بِتْساعْدك تِرْتاح؟

2. قَدّيْش مْهِمّ تْجرِّب أَنْشِطة وهِوايات جْديدة بْحَياتك؟

3. شو دوْر التَّواصُل مع الأَصْحاب بِهِواياتك؟

4. كيف بِتْوازِن بيْن هِواياتك وبيْن شِغْلك أَوْ مسْؤوليّاتك اليَوْمية؟

5. شو هِيِّ الهِوايات أَوْ الأَنْشِطة الشّعْبية بِبلدك؟

6. كيف بِتْشوف العلاقة بيْن الهِوايات والنّمو الشّخْصي؟

7. بِتْحِبّ الهِوايات الدّاخْلِية وَلّا الخارْجية؟ وليْش؟

8. كيف بْتِكْتِشف هِوايات أَوْ أَنْشِطة جْديدة لتْجرِّبا؟

1. What hobbies do you enjoy, and how do they help you relax?
2. How important is it to try new activities and hobbies in your life?
3. What role does socializing with friends play in your hobbies?
4. How do you balance your hobbies with your work or daily responsibilities?
5. What hobbies or activities are popular in your country?
6. How do you see the relationship between hobbies and personal growth?
7. Do you prefer indoor or outdoor hobbies? Why?
8. How do you discover new hobbies or activities to try?

# التّاكْسيّات الجماعية بِبَيْروت
## Shared Taxis in Beirut

## In this episode...

Charbel and Omar explore a unique aspect of transportation in Beirut: shared taxis, known locally as "service." They explain how these collective taxis work, providing an affordable and social way to get around the city. The duo shares funny and memorable experiences from their rides, touching on how this system has become an integral part of daily life in Beirut. Whether you're a local or visiting the city, riding in a "service" is more than just a trip—it's a glimpse into the heart of Beirut's culture. Tune in for tips and stories about navigating the city with this iconic mode of transport!

## Vocabulary

| | |
|---|---|
| economic crisis | أَزْمِة إِقْتِصادية |
| sometimes | أَوْقات |
| gasoline, petrol | بَنْزين |
| I agree with you | بْوافْقك بِالرّأي |
| collective taxi | تاكْسي جماعي |
| transportation | تنقُّل |
| line, route [for buses] | خطّ (خْطوط) |
| passengers | راكِب (ركّاب) |
| symbol | رمْز (رُموز) |
| to fill a gap | سدّ (يْسِدّ) فراغ |
| smooth, easy | سلِس |
| "service" [colloquial term for a collective taxi] | سيرْڤيس |
| driver | شوْفور (شوْفورية) |
| honestly | صراحة |
| traffic jam | عجْقة |
| expensive | غالي |
| trip, journey | مِشْوار (مشاوير) |
| trend, fashion | موْضة |
| transportation system | نِظام نقِل |
| license plate | نمْرة |

# Transcript

**شربِل:** مَرحبا! اليوْم رح نِحْكي عن جزِء مُميّز مِن وَسائِل النّقِل بِبَيْروت: التّاكْسِيّات الجماعية، أوْ مِتِل ما مِنسمِّيا هوْن "السّيرْفيس". أنا شرْبِل، ومعي صديقي عُمر. كيفك يا عُمر؟

Charbel: Hello! Today we're going to talk about a unique part of transportation in Beirut: shared taxis, or as we call them here, "service." I'm Charbel, and with me is my friend Omar. How are you, Omar?

**عُمر:** أهْلا شرْبِل! حمْدِلله، كيفك إنْتَ؟

Omar: Hello Charbel! Thank God, how are you?

**شرْبِل:** مْنيح، ميرْسي. التّاكْسِيّات الجماعية جزِء مْهِمّ مِن حَياتْنا بِبَيْروت. عنّا بِبَيْروت باصات وتاكْسِيّات عادية، بِسّ ما عِنّا تْرانات. ومع هيْك، التّاكْسِيّات الجماعية طريقة مُميّزة ورْخيصة للتّنقُّل بالْمدينة.

Charbel: I'm good, thank you. Shared taxis are an important part of our life in Beirut. We have buses and regular taxis in Beirut, but we don't have trains. However, shared taxis are a unique and cheap way to get around the city.

**عُمر:** مظْبوط. التّاكْسِيّات الجماعية بْتِشْتِغِل بِهالطّريقة: بْتوقف عالطّريق وبِتْقشِّر بالْإيد لتاكْسي بِنُمْرة حمْراء. الشّوْفور بِيِسْألك لوَيْن رايِح؟ وإذا كِنت على طريقو، بْياخْدك. مُمْكِن ترْكب مع ناس تانْيين رايْحين بِنفْس الإتِّجاه، والرِّحْلة أرْخص لأنّو هيْك فِكِرْتا وأوْقات ما بْياخْدك لأنّو مثلاً إنْتَ رايِح لمحلّ بْعيد و ما معو ركّاب.

Omar: That's right. Shared taxis work like this: you stand on the road and wave to a taxi with a red license plate. The driver asks you where you're going, and if it's on his route, he'll take you. You might ride with other people going in the same direction, and the trip is cheaper because that's the idea. Sometimes he won't take you if you're going somewhere far or if he doesn't have any passengers.

**شرْبِل:** قبِل الأزْمة الإقْتِصادية، كان رُكوب السّيرْفيس كْتير رْخيص. المِشْوار كان يُكلِّف بيْن الألْفيْن لتْلات ألاف ليرة لِبْنانية. وكان سِعْر كْتير مْنيح للِّبْناني!

Charbel: Before the economic crisis, taking a "service" was very cheap. The fare was between 2,000 and 3,000 Lebanese pounds—a very good price for the Lebanese!

**عُمر:** صحيح، بسّ للأسف كْتير تْغيّر الوَضِع بعْد الأزْمِة. و حتّى خِلال أزْمِةْ البنْزين، كْتير مِن شوْفوريةْ السيّرْفيس كان عِنْدُن صُعوبِة بِتِعْباية سيّاراتُن بالبنْزين. صار الوَضِع صعب للّي بيسوقوا وللرّكّاب أسْعار المشاوير غِلْيِت، وأوْقات كان لازِم تُنْطُر وَقِت طَويل لْتْلاقي تاكْسي جماعي يْكون رايِح على طريقك.

Omar: That's true, but unfortunately, the situation has changed a lot since the crisis. Even during the gasoline crisis, many service drivers had difficulty filling up their cars with gas. The situation became tough for both drivers and passengers. Fares increased, and sometimes you had to wait a long time to find a shared taxi going your way.

**شرْبِل:** مع كلّ هالتّحدّيّات، التّاكْسيّات الجماعية بِقْيِت جِزء أساسي مِن نِظام النّقلِبِبَيْروت. وكمان، هِيِّ تجْرِبة إجْتماعية إذا بدّك فينا نْقولا! إنّو بْتِلْتِقي مع ناس مِن كلّ المِيْلات ومِن كلّ الطّوايِف ومِن كلّ المناطِق يَعْني شي هيْك experience حِلْوِة للّبْناني ويَعْني ما بْشوف أنا في بلد تاني فيو هَيْدا...هَيْدا النّوْع مِن النّقِل.

Charbel: Despite all these challenges, shared taxis remained an essential part of the transportation system in Beirut. And they're also a social experience if you think about it! You meet people from all walks of life, from all sects, and from all regions—it's a really nice experience for the Lebanese. I don't think there's another country that has this kind of transportation.

**عُمر:** صحّ شرْبِل! بْوافْقك بالرّأي، مع إنّو أوْقات هَيْدا الشّي مِش دايْماً مُريح. في أوْقات لازِم تُنْطُر كْتير لْتْلاقي سيرْفيس رايِح على طريقك وخاصّةً وَقِت العِجْقة يِمْكِن هَيْدا الشّي يْكون شْوَيّ مِزْعِج.

Omar: That's true, Charbel! I agree with you, even though sometimes it's not always comfortable. Sometimes, you have to wait a lot to find a service going your way, especially during traffic, which can be a bit annoying.

**شرْبِل:** صحّ! وأوْقات حتّى لَوْ لْقيت بيكون التّاكْسي مِلْيان. بِتْذكّر مرّة في شوْفور بدّو ياخِدْني بالقوّة مع إنّو السّيّارة كانِت مِلْيانة وكان في أرْبْعة قاعْدين وَرا، وبدّو يْقعِّدْني حدّ القاعِد قِدّام يَعْني! كان شي يَعْني مِش مظْبوط.

Charbel: Exactly! And sometimes, even when you find one, the taxi might be full. I remember once a driver tried to force me into the car even though it was full, with four people already sitting in the back, and he wanted to make me sit in front next to the other passenger! It was just not right.

**عُمر:** عنجدّ شي بيضحّك! وبقْدُر إتْخايَل لأنّو هَيْدا الشّي صار معي كمان. وعِندي قِصّة بِتْضحّك أكْتر كمان، مرّة راكِب وِصِل على طريقو على وِجِهْتو فتح الباب وبلّش يِرُكُض بلا ما يِدْفع للشّوْفور! إفا شو بدّك يَعْمِل الشّوْفور! بِيْتْرُك السِّيّارة وبْيِرُكُض وَرا وأنا ضلّيْت لَوَحْدي بالسّيّارة لَوَقِت طَويل، وصراحة هَيْدا الشّي صدمني.

Omar: That's really funny! I can imagine because this has happened to me too. And I have an even funnier story: once, a passenger got to his destination, opened the door, and started running without paying the driver! So, what did the driver do? He left the car and ran after him, and I was left alone in the car for a long time. Honestly, it shocked me.

**شرْبِل:** يَعْني قُصّة كْلاسيكية! وكمان، ما مْنِقْدِر نِنْسى إنّو كان في موْضة إنّو التّاكْسيّات الجماعية بِنقّو المرْسيْدس الموْديْل ألْف وتِسِعْمية وتمانين. بيسمُّوَا عنّا المرْسيْدس لفّ هيِّ E-كْلاس... E-كْلاس مِتيْن. وما بعْرف ليْه بيسمُّوَا مرسيْدس لفّ! برْكي كِرْمال الأضْوية جايين مبْرومين أوْ هيِّ معْقول بِتْلِفّ كْتير دوْلابا، لأنّو بِتْذكّر السِّيّارة كانِت كْتير بِتْلِفّ. وصراحة السِّيّارة هيْك صارِت رمْز لبَيْروت خاصّةً.

Charbel: That's a classic story! Also, we can't forget that there used to be a trend where shared taxis chose Mercedes models from 1980. We call them Mercedes 'Laff' here–they're E-Class 200. I don't know why they call them Mercedes 'Laff'! Maybe because the lights are rounded or it turns a lot, because I remember the car used to turn a lot [i.e., had a tight turn radius]. Honestly, this car has become a symbol of Beirut especially.

**عُمر:** مظْبوط شرْبِل! بسّ ما بيسمُّوَا مرسيْدس، عنّا بِبَيْروت بيسمُّوا "مارْسادِس"! وهيِّ صارِت جزِء مِن حَياتْنا اليَوْمية، ومع الوَقِت صارِت كمان تُعْتبر مِن التّرُاث عنّا بِبَيْروت. الباصات العامّة موْجودة رُغْم إنّو مِنّا كْتير شعْبية وما كْتير بيحبّوه العالم. بسّ هيِّ كمان وَسيلِة رْخيصة للتّنقُّل، عِنْدا خْطوط محْدودة وما بِتْروح وين مكان. بسّ كمان مُمْكِن تْكون إقْتِصادية وبِتْوفِّر، بسّ صراحة مِش سِلْسِة مِتِلالسّيرْڤيس.

Omar: That's true, Charbel! But they don't just call it "Mercedes" in Beirut; they call it "Marsadis!" And it's become a part of our daily life, and over time, it's also become a part of Beirut's heritage. Public buses exist, although they're not very popular and people don't like them much. But they're also a cheap way to get around, with limited routes that don't go everywhere. But they can be economical and save money, though honestly, they're not as convenient as the service.

**شَرْبِل:** صحّ عُمر، الباصات إلا طابعا الخاصّ وبتْغطّي كْتير مِن المدينة وحتّى برّات بَيْروت. بسّ بْتِشْتِغِل بِجداوِل وخْطوط ثابِتة إذا بدّك. والتّاكْسِيّات العادية كمان خِيار، بسّ أوْقات معْقول تْكون غالْية إذا كِنِت لحالك أوْ المِشْوار بْعيد.وحتّى صار في applications كْتير لتُطْلُب تاكْسي.

Charbel: That's true, Omar. Buses have their own character and cover a lot of the city and even outside Beirut. But they operate on fixed schedules and routes if you want. Regular taxis are also an option, but sometimes they can be expensive if you're alone or the trip is far. There are also many apps now to order a taxi.

**عُمر:** أيْه! يَلّي عم تْقولو كْتير مظْبوط! بسّ أنا صراحة بْحِسّ إنّو نِظام السّيرْفيس بيسِدّ فراغ كْتير بين الباصات والتّاكْسِيّات الخاصّة يَلّي تُعْتبر شْوَيّ غالْية بِبَيْروت. وصراحة، أنا بِعْتِبرا طريقة رائْعة للتّنقُّل ومِش بسّ للتّنقُّل بسّ هِيّ طريقة لتِتْعرّف على ناس جْداد، وبِتْوفِّر مصاري. وفوْق هَيْدا كِلّو دايْماً بْيِطْلعْلك مُغامرة.

Omar: Yeah! What you're saying is very true! But honestly, I feel that the service system fills a big gap between buses and private taxis, which are a bit expensive in Beirut. Honestly, I consider it a great way to get around and not just for transportation, but it's a way to meet new people and save money. On top of all that, you always get an adventure.

**شَرْبِل:** يَعْني بدّنا نْقول يَعْني إذا زِرْتوا بَيْروت جرّبوا السّيرْفيس أوْ التّاكْسي الجماعي. مِش بسّ مِشْوار هِيّ تجْرُبة يِمْكِن تِطْلعوا بِقُصّة حِلْوة تْخبْرُوا مِتِل ما صار معْنا.

Charbel: So we want to say that if you visit Beirut, try the service or shared taxi. It's not just a ride; it's an experience. You might come out with a nice story to tell, just like what happened to us.

**عُمر:** شُكْراً لإِلك شرْبِل. وميرْسي للْمُسْتمِعين. المرّة الجاية رح نِحْكي عن جَوانِب تانْية مِن حَياتْنا بِبَيْروت. لَوَقْتا، ديروا بالْكُن على حالكُن واسْتِمْتْعوا بالرِّحْلة!

Omar: Thank you, Charbel. And thank you to our listeners. Next time, we will talk about other aspects of our life in Beirut. Until then, take care of yourselves and enjoy the ride!

## Comprehension Questions

١. شو هِيِّ التّاكْسِيّات الجماعية بِبَيْروت وشو مِنْسمِّيا بِالْعامية؟

٢. كيف بْتِشْتِغِل التّاكْسِيّات الجماعية بِبَيْروت؟

٣. قدّيْ كان يْكَلِّف رُكوب التّاكْسي الجماعي قبل الأزْمة الإقْتصادية؟

٤. كيف أثّرِت أزْمةْ البِنْزين على شوْفورِيةْ التّاكْسِيّات الجماعية؟

٥. لِيْش تُعْتبر التّاكْسِيّات الجماعية جزء أساسي مِن نِظام النّقل بِبَيْروت؟

٦. شو هِيِّ بعْض التحدِّيات اللي بيواجِها الرُّكاب بِاسْتِخْدام التّاكْسِيّات الجماعية؟

٧. لِيْش التّاكْسِيّات الجماعية بِبَيْروت بْتِسْتعْمِل مرْسِيدس موْدِيْل أَلْف وتِسِعْمِية وتِمْانين؟

٨. شو هِيِّ البدايِل التّانْية للنّقِل العامّ بِبَيْروت وليْش السّيرْفيس بْيِبْقى خِيار مُفضّل؟

1. What are collective taxis in Beirut and what do we call them in colloquial language?
2. How do collective taxis work in Beirut?
3. How much did it cost to ride a collective taxi before the economic crisis?
4. How did the gasoline crisis affect collective taxi drivers?
5. Why are collective taxis considered an essential part of the transportation system in Beirut?
6. What are some of the challenges passengers face when using collective taxis?
7. Why do collective taxis in Beirut use Mercedes models from the 1980s?
8. What are the other alternatives for public transportation in Beirut, and why does the service remain a preferred option?

## Discussion Questions

١. هل سبق وسْتعْملِت تاكْسي جماعي بِبَيْروت؟ خبِّرْنا عن تجْرُبْتك.

٢. كيف بِيخْتِلِف نِظام النّقِل العامّ بِبَيْروت عن نِظام النّقِل العامّ بِبلدك؟

٣. شو هِيِّ الصُّعوبات اللي بِتْواجِها بالنّقِل العامّ بِبلدك؟

٤. هل بِتْفضِّل إسْتِعْمال التّاكْسيّات الجماعية وَلّا التّاكْسيّات الخاصّة؟ لِيْش؟

٥. كيف بِتْأثّر الأزَمات الإقْتِصادية على وَسائِل النّقِل بِبلدك؟

٦. هل بِتْحِبّ تِتْعرّف على ناس جْداد مِن خِلال رِحْلاتك؟ خبِّرْنا عن قُصّة صارِت معك.

٧. شو هِيِّ وَسائِل النّقِل المُفضّلة عِنْدك بمدينْتك؟ وليْش؟

٨. إذا زِرِت بلد جْديد، بِتْحِبّ تْجرِّب وَسائِل النّقِل المحلّية؟ لِيْش أوْ ليْش لا؟

1. Have you ever used a collective taxi in Beirut? Tell us about your experience.
2. How does the public transportation system in Beirut differ from the public transportation system in your country?
3. What difficulties do you face with public transportation in your country?
4. Do you prefer using collective taxis or private taxis? Why?
5. How do economic crises affect transportation methods in your country?
6. Do you like meeting new people during your travels? Share a story that happened to you.
7. What are your favorite means of transportation in your city? Why?
8. If you visit a new country, do you like to try the local transportation? Why or why not?

# التّسوُّق والموْضة بِلِبنان
## Shopping and Fashion in Lebanon

## In this episode...

Charbel and Farah talk about the vibrant world of fashion and shopping in Lebanon. From the high-end boutiques and international brands in Beirut to the local designers like Elie Saab and Zuhair Murad, Lebanon has established itself as a hub for fashion lovers. They also explore the lively street markets, where unique handmade items and traditional Lebanese garments can be found. With a strong fashion culture and a growing beauty industry, shopping in Lebanon offers something for everyone, from luxury seekers to those looking for hidden gems at affordable prices.

## Vocabulary

| | |
|---|---|
| fashion; outfits | أَزْياء |
| me too | أنا كمان |
| accessories | أَكْسِسْوارات |
| brand | بْراند |
| shopping | تسوُّق |
| design | تصْميم (تصاميم) |
| sale, discount | تِنْزيل أسْعار |
| handicrafts | حِرف يَدَوية |
| map | خريطة |
| market | سوق (أسْواق) |
| popular market, traditional market | سوق شعْبي |
| beauty salon | صالوْن التِّجْميل |
| beauty industry | صِناعةْ الجّمال |
| cosmetic clinic | عِيادةْ التِّجْميل |
| luxury | فاخْرة |
| look, style | لوك |
| jewelry | مُجَوْهرات |
| shopping center, mall | مركز تسوُّق |
| designer | مُصمِّم |
| fashion | موْضة |

## Transcript

**شَرْبِل:** هاي، كيفْكُن؟ اليوْم رح نِحْكي عن مَوْضوع مُثير وهيْك مُهِمّ خاصّةً يَلّي بيحِبّوا الشوْپينْغ والتّسوّق. رح نِحْكي عن الموْضة بِلِبْنان، معْكُن شرْبِل ومعي اليوْم صديقْتي فرح. كيفِك فرح؟

Charbel: Hi, how are you all? Today we're going to talk about an exciting and important topic, especially for those who love shopping. We'll be talking about fashion in Lebanon. I'm Charbel, and with me today is my friend Farah. How are you, Farah?

**فرح:** أهْلا شرْبِل، أنا مْنيحة، ميرْسي مْحمّسِة نِحْكي عن التّسوّق والموْضة شغْلتيْن كْتير بْحِبُّن.

Farah: Hi, Charbel! I'm good, thanks. I'm excited to talk about shopping and fashion, two things I absolutely love.

**شرْبِل:** ليْكي أنا كمان، لِبْنان عِنْدو إذا بدّك مشهد تسوُّق نابِض بالْحَياةْ مع خلْطة شْوَيّ مِن الـ brandsومحلّات المُصمّمين المحلّيّين والأسْواق الحَيَوية، يَعْني كْتير مُناسِب لمُحِبّين الموْضة.

Charbel: Me too! Lebanon has, if you want, a vibrant shopping scene with a mix of brands, local designer stores, and lively markets, which is perfect for fashion lovers.

**فرح:** أكيد. بَيْروت خْصوصةً هِيّ مركز للتّسوّق وللْموْضة. عِنّا مطارِح مِتِل أسْواق بَيْروت، ABC Verdun، وشَوارِع كْتير فيا malls كْبار.

Farah: Absolutely. Beirut, in particular, is a hub for shopping and fashion. We have places like Beirut Souks, ABC Verdun, and many streets with large malls.

**شرْبِل:** صحّ، وما نِنْسى أكيد المُصمّمين المحلّيّين يَلّي عِمْلوا إلْن إسْم عالميّاً. فينا نِذكُر إيلي صعْب، زُهيْر مُراد، وربيع كَيْروز وغَيْرُن وحطّوا لِبْنان على خريطةْ الموْضة العالمية.

Charbel: That's right, and we shouldn't forget the local designers who have made a name for themselves globally. We can mention Elie Saab, Zuhair Murad, and Rabih Kayrouz, among others, who have put Lebanon on the global fashion map.

**فرح:** عنْجدّ. تصامیمُن رائْعة وبتعْکُس المَوْهِبة الکْبیرة اللي عنّا. لیْك التّسوُّق بلِبْنان experienceكْتیر مْمیَّزة لأنّو بتْشوف مزیج مِن الموْضة العالمیة والمحلّیة.

Farah: Indeed. Their designs are amazing and reflect the great talent we have. Shopping in Lebanon is a very unique experience because you see a mix of global and local fashion.

**شرْبِل:** ومِش بسّ عن الموْضة الـluxury الفاخْرة. عنّا أسْواق شعْبیة یَعْني مِتل بمنْطِقة برْج حمّود، عنّا أسْواق شعْبیة بطْرابُلُس، بجْبیْل، وبالبِترون. هَیْدي المطارح إذا بدّك مِثالیة لتْلاقي قُطع غریبة، قُطع أثریة في کْتیر حِرف یَدَویة حتّى موْضة قدیمة عبیّات، طرْبوش کِلّ شي خصّو بالثّقافة اللِّبْنانیة. حتّى في أسْواق للدّهب یَعْني هیْك محلّات بیْجي هیْك شارِع ومحلّات دهب حدّ بعْضا. شي کْتیر حِلو یَعْني.

Charbel: And it's not just about luxury fashion. We also have traditional markets like in the Burj Hammoud area, as well as markets in Tripoli, Byblos, and Batroun. These places are ideal for finding unique pieces, antiques, and lots of handmade crafts, even vintage fashion like abayas, tarbooshes, anything related to Lebanese culture. We also have gold markets, where you can find street after street of jewelry shops—it's really something special.

**فرح:** بْحِبّ هالأسْواق عنْجدّ فیك تْلاقي فیا إشْیا غریبة وحِلْوة بأسْعار کْتیر مْنیحة. وزْیادة عن هیْك هِيّ طریقة بتْسلّي لتْقضّي النّهار ونبرْمُر بین العالم ونْغیرِّ جوّ.

Farah: I love those markets. You can find unique and beautiful things at great prices. Plus, it's a fun way to spend the day, wandering around and enjoying a change of scenery.

**شرْبِل:** أکید. یَلّا نِحْکي عن الذّوْق بالموْضة بلِبْنان. النّاس هوْن بْیِهْتمّوا کْتیر بمظْهرُن. یَعْني حتّى إذا کانِت ضهْرة عادیة أوْ حتّى مُناسبة رسْمیة، بتْشوفي اللِّبْنانیة لابْسین بطریقة سوبّر مْرتّبة. ما بیحِبّوا یْکونوا هیْك یَعْني إذا في شي بدُّن یْروحوا على السّوبرْمارکِت، بتْلاقي لِبْسوا تْیاب مْرتّبة زبْطوا حالُن بسّ لمّا یْبیّنوا هیْك مْبهْدلین.

Charbel: For sure. Now let's talk about fashion taste in Lebanon. People here really care about their appearance. Even if it's a casual outing or a formal event, you'll see Lebanese people dressed very neatly. They don't like going out looking unkempt, even if they're just going to the supermarket—they'll dress well and make sure they look presentable.

**فرح:** هَيْدا مَظْبوط، الموضة جزء كْبير مِن ثقافْتِنا. اللّبْنانيّين دايْماً بيحِبّوا يِلِبْسوا أحْلى شي عِنْدُن يْبَيّْنوا بأفْضَل شكِل. وفي كْتير إهْتِمام بالتّفاصيل، مِتِل التّياب مِتِل الـ make up مِتِل الأكْسِسْوارات وحتّى الشّوز وخاصّةً النّسْوان.

Farah: That's true. Fashion is a big part of our culture. Lebanese people always like to wear their best to look their best. There's a lot of attention to detail, from clothes to makeup, accessories, and even shoes, especially for women.

**شرْبِل:** ولمّا نِحْكي عن الأكْسِسْوارات يَعْني عِنّا مُصمّمين مُجَوْهرات بيجنّنوا. في مِتِل الزُّغَيْب، النّصولة، يَعْني في كذا حدا يَعْني ما بِدّي سمّي الكِلّ... ما بِدّي سمّي وإنْسى عالم.

Charbel: And speaking of accessories, we have some amazing jewelry designers here. Like Zoughaib and Nsouli, and many others. I don't want to name everyone and forget someone.

**فرح:** صحّ، ومِش بسّ التّياب يا شرْبِل والمُجَوْهرات. عِنّا صناعةِ الجّمال كْتير مِزْدِهْرة بِلِبْنان. عِنّا الصّالونات التّجْميل، عِيادات التّجْميل بْيِهْتمّوا مِن الشّعِر للْبشرة، كِلّ شي.

Farah: Right, and it's not just about clothes and jewelry, Charbel. The beauty industry in Lebanon is booming. We have beauty salons and cosmetic clinics that take care of everything from hair to skin.

**شرْبِل:** كِلّو هَيْدا جزء مِن النّهج والفِكِر اللّبْناني للشّعور بالرّاحة والجّمال. وما نِنْسى عنّا sale مَوْسِمي. يَعْني عِنّا إذا بدّكُن تِنْزيل أسْعار. هالْفِترة التّسوّق هِيّ شي أساسي النّاس وأنا مِنّن أكيد يَعْني، بْيِطْلعوا لَيْلاقوا هيْك اللي بدّن يِشْتروا بسّ بِسِعِر أقَلّ. يَعْني هَيْدا الفِترة بِتْكون كْتير عاجْقة بالـmalls وكِلّ محلّات التّسوّق.

Charbel: All of this is part of the Lebanese mindset of feeling good and looking good. And we can't forget about seasonal sales. If you want discounts, this is the time when shopping becomes essential. People, and I'm definitely one of them, go out to find what they want at lower prices. It's a busy time in malls and shopping areas.

**فرح:** ميّة بالميّة شرْبِل. الـ sale مَوْضوع كْتير كْبير بِلِبْنان. كِلّ العالم بْتِنْطُر الـsale مِن season لـseason إنْ كان بالصّيْف أوْ بالشّتي، وبيكون عَيْنُن عَ محلّات special

تَيْروحوا لعِنْدُن تْيَجدِّدوا الـlook الجْديد شو في نازِل جْديد تْيَغَيْروا وبِذات الوَقِت ما يِتْكلّفوا بمَبالغ كْبيرة.

**Farah:** Absolutely, Charbel. Sales are a big deal in Lebanon. Everyone waits for the sales from season to season, whether it's summer or winter, and they keep an eye on certain stores so they can update their look without spending too much.

**شرْبِل:** عنْجدّ يَعْني، أحْلى شي بهالْفِتْرة التّسوُّق بلِبْنان ومِش بسّ لإِلْنا يَعْني نِحْنا العايْشين هوْن. في كْتير عالم سُوّاح إذا بدّك بْيِجوا خِصّيصة لَيِشْتِروا مِن عِنّا أوْ يِتْسوّقوا عِنّا وهَيْدا push كْبير ودفْعة كْبيرة للإقْتِصاد اللّبْناني.

**Charbel:** Honestly, the best part of shopping in Lebanon isn't just for us locals. We have a lot of tourists who come here specifically to shop, which is a huge boost for the Lebanese economy.

**فرح:** أكيد شرْبِل، هَيْدا شي كْتير حِلو عِنّا بلِبْنان لأنّو مِن كِلّ البِلْدان العربية بْيِجوا لعِنّا لهوْن تَيْشوفوا الموْضة، تَيْشوفوا شو في طالع specially، new collection مِن الـdesigners اللي بيصمِّموه أزْياء هَيْدا شي بيكبِّرْنا وبيخلّي لِبْنان بأفْضل صورة بِـ ... specially بالشّوْبينْغ وبالأزْياء.

**Farah:** For sure, Charbel. It's great because people from all over the Arab world come here to see the fashion, to check out the latest trends, especially the new collections from designers. This helps elevate Lebanon's image, especially when it comes to shopping and fashion.

**شرْبِل:** مِيّة بالْمِيّة، مِيّة بالْمِيّة اللي عم تْقولي. شو بِدّي قول؟ ميرْسي لمُشاركْتِك معي يا فرح. كان حديث كْتير حِلو وميرْسي لَيّ عم يِسْمعْنا وانْشالله تْكونوا نْبسطْوا وسْتمْتعْتوا بالْحديث عن التّسوُّق والموْضة بلِبْنان.

**Charbel:** Absolutely, 100% to what you're saying. What can I say? Thank you for joining me, Farah. It was a really nice conversation, and thank you to everyone listening. Hopefully, you enjoyed and had fun with our conversation about shopping and fashion in Lebanon.

**فرح:** شُكْراً إلك يا شرْبِل، وشُكْراً لكِلّ حدا عم يِسْمعْنا. وانْشالله المرّة الجاية مْنِلْتِقي بمَوْضوع جْديد. لَوَقْتا، تْسَوّقوا وسْتمِتْعوا specially بلِبْنان.

**Farah:** Thank you, Charbel, and thanks to everyone listening. Hopefully, next time we'll meet with a new topic. Until then, shop and enjoy! Especially in Lebanon.

## Comprehension Questions

١.  شو هُوّ مَوْضوع الحلْقة اللي حِكْيوا عنّو شرْبِل وفرح؟

٢.  شو هِيّ المناطِق الشّهيرة للتّسوُّق في بَيْروت؟

٣.  مين هِنّي المُصَمِّمين اللّبْنانِيّين اللي حِكي عنُّن شرْبِل وفرح؟

٤.  شو بيمَيِّز تجْرِبة التّسوُّق في الأسْواق الشّعْبية بلِبْنان؟

٥.  كيف بْيِهْتمّ النّاس بلِبْنان بمظْهرُن حسب حديث شرْبِل وفرح؟

٦.  شو هِيّ الأكْسِسْوارات اللي ذكرُوَا بِالْحديث؟

٧.  كيف بْيوصْفوا شرْبِل وفرح تأْثير sale أَوْ تنْزيلات الأسْعار على النّاس بلِبْنان؟

٨.  لَيْش بْيِجي سُوّاح مِن بلْدان عربية لَيِتْسَوّقوا بلِبْنان؟

1. What is the topic of the episode that Charbel and Farah discussed?
2. What are the famous shopping areas in Beirut?
3. Who are the Lebanese designers mentioned by Charbel and Farah?
4. What makes the shopping experience in Lebanon's traditional markets unique?
5. How do people in Lebanon take care of their appearance according to Charbel and Farah?
6. What accessories were mentioned in the discussion?
7. How do Charbel and Farah describe the impact of sales or price reductions on people in Lebanon?
8. Why do tourists from other Arab countries come to shop in Lebanon?

## Discussion Questions

1. شو هِيّ المحلّات المُفَضّلة عِنْدك للتّسوُّق بِبلدك؟

2. كيف بِتْشوف تأْثير المُصمِّمين المحلّيِّين على صِناعةْ المَوْضة بِبلدك؟

3. عِنْدك إهْتِمام بالْمَوْضة؟ إذا أَيْه، شو هُوّ سْتايْلك المُفَضّل؟

4. كيف بِتْشوف دوْر الأَسْواق الشّعْبية بالْحِفاظ على التّراُث الثّقافي؟

5. شو هُوّ تأْثير sale أَوْ تِنْزيلات الأَسْعار على عادات التّسوُّق عِنْدك؟

6. كيف بِتْعبِّر الأَكْسِسْوارات عن شخْصيتك بالْمَوْضة؟

7. شو هِيّ تجرِبْتك مع التّسوُّق بِأماكِن جْديدة أَوْ بِلْدان مِخْتِلْفة؟

8. كيف بِتأَثِّر المَوْضة بِبلدك على الزُّوار أَوْ السُّواح مِن بِلْدان تانْية؟

1. What are your favorite places to shop in your country?
2. How do local designers impact the fashion industry in your country?
3. Are you interested in fashion? If yes, what is your favorite style?
4. How do traditional markets play a role in preserving cultural heritage?
5. What is the impact of sales or price reductions on your shopping habits?
6. How do accessories express your personality in fashion?
7. What is your experience with shopping in new places or different countries?
8. How does fashion in your country influence visitors or tourists from other countries?

# تَأْثيرالثّقافات على لبْنان

## The Influence of Cultures on Lebanon

### In this episode...

Omar and Charbel discuss the rich cultural influences that have shaped Lebanon throughout its history. From the Ottoman rule, which left its mark on language, cuisine, and infrastructure, to the French mandate, which introduced new educational systems, legal frameworks, and architectural styles, Lebanon's cultural tapestry is a diverse blend. They also touch on the impact of Syria, both politically and culturally, and how Lebanon's strategic location has made it a crossroads for many civilizations. Together, these influences have created a unique and resilient cultural identity for the Lebanese people.

## Vocabulary

| | |
|---|---|
| mandate | إنْتِداب |
| infrastructure | بِنْية تحْتية |
| influence, impact | تأْثير |
| education | تعْليم |
| roots | جُذور |
| civilization | حضارة |
| human rights | حُقوق الإنْسان |
| rule, governance | حِكْم |
| politics | سِياسة |
| style, design | طِراز |
| social customs | عادات إجْتِماعية |
| language | لُغة |
| dialect | لهْجة |
| blend, mix | مزيج |
| cuisine | مطْبخ |
| musical modes, scales | مقامات |
| aspect, side | ناحْيِة |
| system | نِظامِ (أنظِمة) |
| architecture | هنْدسة مِعْمارية |
| identity | هَوية |

## Transcript

**عُمر:** مَرْحبا! اليوْم رح نِحْكي عن مَوْضوع مْهِمّ ومُثير لِلْإهْتِمام، تَأْثير الثَّقافات المِخْتِلْفِة على لِبْنان. أنا عُمْر ومعي اليوْم صديقي شرْبِل. كيفك اليوْم يا شرْبِل؟

**Omar:** Hello! Today we're going to talk about an important and interesting topic: the influence of different cultures on Lebanon. I'm Omar, and with me today is my friend Charbel. How are you today, Charbel?

**شرْبِل:** والله يا عُمر فاجأت المُستمِعين! أنا مْنيح وهيْك كمان إذا بدّك حمّسْتْنا نِحْكي شْوَيّ ونْخبِّر المُسْتمِعين عن التَّأْثيرات الثَّقافية اللي تْشكّلِت بِلِبْنان.

**Charbel:** Well, Omar, you surprised the listeners! I'm good, and you've also got us excited to talk a bit and tell the listeners about the cultural influences that have shaped Lebanon.

**عُمر:** أكيد، لِبْنان معْروف بِتاريخو العريق وتعدُّد الثَّقافات اللي قطعِت عْليْه. رح نْبلِّش الحديث اليوْم بِالْحِكْم العثْماني يَلّي ضلّ وسْتمرّ لفتْرِةْ أكْتر مِن ٤٠٠ سِنِة بِلِبْنان مِن القرْن السّادِس عشر لحتّى نِهايةْ الحرْب العالمية الأولى.

**Omar:** Absolutely, Lebanon is known for its rich history and the diversity of cultures that have passed through it. We'll start today's discussion with the Ottoman rule, which lasted for more than 400 years in Lebanon, from the 16th century until the end of World War I.

**شرْبِل:** صحّ، ليْك الحِكْم العثْماني كان إلو تأْثير كْبير على لِبْنان، يَعْني خُصوصاً مِن النّاحِية الإدارية والبِنْية التَّحْتية. العثْمانيّين عِمْلوا طُرُق وجْسورة وإذا بدّك حسّنوا شبكات الماي، وكمان اللّغّة التّرْكية أثّرِت على اللّهْجِة اللّبْنانية، ما بدْنا نِنْكُر هَيْدا الشّي، لِأنّو بعْض الكلْمات اللي مْنِسْتعْمِلا اليوْم هيِّ فينا نْقول أصْلاً تِرْكي.

**Charbel:** Right, the Ottoman rule had a big impact on Lebanon, especially from an administrative and infrastructure perspective. The Ottomans built roads and bridges, improved water networks. Also, the Turkish language has influenced the Lebanese dialect—we can't deny this because some of the words we use today are originally Turkish.

**عُمر:** شرْبِل! ومِش بسّ هيْك، العثْمانية كمان تركوا تأْثير على المطْبخ اللّبْناني مثلاً الحِلو مِتِل البِقْلاوة وأطْباق مِتِل الكِبّة والمشاوي إلا جُذور عثْمانية، وزِيادة عن هيْك

الأنْماط الموسيقية والمقامات يَلّي مْنِسْمعا اليوْم بِالموسيقى اللِّبنانية كمان هِيِّ ذاتا إلا جُذور عِثْمانية.

**Omar:** Charbel! And not only that, the Ottomans also left an influence on Lebanese cuisine. For example, sweets like baklava and dishes like kibbeh and grilled meats have Ottoman roots. Additionally, the musical styles and "maqamat" (melodic modes) that we hear today in Lebanese music also have Ottoman origins.

**شرْبِل:** مظْبوط، وليْك بعْد إذا بدْنا نْكفّي بِهالتّأْثيرات، في بعْد الحِكْم العِثْماني لِبْنان نْتقل لِفتْرة مِن الإنْتِداب الفرنْسي بعد الحرْب العالمية الأولى. الفرنْسِيّين كانوا إلُن تأْثير كْبير على ...بدْنا نحْكي عن التّعْليم، النِّظام القانوني، الهنْدِسة المعْمارية. لهلّأ مِنْشوف تأْثير الثّقافة الفرنْسية بعْدا بِلِبْنان.

**Charbel:** That's true. And if we continue with these influences, after the Ottoman rule, Lebanon transitioned to the period of the French Mandate after World War I. The French had a significant influence on, let's say, education, the legal system, and architecture. Even today, we can still see the influence of French culture in Lebanon.

**عُمر:** شرْبِل، مظْبوط يَلّي عم بِتْقولو، ونِحْنا لِبْنان بلد فْرانْكوْفوْني ومِتِل ما قلِت التّأْثير كان كْتير كْبير بِالْقِطاع التّعْليمي صار عنّا كْتير مِن المدارِس يَلّي بِتْعلِّم اللُّغة الفرنْسية تأْسّسِت بِهَيْدا الوَقِت وكمان مِنْشوف تأْثير الفرنْساوية عَ اللِّغّة اللِّبْنانية بِحدّ ذاتا، كْتير بِلِبْنان بْيِحْكوا فرنْسي وبْيِخْلِطوا بين الفرنْسي والعربي بالْحديث اليَوْمي.

**Omar:** Charbel, what you're saying is true. Lebanon is a Francophone country, and as you said, the influence was very significant in the educational sector. Many schools that teach French were established during this time, and we also see the influence of French on the Lebanese language itself. Many in Lebanon speak French and mix it with Arabic in their daily conversations.

**شرْبِل:** صحّ! وإذا بدْنا نِحْكي شْوَيّ عن الهنْدِسة المعْمارية، مِنْشوف بْيوت ومباني بِبَيْروت وحتّى بِمناطِق تانْية، بْتِعْكُس طِراز الفرنْسي يَعْني أوّل ما تِطلّع عْلَيا بِتْقول: لأ، هَيْدا بيْت فرنْسي. كمان الفرنْساوية فوّتوا مفاهيم حُقوق الإنْسان والحُرِّيّات ساعدِت شْوَيّ إذا بدّك تِشْكيل الهَوية الوَطنية اللِّبْنانية وكان إلُن دوْر كْبير بِـ... يْطَوّروا الثّقافة الأدبية والفنّية بِلِبْنان.

**Charbel:** Right! And if we talk a bit about architecture, we can see houses and buildings in Beirut and other areas that reflect the French style. The first thing you say when you look at them is, "This is a French house." The French also introduced concepts of human rights and freedoms, which somewhat helped shape the Lebanese national identity and played a big role in developing Lebanon's literary and artistic culture.

**عُمَر:** صحّ وبعْد الفرنْسِيِّين كان في تأْثير سوري على لبْنان خُصوصاً بفترْةِ الحرْب الأهْلية وما بعْدا. السّوريّين كان إلُن تأْثير على السِّياسةِ والأمْنِ بلبْنان وكوْنُن بلد قريب والبلديْن بيْتشاركوا الحْدود.

**Omar:** True, and after the French, there was a Syrian influence on Lebanon, especially during the civil war and after it. The Syrians had an impact on politics and security in Lebanon, given that the countries share borders and have a close relationship.

**شرْبِل:** ليْك صحّ وما بدّنا ننْكُرعلاقة بيْن لبْنان وسوريا مْعقّدة شْوَيّ وتاريخا طَويل. السّوريّين ساهموا بتشْكيلِ الحَياةْ السِّياسية بلبْنان لسنَواتِ طَويلةِ بعد الحرب، ومع كلِّ هالتّحدِّيّاتِ العلاقة أثّرت على الثّقافةِ واللّهْجةِ اللّبْنانية. كمان في تأْثيرات سورية إذا بدّك هيْك عطيو شْوَيّ عَ المأْكولات حتّى لوْ شي بسيط على العاداتِ الإجْتماعية.

**Charbel:** That's right, and we can't deny that the relationship between Lebanon and Syria is a bit complex and has a long history. The Syrians contributed to shaping political life in Lebanon for many years after the war. Despite all these challenges, the relationship also influenced Lebanese culture and dialect. There are also Syrian influences, if you will, on food and even on some social customs, although in a minor way.

**عُمَر:** بالنِّهايةِ شرْبِل لبْنان مزيج مِن هالتّأْثيرات الثّقافية مِن العثْمانيِّين للفرنْسِيِّين للسّوريِّين ولكْتير حضارات قطعِت قبْلُن بالتّاريخ القديم. كلِّ واحْدةِ مِنُن تركِت بصْمِتا على لبْنان وخلقِت بلد مُتنوّع غني ثقافيّاً دينيّاً وحضاريّاً. وما ننْسى إنّو اللّبْنانيّين نفْسُن كان إلُن دوْر كْبير بالتّفاعُل مع هالثّقافات وإسْتيعابا وإضافةِ لمساتُن الخاصّة عْلَيا.

**Omar:** In the end, Charbel, Lebanon is a blend of these cultural influences—from the Ottomans to the French to the Syrians and many other civilizations that passed through in ancient history. Each one of them left its mark on Lebanon, creating a country that is diverse, rich in culture, religion, and civilization. And let's not forget that the Lebanese themselves played a big role in interacting with these cultures, absorbing them, and adding their own touches.

**شَرْبِل:** مَظْبوط عُمر. لِبْنان شعْب... اللِّبْنانية شعْب جبّار، شعْب بْيِقْدر يِتْحمّل كلّ هالصُّعوبات مِتِل ما عم نْشوف. ونِحْنا حْكينا عن فتْرة قصيرة مِن هوْل اللي مرقوا عنّا عَ لِبْنان بسّ نِحْنا ما نِنْسى في تاريخ عريق لِلِبْنان، هُوِّ كان أساس بالْفينيقية وبيْن كلّ هالْحضارات اللي مرقِت وبيْن كلّ هالْحُروب اللي قطعِت عْليْه كلّو بيولّد ثقافات وبيولِّد شعِب جبّار، شعْب مْحِبّ، شعِب قَوي، شعِب صامِد وبتْمنّى إنّو يْضلّ هيْك ويوصل للّي بدّو ياه. عُمر thank you لإلك إنْتَ بلّشِت هالحلْقة اليوْمِر. أنا رح إخْتِما. ميرْسي لكِلّ اللي عم يِسْمعونا. مَوْضوع هيْك لَوْ إنّو قطعْنا عْليْه بسيط بسّ هُوِّ جزْء كْبير مِن الثّقافة بلِبْنان، بتْمنّى تْكونوا نْبسطّوا وتْعرّفْتوا أكْتر على هالثّقافة اللِّبْنانية لَوَقْتا تْتِهوا عَ حالْكُن ومْنِلْتِقي بمَوْضوع تاني.

Charbel: That's true, Omar. The Lebanese people are resilient—they've managed to endure all these hardships, as we can see. We've talked about a brief period of those who have passed through Lebanon, but we mustn't forget that Lebanon has a rich history, dating back to the Phoenicians. Among all these civilizations and wars that have crossed through, they've all contributed to a strong, loving, resilient, and proud people. I hope they continue this way and achieve what they aspire to. Omar, thank you for starting today's episode. I'll wrap it up. Thank you to everyone who's listening. This topic, although we touched on it briefly, is a big part of Lebanese culture. I hope you enjoyed it and got to know more about Lebanese culture. Until then, take care, and we'll meet again with another topic.

## Comprehension Questions

١. كيف أثّرِت الثّقافة العِثْمانية على الموسيقى اللِّبْنانية؟

٢. كيف أثّرِ الحِكْم العثْماني على لِبْنان مِن النّاحْيِة الإدارية والبِنْيِة التّحْتية؟

٣. شو هِيِّ الأطْباق اللِّبْنانية اللي قال عُمر إنّو جُذورا عِثْمانية؟

٤. كيف وَصف شرْبِل تأثِير الإنْتِداب الفرنْسي على لِبْنان، خاصّةً مِن ناحْيِة التّعْلِيم والهِنْدِسة المعْمارية؟

٥. شو هُوّ تأثِير اللُّغة الفرنْسية على اللّهْجة اللِّبْنانية حسب عُمر؟

٦. كيف أثّرِت العلاقة المعْقّدة بيْن لِبْنان وسوريا على الثّقافة واللّهْجة اللِّبْنانية؟

٧. كيف بْيوصُف عُمر دوْر اللِّبْنانيّين بالتّفاعُل مع الثّقافات اللي مرقِت عْلَيْنْ؟

٨. ليْش شرْبِل بْيِعْتِبِر اللِّبْنانيّين "شعِب جبّار"؟ شو هِيِّ الأسْباب اللي ذكرا؟

1. How did Ottoman culture influence Lebanese music?
2. How did Ottoman rule impact Lebanon in terms of administration and infrastructure?
3. What are the Lebanese dishes that Omar mentioned have Ottoman roots?
4. How did Charbel describe the influence of the French mandate on Lebanon, especially in terms of education and architecture?
5. What is the impact of the French language on the Lebanese dialect according to Omar?
6. How did the complex relationship between Lebanon and Syria affect Lebanese culture and dialect?
7. How does Omar describe the role of the Lebanese people in interacting with the cultures that influenced them?
8. Why does Charbel consider the Lebanese people "a strong people"? What reasons did he mention?

## Discussion Questions

1. كيف بِتْشوف تَأْثير الثّقافات المِخْتِلْفِة على بلدك؟ شو هِيِّ الثّقافات اللي أثّرِت عْليْه؟

2. شو هِيِّ الأطْباق التّقْليدية بِبلدك اللي جُذورا مُمْكِن تْكون مِن ثقافات تانْيِة؟

3. كيف بِتْشوف تَأْثير الإنْتِداب أَوْ الإسْتِعْمار على التُّراث الثّقافي والمعْماري بِلدك؟

4. بِتْحِسّ إنّو اللُّغة الأَجْنبية أثّرِت على اللّهْجِة المحلّية بِبلدك؟ كيف؟

5. كيف بِتْشوف العلاقة بينْ بلدك والدُّوَل المُجاوْرة؟ أثّرِت شي على الثّقافِة أَوْ اللّهْجِة المحلّية؟

6. كيف بِتْشوف دوْر الشّعِب بالتّفاعُل مع الثّقافات اللي مرقِت على بلدك؟

7. بِتْحِسّ إنّو بلدك بْيِقْدر يْحافِظ على هَويتو الثّقافية رُغْم التَّأْثيرات الخارْجية؟ كيف؟

8. كيف مُمْكِن نِتْعلّم مِن التّجارُب التّاريخية لتعْزيز التّنَوُّع الثّقافي بِبلْدنا؟

1. How do you see the influence of different cultures on your country? What cultures have had an impact on it?
2. What are the traditional dishes in your country that might have roots in other cultures?
3. How do you see the impact of colonialism or mandates on your country's cultural and architectural heritage?
4. Do you feel that a foreign language has influenced the local dialect in your country? How?
5. How do you see the relationship between your country and neighboring countries? Has it affected the local culture or dialect?
6. How do you view the role of your people in interacting with the cultures that have influenced your country?
7. Do you think your country can maintain its cultural identity despite external influences? How?
8. How can we learn from historical experiences to enhance cultural diversity in our country?

# صِناعةُ الصّابون العُضوي بِلِبْنان
## Organic Soap Making in Lebanon

### In this episode...

Charbel and Farah discuss the growing industry of organic soap and shampoo production in Lebanon. Rooted in traditional methods, Lebanese artisans have been crafting natural soaps using olive oil, laurel leaves, and other local ingredients for generations. Charbel and Farah explore how these handmade products are gaining popularity today, not only for their benefits to skin and hair but also for their eco-friendly and sustainable nature. The episode also highlights the economic boost this industry provides to small businesses and local farmers, making it both a cultural and environmental win for Lebanon.

## Vocabulary

| | |
|---|---|
| shapes and colors | أَشْكال وأَلْوان |
| environmental sustainability | إِسْتِدامةِ بيئية |
| skin | بشرة |
| artisan | حِرافي |
| moist, moisturized | رُطِب |
| olive oil | زيْت الزّيْتون |
| soap | صابون |
| traditional soap | صابون بلدي |
| eco-friendly | صديق للْبيئة |
| organic | عُضوي |
| care | عِنايةِ |
| benefits | فَوايِد |
| local | محلّي |
| farmer | مُزارِع |
| sustainable | مُسْتدام |
| natural ingredients | مُكوّنات طبيعية |
| product | منْتوج |
| soft | ناعِم |
| workshop | وَرْشِةْ عمل |
| laurel leaves, bay leaves | وَرق الغار |

# Transcript

**شربِل:** هاي، اليوْم رح نِحْكي عن صِناعة مُثيرة وهيْك مِزْدِهْرة بلِبْنان، مأخوذةِ مِن جْدودْنا هِيِّ صِناعةْ الصّابون والشّامْبو الـ organic أوْ العُضْوي. أنا شرْبِل ومعي رْفيقْتي فرح؟

**Charbel:** Hi, today we're going to talk about an exciting and blooming industry in Lebanon, passed down from our ancestors: organic soap and shampoo making. I'm Charbel, and with me is my friend Farah. How are you, Farah?

**فرح:** أهْلا شرْبِل، كْتير مْحمّسِة نِحْكي عن مَوْضوع صِناعةْ الصّابون والشّامْبو الـ organic بلِبْنان. عم تِكْتِسِب كْتير إهْتِمام بالْفتْرة الأخيرة.

**Farah:** Hi Charbel, I'm very excited to talk about organic soap and shampoo making in Lebanon. This topic has gained a lot of interest recently.

**شرْبِل:** أكيد، لِبْنان عِنْدو تاريخ طَويل باسْتِخْدام هَيْدي المكُوّنات الطّبيعية بمنْتوجات العِنايةِ الشّخْصية. الصّابون الطّبيعي المصْنوع مِن زيت الزّيْتون أوْ وَرق الغار الأوكاليبْتُس ومُكوّنات طبيعية تانْية كان جزءٍ مِن تقاليدْنا لقُرون يَعْني.

**Charbel:** Absolutely, Lebanon has a long history of using these natural ingredients in personal care products. Natural soap made from olive oil or laurel leaves, eucalyptus, and other natural ingredients has been a part of our traditions for centuries.

**فرح:** صحّ، إسْتِعْمال زيت الزّيْتون بصِناعةْ الصّابون مْميّز كْتير. زيت الزّيْتون كان دايْماً مَوْجود بِبْيوتْنا اللُّبْنانية، مِش بسّ للطّبْخ، كمان للعِنايةِ بالْبشرة معْروف بِفَوايْدو للْبشرة.

**Farah:** Yes, the use of olive oil in soap making is very special. Olive oil has always been present in Lebanese homes, not just for cooking but also for skincare due to its well-known benefits for the skin.

**شرْبِل:** صحّ، والصّابون التّقْليدي مِن طْرابْلُس المعْروف بالصّابون البلدي مشْهور بِجودْتو العالْية ومُكوِّناتو الطّبيعية. بْيِتْصنّع هيْك بطريقة تقْليدية ويمْكِن تِسْخين الماي وإضافةِ زُيوت عِطْرية مِتِل الأوكاليبْتُس وهَيْدي القِصص إلا فَوايد كمان إضافية.

**Charbel:** Right, and traditional soap from Tripoli, known as "baladi" soap, is famous for its high quality and natural ingredients. It's made in a traditional way, often by heating water and adding essential oils like eucalyptus, which have additional benefits.

**فرح:** شرْبِل العملية كْتير حِلْوة، الخليط بْيِنْصبّ بْقوالِب لَيِجمد لكذا أُسْبوع. النّتيجِة هيِّ صابون طبيعي بِناسِب كلّ أنْواع البشرة. أنا بِسْتخدِمو مِن سْنين وهُوّ فِعْلاً ساعد بشِرْتي تِبْقى ناعْمِة ورُطْبة.

**Farah:** Charbel, the process is very interesting. The mixture is poured into molds and left to harden for several weeks. The result is natural soap suitable for all skin types. I've been using it for years, and it has really helped keep my skin soft and moisturized.

**شرْبِل:** حتّى أنا بِسْتعْمِل هَيْدا الصّابون، وصراحة لاحظِت إنّو بشرْتي تْغيّرِت صارِت أحْسن، خفّ. إذا بدّك هيْك كانت كْتير جافّة خفّ الجفاف فيا مِن وَرا هَيْدا الصّابون ولأنو خلص بطّلِت إسْتعْمِل الصّابون التّجاري. وليْكي بِتْلاحْظي هلّأ مع هالصّناعة عم تِرْجع تْصير أكْتر trendy، عم بْيَعمْلوا أشْكال وألْوان مِنُّن لهالصّابون عنْجدّ شي كْتير حِلو. ومِش بسّ الصّابون بدْنا نِحْكي عنّو كمان في إتِّجاهْ زايِد للشّامْبو الـorganic كمان بِلِبْنان، الصّناعة الطّبيعي.

**Charbel:** I also use this soap, and honestly, I've noticed that my skin has improved—it's become better, and the dryness has reduced. If you will, my skin was really dry, and the dryness decreased because of this soap, and I stopped using commercial soap. And you'll notice now that this kind of artisanal soap is becoming more trendy. They're making different shapes and colors, and it's really nice. And we're not just talking about soap; there's also a growing trend towards organic shampoo in Lebanon, natural products.

**فرح:** صحّ الشّامْبو الطّبيعي مصْنوع مِن مُكوّنات طبيعية مِتِل زيت الزّيْتون والرّوزماري، بابونج عم بِتْصير أكْتر شعْبية. هالشّامْبو شي خَيالي صراحة، ما فيو مَواد كِمْيائية وبِتْكون أفْضل لشعِرْنا.

**Farah:** Yes, natural shampoo made from ingredients like olive oil, rosemary, and chamomile is becoming more popular. This shampoo is amazing because it doesn't contain chemicals and is better for our hair.

**شربِل:** مِيّة بالمِيّة، يَعْني فينا نْقول فَوايِد إسْتِخْدام هَيْدا الشّامْبو كْتيرة. حتّى بيساعِد تْتْحافْظي على الزّيْت الطّبيعي بالشّعْر، حتّى لاحَظِت إنّو بيقلّل الحساسية تبع فَرْوِةْ الرّاس، حتّى بْيِجي الـcover تبعو، التّغْليف مَحْطوط إنّو صديق لِلْبيئة.

Charbel: Absolutely, the benefits of using this shampoo are many. It helps maintain the natural oils in the hair, reduces scalp sensitivity, and even the packaging is environmentally friendly.

**فرح:** وما نِنْسى الأثر الإقْتِصادي. كْتير مِن هالأَعْمال الصّغيرة بِلِبْنان عم تِزْدِهِر مِن خِلال إنْتاج الصّابون والشّامْبو الطّبيعي. وبِهالطّريقة بيكونوا عم بْيِسْتعِمْلوا مُكوّنات محلّية، وحتّى بْيِدْعموا المُزارعين المحلّيّين وبِشجّعوا الزّراعة على المدى الطّويل.

Farah: And we shouldn't forget the economic impact. Many small businesses in Lebanon are thriving through the production of natural soap and shampoo. They use local ingredients and support local farmers, encouraging sustainable agriculture in the long term.

**شربِل:** صحّ هَيْدي نِقْطة كْتير مْهِمّة، وإنّو دعْم هالأَعْمال بيساعِد على تعْزيز الإقْتِصاد المحلّي وتِشْجيع المُمارسات المُسْتدامة. أنا شخْصيّاً بْحِبّ زور هالأَسْواق المحلّية وإشْتِري هَيْدا الصّابون المصْنوع يَدَوِيّاً. بيخلّيني أشْعُر بِهيْك بِرِضا داخْلي إنّو عم بيدْعم الحِرافيّين المحلّيّين.

Charbel: That's a very important point. Supporting these businesses helps boost the local economy and promotes sustainable practices. Personally, I love visiting local markets and buying handmade soap. It gives me a sense of satisfaction knowing I'm supporting local artisans.

**فرح:** أكيد، ومُؤخّراً في علامات تِجارية معْروفة هلّأ كْتسبت شِهْرِتا المحلّية والدُوَلية، مِتِل خان الصّابون، اللي قِدْروا يُعْرْضوا جمال وفَوايِد صِناعِةْ الصّابون اللّبْناني التّقْليدي لْلْعالم.

Farah: Absolutely, and recently, some well-known brands have gained both local and international recognition, like Khan Al Saboun, which has showcased the beauty and benefits of traditional Lebanese soap making to the world.

**شربل:** كمان بعد شغْلِة، لاحظِت إرْتِفاع إذا بدِّك بالدَّوْرات اللي بِتْساعِد النّاس إنّو يِتْعلَّموا كيف يَعْمُلوا صابون وشامْبو حتّى هنّي لحالُن بالبِيْت. وهَيْدا النّشاط كْتير بيسلّي وحتّى تعْليمي يَعْني وْبيِرْبُط النّاس بِتُراثْنا والثّقافِة وتقاليدْنا القديمة.

**Charbel:** Another thing I've noticed is the rise in workshops that help people learn how to make soap and shampoo at home. This activity is not only fun but also educational, connecting people with our heritage and traditional practices.

**فرح:** صحّ، هديك السِّنِة حْضِرت workshop من هالنّوْع. كانِت التّجْرِبِة كْتير رائْعة. تْعلَّمِت كيف إدْمُج هالمُكوّنات المِخْتِلْفِة مع بعْضا لأعْمُل صابون أوْ شامْبو. وهَيْدا الشّي عنْجدّ هيْك عطاني حِرفية تقْليدية.

**Farah:** Yes, last year I attended such a workshop. It was a fantastic experience. I learned how to combine different ingredients to make soap and shampoo. It really gave me a traditional craft skill.

**شربل:** هَيْدا شي كْتير حِلو. صِناعِةْ الصّابون والشّامْبو العُضْوي بِلِبْنان هُوّ مزيج مِثالي بيْن التّقْليد والحداثِة بِتْحافِظ على تُراثْنا الثّقافي وبِتْشجِّع الصّحّة والإسْتِدامِة البيئية حتّى.

**Charbel:** That's wonderful. Organic soap and shampoo making in Lebanon is a perfect blend of tradition and modernity, preserving our cultural heritage while promoting health and environmental sustainability.

**فرح:** مِيّة بالْمِيّة، كْتير حِلو نْشوف كيف هالصّناعة عم تِتْطّور.

**Farah:** Absolutely, it's great to see how this industry is evolving.

**شربل:** انْشالله، انْشالله! ميرْسي فرح للمُشاركِة الحِلْوة وانْشالله المُسْتِمعين اللي تابعونا اليوْم نْبسطوا بِهَيْدا الحديث وتْحمّسوا وتْعرّفوا أكْتر عن الصِّناعة... صِناعِةْ الصّابون والشّامْبو بِلِبْنان. انْشالله نِلْتِقي بمَوْضوع جْديد next time.

**Charbel:** Hopefully, it will keep growing! Thanks for this lovely conversation, Farah, and I hope our listeners enjoyed it, got excited, and learned more about soap and shampoo making in Lebanon. We'll meet again with a new topic next time.

**فرح:** thank you شربِل، و thank you لكِلّ اللي تابعونا.

**Farah:** Thank you, Charbel, and thank you to everyone who tuned in.

## Comprehension Questions

١. شو هُوِّ مَوْضوع الحلْقة اللي حِكْيوا عنّو شرْبِل وفرح؟

٢. لِيْش يُعْتبر زيْت الزِّيْتون مُكَوِّن أساسي بِصِناعِةْ الصّابون التّقْليدي بِلِبْنان؟

٣. كيف بتْتِمّ عملية صِناعِةْ الصّابون بطْرابْلُس؟

٤. شو هِيِّ فوايِد الصّابون الطّبيعي على البشرة حسب تجْرِبِةْ فرح وشرْبِل؟

٥. لِيْش عم بتْصير صِناعِةْ الشّامْبو العُضْوي أكْتر شعْبية بِلِبْنان؟

٦. كيف بيساهِم إنْتاج الصّابون والشّامْبو الطّبيعي بِدعْم الإقْتِصاد المحلّيّ؟

٧. شو هِيِّ العلامة التّجارية اللّبْنانية المعْروفِة اللي كْتسبِت شِهْرة محلّية ودُوَلية بِصِناعِةْ الصّابون؟

٨. لِيْش تُعْتبر الوَرْشات التّعْليمية لِصِناعِةْ الصّابون والشّامْبو نشاط مْهِمّ ومُفيد؟

1. What is the topic of the episode that Charbel and Farah talked about?
2. Why is olive oil considered a key ingredient in traditional soap making in Lebanon?
3. How is the soap-making process done in Tripoli?
4. What are the benefits of natural soap for the skin according to Farah and Charbel's experience?
5. Why is organic shampoo production becoming more popular in Lebanon?
6. How does producing natural soap and shampoo support the local economy?
7. What is the well-known Lebanese brand that gained local and international fame in soap making?
8. Why are educational workshops for soap and shampoo making an important and useful activity?

## Discussion Questions

١. جرّبِت إسْتِعْمال الصّابون أوْ الشّامْبو العُضْوي مِن قبِل؟ كيف كانِت تجْرِبْتك؟

٢. شو هِيِّ فَوايِد إسْتِعْمال المنْتوجات الطّبيعية للْعِناية الشّخْصية برأْيَك؟

٣. كيف بتْشوف تأْثير صِناعةْ المنْتوجات الطّبيعية على الإقْتِصاد المحلّي؟

٤. عِنْدك أيّ قُصص عن تجْرِبِة شخْصية مع صِناعةْ المنْتوجات الطّبيعية؟

٥. شو هِيِّ النّصايِح اللي بْتعْطِيا للْأشْخاص اللي حابّين يْجرُّبوا صِناعةْ الصّابون بِالْبيْت؟

٦. كيف بتْشجِّع النّاس على إسْتِعْمال المنْتوجات الطّبيعية بدل مِن التّجارية؟

٧. شو هِيِّ المكوِّنات الطّبيعية اللي بتْفضِّلا بمنْتوجات العِناية الشّخْصية؟

٨. كيف بتْشوف تطوُّر صِناعةْ المنْتوجات الطّبيعية بلِبْنان مُقارنةً بِبلدك؟

---

1. Have you ever tried using organic soap or shampoo before? How was your experience?
2. What are the benefits of using natural personal care products in your opinion?
3. How do you see the impact of natural product industries on the local economy?
4. Do you have any personal stories about experiences with making natural products?
5. What advice would you give to people who want to try making soap at home?
6. How do you encourage people to use natural products instead of commercial ones?
7. What natural ingredients do you prefer in personal care products?
8. How do you see the development of natural product industries in Lebanon compared to your country?

# مَوْسم الزَّيْتون وزِيْت الزَّيْتون
## The Olive Season and Olive Oil

### In this episode...

Charbel and Omar talk about the beloved tradition of olive harvesting and olive oil production in Lebanon. They reminisce about family gatherings during the olive harvest season, which runs from October to December, and the important role it plays in Lebanese culture. They also discuss the process of pressing olives to produce high-quality olive oil, a staple in Lebanese cuisine. Through their stories, you'll get a glimpse of how this tradition brings communities together and how olive oil continues to be a symbol of heritage and pride for Lebanon.

## Vocabulary

| | |
|---|---|
| land, earth | أَرْض |
| orchard | بِسْتان |
| neighbors | جيران |
| harvest | حْصاد |
| smell, aroma | ريحة |
| agricultural | زِراعي |
| green olives | زيْتون أخْضَر |
| tree | شجْرة (أشْجار) |
| plate, dish | صحِن |
| fresh | طازة |
| process | عملية |
| health benefits | فَوايِد صُحّية |
| harvesting, gathering and pickling time | قْطاف |
| pickling | كبيس |
| stage (of a process) | مرْحلِة |
| press (for olive oil) | معْصِرة |
| salt | مِلح |
| season | مَوْسِم (مَواسِم) |
| preserved foods | مونِة |
| pure | نقي |

## Transcript

**شَرْبِل:** مرحبا يا جماعة! اليَوْم رح نِحْكي عن جِزءٍ مُهِمّ كْتير مِن تُراثْنا الزِّراعي بِلِبْنان: مَوْسِمِ الزَّيْتون وزيْت الزَّيْتون. شَرْبِل مَعْكُن، واليَوْم رْفيقي عُمَر معي. كيفك يا عُمَر؟

**Charbel:** Hello everyone, today we're going to talk about a very important part of our agricultural heritage in Lebanon: the olive season and olive oil. I'm Charbel, and today my friend Omar is with me. How are you, Omar?

**عُمَر:** أهْلا شَرْبِل، شْتَقْنا. أنا مْنيح، إنْتَ كيف؟ والله هَيْدا المَوْضوع كْتير غالي عَ قَلْبي وبِذكِّرْني بإيّام ما كِنّا نِطْلَع عِنْد جِدّي عَ الجَبَل بِمَوْسِم القْطاف، لنِعْمِل... لنُقْطُف الزَّيْتون ونعْمِل زيْت زيْتون.

**Omar:** Hello Charbel, I missed you! I'm good, how are you? This topic is really close to my heart and reminds me of the days when we used to go up to my grandfather's place in the mountains during the harvest season to pick olives and make olive oil.

**شَرْبِل:** عنْجَدّ، مَوْسِم الزَّيْتون هُوّ وَقْت كْتير مْمَيِّز بالسِّنِة. هُوّ مِش بَسّ جِزءٍ مِن التُّراث الزِّراعي إذا بدّك بِلِبْنان، بَسّ كمان هُوّ بْيِجْمَع العَيْلِة والجّيران بِوَقْت الحصاد إذا بدّك أوْ وَقْت القْطاف. بْتَعْرِف يا عُمَر إنّو مَوْسِم الزَّيْتون بيبلِّش عادةً بِشهْر أُكْتوبِر وبيضَلّ لشهْر ديسمْبِر وهَيْدا الوَقْت بيكون مِلْيان نشاط وحَيَويِة بالضِّيَع بِلِبْنان.

**Charbel:** Indeed, the olive season is a very special time of the year. It's not just a part of Lebanon's agricultural heritage, if you will, but it also brings together family and neighbors during the harvest time, or as we call it, the picking time. You know, Omar, the olive season usually starts in October and lasts until December, and this time is full of activity and energy in the villages of Lebanon.

**عُمَر:** أيْه! اللي عم بِتْقولو مِيّة بالمِيّة مظْبوط، وأنا عِنْدي ذِكْرَيات كْتير حِلْوِة مِن وَقْت القْطاف. كِنّا نْروح كِلّ العَيْلِة عَ البِسْتان ونْقضّي نْهار كِلّو عم نْجمِّع زيْتون. الجَوّ بيكون رائِع والشَّمْس دافْيِة وكِلّ حدا بيكون عِنْدو وظيفِة يَعْمِلا. في ناس بِتْكون عم بِتْقطِّف في ناس عم بِتْلِمّ وتْضُبّ بالكْياس.

**Omar:** Yeah! What you're saying is absolutely true, and I have many fond memories of the harvest time. The whole family would go to the orchard and spend the entire day gathering olives. The weather would be great, the sun warm, and everyone had a job to do. Some would be picking, some gathering, and others packing the olives into sacks.

**شَرْبِل:** مِيّة بالمِيّة اللي عم تِحكي. أنا كمان عِنْدي كْتير ذِكْرَيات حِلْوة بِمَوْسِم الزّيْتون. بْتِذكّر مرّة كنّا عم نْجمّع الزّيْتون، وْقِعْنا بِمَوْقِف هيْك بيضحّك إذا بدّك.كان في شجْرة كْبيرة وعالْية كْتير، وأنا جرّبِت أطْلع عْلَيا لأَقْطُف الزّيْتون مِن فوْق. وفجْأة فقدِت التّوازُن تبعي ووْقِعِت. بسّ لحظّي الحِلو إنّو كان في هَيْدي الحصيرة اللي بيحُطُّوا، يَعْني خفّفِت الإصابة. وكانِت العَيْلة كِلّا هيْك بين عِتْلاني همّ وبيْن بدا تِضْحك وبين عم بْتعيّط عْلَيّ إنّو إمّي ليْش شو طلّعْني لفوْق. قطعِت عَ خيْر وَقْتا وهيْك ذِكْرى بْتِضلّ بِعقْلي.

Charbel: Exactly, what you're saying is true. I also have many great memories from the olive season. I remember once when we were picking olives, we had a funny incident. There was this big, tall tree, and I tried to climb it to pick the olives from the top. Suddenly, I lost my balance and fell. Luckily, there was a mat they put down, which softened the fall. And the whole family was kind of between being worried, wanting to laugh, and yelling at me, like my mom, saying why did I go up there. Thankfully, it ended well, and this is a memory that always stays with me.

**عُمر:** أيْه والله يا شرْبِل ضحّكِتْني بهالْخبْرية وحتّى صايْرة معي وبيعْرِف كذا شخْص صايْرة معو. مَوْسِم الزّيْتون عنّا عنْجدّ مِتل ما بيقولوا مِن التّقاليد الكْتير مُرسّخة بِثقافِتْنا وجُذورْنا. وعلى فِكْرة ما كانِت المُهِمّة تِخْلص بسّ بالْحصاد. لأنّو المرْحلة اللي بْتِجي بعد الحصاد هيِّ مرْحلة كْتير مْهِمّة وهيِّ عصْر الزّيْتون ولَيطْلعلْنا زيْت الزّيْتون كِرْمال المونة ونِسْتعْمِلا بِفصل الشّتي.

Omar: Oh Charbel, that story made me laugh, and it's even happened to me, and I know others who've experienced it too. The olive season is truly, as they say, one of the deeply rooted traditions in our culture and heritage. By the way, the task doesn't end with the harvest. The next stage, which is very important, is pressing the olives to get the olive oil for storage and use during the winter.

**شَرْبِل:** عنْجدّ العملية كِلّا هيْك مُثيرة إذا بدّك بين إنّو توصل ...يوصل الزّيْتون على المعْصرة بيتِمّ غسْلا وتِنْقايِتا وتْنْضيفا، بعْديْن حتّى تِنْعصر لَيسْتخِرْجوا الزّيْت. أوّل

مرّة شِفِت فيا العملية كانت عنْجَدّ هيْك مدْهوش والزّيْتون إنّو كيف الزّيْتون بِيْتْحوّل لزيْت نقيّ وهيْك دهبي وبتْحِسّ الرّيحة عنْجَدّ رائْعة بِتْتْلي الدّني.

**Charbel:** Indeed, the whole process is quite fascinating if you will—from when the olives arrive at the press, they get washed, sorted, and cleaned, and then they are pressed to extract the oil. The first time I saw the process, I was really amazed at how the olives are transformed into pure, golden oil with a smell that's truly wonderful.

**عُمر:** على فِكْرة شرْبِل، أنا بعكس أغْلبيّة العالم يَلّي بْيِنْطروا شْوَيّ على زيت الزّيْتون لكانِت خفّت حِدّيتو. بعدْني بِتْذكّر إنّو مِن أطْيَب الطّعْمات اللي دايقا هُوّ زيْت الزّيْتون الطّازة يَلّي بعْدو ضاهِر مِن المعْصرة. كان يِبْقى لَوْنو أخْضر كْتير قوي هيْك لَوْنو أخْضر فائِع. وكان عِنْدو طعْمة مُميّزة وريحتو قَوية بسّ بذات الوَقِت مِلْيانة aromas مِتِل ما كِنّا... مِتِل ما عم بْتْذكّر. مِش غريب إنّو زيت الزّيْتون كْتير بْيُسْتعْمل بالْمطْبخ اللّبْناني وهَيْدا شي بِتْخايل فينا نِرِبْطو بكمّيّة أشْجار الزّيْتون اللي عِنّا ياها وبِهيْدي التّقاليد يَلّي أغْلبيّة العيَل اللّبْنانية بعْدا لهلّأ مُحافْظة عْلَيا.

**Omar:** Actually, Charbel, unlike most people who wait a bit for the olive oil to lose its sharpness, I still remember that one of the best tastes I've had was freshly pressed olive oil, right out of the press. It was a very strong green color, vibrant, with a distinctive taste and a strong aroma, but at the same time, it was filled with complex aromas, as I recall. It's no surprise that olive oil is so widely used in Lebanese cuisine, and I think we can link this to the abundance of olive trees we have and the traditions that many Lebanese families still preserve.

**شرْبِل:** مِيّة بالْمِيّة يا عُمر، زيْت الزّيْتون هُوّ جزء مِن هَوِيّتْنا الغِذائية إذا بدّك. هُوّ شي أساسي ويُسْتعْمل إذا بدّك بأغْلبيّة الطّبِخ، يَعْني مِش بسّ نَيّ حتّى نَيّ بْينْطبخ فيه يَعْني. وما نِنْسى إنّو عِنْدو كمان فَوايِد صُحّية كْتير وبيساعِد على تِحْسين الصّحّة صحّةْ القلْب والشّرايين.

**Charbel:** Absolutely, Omar, olive oil is a part of our culinary identity if you will. It's something essential and is used in most of our cooking, not just raw but also in cooked dishes. And let's not forget that it also has many health benefits, helping to improve heart and vascular health.

**عُمَر:** مَظْبوط! اللي عم تِحْكي مُثْبَت عِلْمِيّاً على فِكْرة وخاصَّةً إِنّو بِلِبْنان قْدِرْنا نِنْتُج من أَعْلى نَوْعِيّات الزِّيْت الزَّيْتون بِالْعالَم. وحَصَدْنا كْتير جَوايِز وبَعْدِنا لِهَلّأ عم نْطَوِّر بِهَيْدي الصِّناعة والزِّراعة. وعلى فِكْرة غير مَوْضوع زيْت الزَّيْتون في الزَّيْتون بِحَدّ ذاتو. ونِحْنا عادةً بْلِبْنان مْنَعْمِل... مِنْسَمِّيا مْنِكْبُس الزَّيْتون. كِلّ عَيْلة لِبْنانية عِنْدا طريقْتا الخاصّة بَسّ إِجْمالاً بِيزيدوا مَوادّ على الزَّيْتون مِتِل اللّيْمون مِتِل الحامُض مِتِل الفُلْفُل الحارّ الأَعْشاب وأَكيد زيْت الزَّيْتون وبِيتِرْكوا فَتَرات شْوَيّ طَويلة يَعْني. يِمْكِن بِدّك شهر لتِقْدِر تِسْتَعِمْلو بَسّ بْيِطْلَع طَعِمْتو وَلّا أَلَزّ خاصَّةً هيْك مع صَحْن لَبْنِة وزيْت زيْتون عَ وِجّا.

**Omar:** True! What you're saying is scientifically proven, and especially in Lebanon, we've managed to produce some of the highest quality olive oils in the world. We've won many awards, and we continue to develop this industry and agriculture. By the way, apart from olive oil, we also have olives themselves. In Lebanon, we usually pickle olives—each Lebanese family has its own method, but in general, they add ingredients like lemon, hot peppers, herbs, and of course, olive oil, and let them sit for a while. It might take about a month before they're ready to eat, but the taste is incredible, especially with a plate of labneh and olive oil on the side.

**شَرْبِل:** يا عَيْني عْلَيْك! ما نِنْسى الحُمُّص كمان ما بْيِتّاكل بلا زيْت. لَيْك عُمر مِتِل ما عم تْقول كبيس الزَّيْتون ما بِيفارِق الطّاوْلة اللِّبْنانية. وفي عِنّا مِتِل إِنّو "الحُبّ القديم بْتِمْشي معك على الخِبْزة والزِّيْتونة" لْتْشوف قَدّي عتيق هالْمِثِل. ومِش بَسّ هيْك عم تِحْكي عن الطُّرُق اللي بْيِنْكبِس فيا الزَّيْتون. بْتِعْرَف يا عُمر إِنّو أنا بْحِبّ الزَّيْتون أَخْضَر. بْتِعْرَف شو يَعْني الزَّيْتون الأَخْضَر؟ هُوَّ بيكون بَعْدو مَقْطوف طازة وبْيِنْقِع بْمايّ وبْيِنْكبِس بِالْمِلِح. طَعِمْتو قَوِية كْتير ومُرّة بَسّ عَنْجَدّ وَلا أَطْيَب. وهات لَخَبِّرك خَبْرِية بْتِضْحَّك عَنّي، أنا وصْغير. هُوَّ في زيْتون الأَخْضَر وزيْتون الأَسْوَد، بْتِعْرَف يا عُمر إِنّو أنا كِنْت مْفَكِّر إِنّو زيْتون الأَسْوَد بْيِجي من غير شَجْرِةٍ مِن الزَّيْتون الأَخْضَر. بَعْدَيْن عِرِفْت إِنّو هِيّ process إِنّو مِتِل كأَنّو بِدّو يِسْتِوي أَكْتَر الزَّيْتون وبْيِنْقطِف بَسّ يْصير أَسْوَد.

**Charbel:** Absolutely! And let's not forget that hummus isn't complete without olive oil. Look, Omar, as you said, pickled olives never leave the Lebanese table. We have a saying that goes, "the old love walks with you on bread and olives," to show how deep this tradition is. And not only that, speaking of how olives are pickled, you know, Omar, that I love green olives. Do you know what green olives are? Green olives are freshly picked and then pickled in water and salt. Their taste is very strong and bitter, but honestly, there's nothing better. Let me tell you a funny story about myself when I was young. There are green olives and black olives, and you know, Omar, I used to think that black olives came from a different tree than green olives. Later, I learned that it's a process—like the olives have to ripen more and are picked when they turn black.

**عُمَر:** كلّنا هيْك يمْكن كنّا مْفكّرين بمرْحلة من المراحل. هلّأ هَيْدي فُرْصة لإلْنا لنْشجِّع المُسْتمعين إنّو يْحافْظوا على هَيْدا التِّقْليد، كمْلوا زراعة أَشْجار الزّيْتون بلبْنان وصناعة زيْت الزّيْتون. لأنّو هَيْدا الشّي بيخلّي الواحد يشْعُر بالإنْتماء. بْتعْرف بيقولوا اللي بيْزرع شجْرة زيْتون بالأرْض ما بْيترْكا. انْشالله هيْك يسْتمرّ هَيْدا التِّقْليد ويْضلّ بثقافتْنا لأنّو هَيْدا الشّي بيفَوِّت الفرح وبيعلِّمك العمل الجّماعي وكمان هُوّ فُرْصة لنشْكُر الأرْض اللي عم تعْطينا خَيْراتا.

Omar: We all probably thought that at some point. Now, this is a great opportunity for us to encourage our listeners to keep this tradition alive, continue planting olive trees in Lebanon, and produce olive oil. This makes one feel connected to the land, and as they say, those who plant an olive tree never leave it. Hopefully, this tradition continues and stays in our culture because it brings joy, teaches teamwork, and is also a way to thank the land for giving us its blessings.

**شرْبِل:** حلو حلو اللي عم تِحْكي يا عُمر! ميرْسي لألك عَ هالْمُشاركة الحِلْوة وانْشالله يْكونوا سْتمْتعوا المُسْتمعين معْنا وشهّيْناهُن على الزّيْت الزّيْتون. انْشالله مْنلْتقي بمَوْضوع جْديد مرّة تانْية وخبْرية جْديدة من لبْنان لَوَقْتا نْتبْهوا عَ حالكُن.

Charbel: What you're saying is beautiful, Omar! Thank you for this lovely conversation, and I hope our listeners enjoyed it and that we made them crave some olive oil. Hopefully, we'll meet again with a new topic and story from Lebanon. Until then, take care of yourselves.

**عُمَر:** شُكْراً إلك شرْبِل وشُكْراً لكلّ يَلّي تابعونا. انْشالله نلْتقى المرّة الجايِة بمَوْضوع جْديد وحْكايات جْديدة من حَياتْنا بلبْنان لَوَقْتا خلّو بالْكُن على حالْكُن وما تِنْسوا تْضيفوا زيْت الزّيْتون على كلّ الأَطْباق.

**Omar:** Thank you, Charbel, and thanks to everyone who joined us. Hopefully, we'll meet again next time with a new topic and a new story from our life in Lebanon. Until then, take care of yourselves and don't forget to add olive oil to all your dishes.

## Comprehension Questions

١. أيْمْتى عادةً بيبلِّش مَوْسِمِ الزّيْتون بِلِبْنان وبأيّ شهرِ بِيْنْتِهِي؟

٢. كيف كانِت ذِكْرَيات عُمر وشرْبِل بمَوْسِمِ الزّيْتون؟

٣. شو هِيِّ المرْحلِة اللي بْتِجي بعِد الحصاد؟ وشو أهمية هالْمرْحلِةْ؟

٤. كيف بيتِمّ إسْتِخْراج زيْت الزّيْتون بالْمعْصرة؟

٥. ليْش عُمر بيفضِّل زيْت الزّيْتون الطّازة يَلّي بْيِطْلع ضُغْري مِن المعْصرة؟

٦. كيف بْتِتِمّ عملية كبيس الزّيْتون بِلِبْنان؟ وشو هِنّي المكوّنات اللي بْيِنْضافوا؟

٧. شو هِيِّ الأخْطاء اللي كان مْفكِّرا شرْبِل عن الفرْق بيْن الزّيْتون الأخْضر والزّيْتون الأسْوَد؟

٨. شو هُوِّ الشُّعور أَوْ الدّرْس اللي بْيِسْتفاد مِن عمليةِ زِراعةِ الزّيْتون بِلِبْنان حسب رأْيِ عُمر؟

1. When does the olive season in Lebanon usually start and in which month does it end?
2. What were Omar and Charbel's memories of the olive season?
3. What is the stage that comes after the harvest? And what is the importance of this stage?
4. How is olive oil extracted in the press?
5. Why does Omar prefer the fresh olive oil that comes straight from the press?
6. How is the process of pickling olives done in Lebanon? And what ingredients are added?
7. What were the mistakes Charbel thought about the difference between green and black olives?
8. What is the feeling or lesson that can be learned from the process of olive cultivation in Lebanon according to Omar?

## Discussion Questions

١. شو هِنّي التّقاليد الزّراعية اللي بِعْدك بْتِتّبعا بِبلدك؟ وكيف بِتْأَثّر هالتّقاليد على حَياتك اليَوْمية؟

٢. في بِبلدك مُنْتج زراعي مْعيّن بيشكِّل جِزءِ كْبير مِن التُّراث والثّقافِة؟ خبِّرْنا عنّو.

٣. شو هِيِّ الذِّكْرَيات المُرْتِبْطة بمَواسم الحصاد أَوْ الأعْياد الزّراعية بِبلدك؟

٤. كيف بِتْأَثّر الفُصول على الزّراعة بِبلدك؟ وبيكون في عِنْدك مَواسِم مْعيّنة مُميّزة؟

٥. لشو بْتعْتِقِد أهميةْ زِراعةْ الأشْجار والمُحافظة على البيئة بِبلدك؟

٦. قدّيْش مْهِمّ الحِفاظ على التّقاليد الزّراعية بِبلدك، خُصوصاً بِظلّ التّقدُّم التّكْنولوْجي؟

٧. كيف بيتِمّ إسْتِخْراج أَوْ تُحْضير المُنْتجات الزّراعية بِبلدك؟ وبِتْحافِظ على الطُّرُق التّقْليدية؟

٨. كيف بِتْحِسّ زِراعةْ وإنْتاج مُنْتج مْعيّن مُمْكِن يْوَحِّد النّاس ويْعزِّز العمل الجّماعي بِبلدك؟

1. What are the agricultural traditions that you still follow in your country? How do these traditions affect your daily life?
2. Is there a particular agricultural product in your country that is a significant part of the heritage and culture? Tell us about it.
3. What are your memories associated with harvest seasons or agricultural festivals in your country?
4. How do the seasons affect agriculture in your country? Do you have specific special seasons?
5. How important do you think it is to plant trees and preserve the environment in your country?
6. How important is it to preserve agricultural traditions in your country, especially with technological advancement?
7. How are agricultural products extracted or prepared in your country? Do you maintain traditional methods?
8. How do you feel that planting and producing a particular product can unite people and enhance teamwork in your country?

# الجِّيل الجْديد ووَسائِل التّواصُل الإجْتِماعي
## The New Generation and Social Media

### In this episode...

Charbel and Farah explore how the new generation is growing up in a world dominated by social media and technology. They discuss how children today spend more time on screens—watching YouTube videos, playing games, and scrolling through TikTok—compared to the outdoor, social activities of the past. Charbel and Farah also reflect on the impact this shift has on children's mental and physical health, while emphasizing the importance of balance between technology use and real-life interactions. They highlight how parents can guide their children toward a healthier relationship with technology.

## Vocabulary

| | |
|---|---|
| the new generation | الجّيل الجْديد |
| to give up, abandon | تْخلّى (يِتْخلّى) عن |
| technological | تِكْنوْلوْجي |
| balance | تَوازُن |
| social interaction | تَواصُل إجْتِماعي |
| privacy | خْصوصية |
| supervision, monitoring | رقابِة |
| to lean on, rely on | ركّى (يْركيّ) على |
| spirit of enthusiasm | روح الحماس |
| screen | شاشِة |
| physical health | صُحّة جسدية |
| mental health | صُحّة عقْلية |
| childhood | طُفولِة |
| lack of movement, physical inactivity | قِلّة الحركِة |
| activities | نشاطات |
| eyesight | نظر |
| face to face | وِجّ لَوِجّ |
| overweight | وزِن زايِد |
| social media | وَسائِل التَّواصُل الإجْتِماعي |
| great tool | وَسيلِة رائْعة |

# Transcript

**شَرْبِل:** هاي، كيفْكُن؟ اليوْم رح نِحْكي عن مَوْضوع هيْك جْديد إذا بدّكُن ومُثير للإهْتِمام: الجيل الجْديد ووَسائِل التَّواصُل الإجْتِماعي. معْكُن شرْبِل ومعي اليوْم صديقْتي فرح. كيفِك يا فرح؟

Charbel: Hi, how are you all? Today, we're going to talk about a new and interesting topic: the new generation and social media. I'm Charbel, and with me today is my friend Farah. How are you, Farah?

**فرح:** هاي شرْبِل، الحمْدلله أنا مْنيحة، إنْتَ كيف؟

Farah: Hi Charbel, thank God I'm good. How are you?

**شَرْبِل:** great، great! صراحة هيْك المَوْضوع اليوْم اللي بدّنا نِحْكي في عن كيف هالجّيل يَعْني صار بسّ إنّو بْيِعْتِمِد على الـtechnology وكِلّ شي خصّو بالـsocial media. يَعْني بِتْلاحْظي كيف هالوْلاد هالأيّام كِلُّن عنْدُن smart phones وآيْبادات، يَعْني بيقضّوا على يوتْيوب وتيك توْك ويَعْني كِلّ الوَقِت!

Charbel: Great, great! Honestly, today's topic is about how this generation relies entirely on technology and everything related to social media. You notice how kids these days all have smartphones and iPads, and they spend all their time on YouTube and TikTok—like, all the time!

**فرح:** صحّ المَوْضوع هَيْدا كْتير تْغيّر عن قبل. اليوْم كِلّ الوْلاد صاروا يْقضّوا وَقِت أكْتر على الشّاشات، شي مِش مقْبول! بْيِحْضروا videos على يوتْيوب، على تيك توْك أوْ حتّى بْيِلْعبوا عَ هالـgames اللي يَعْني مِش حتّى لأعْمارُن.

Farah: Right, this topic has changed a lot from before. Nowadays, kids spend more time in front of screens, which is unacceptable! They watch videos on YouTube, TikTok, or even play games that are not even for their age.

**شَرْبِل:** مِيّة بالمِيّة يَعْني وهَيْدا الشّي ما بعْرف يَعْني، أنا منّي أخِصّائي بسّ أكيد عم يأثّر عْلَيْن بطرُق كْتير يَعْني مثلاً. بدّنا نِحْكي عن كيف هالـtechnology عم بِتأثّر على صحّتْن العقْلية والجَسدية. يَعْني الوْلاد بدل ما يْروحوا يِلْعبوا برّا أوْ يِلْعبوا مع بعْضُن هِنّي بيقضّوا على الشّاشات.

**Charbel:** Absolutely, and this, I don't know, I'm not an expert, but it surely affects them in many ways. For example, we need to talk about how this technology affects their mental and physical health. Instead of going out to play or playing with each other, kids are spending time on screens.

**فرح:** بِتْذكّر نِحْنا لمّا كِنّا صْغار كِنّا نِطْلع نِلْعب بالبِسِكْليتات، بالـskateboard، بالـrollers. يَعْني الشّباب كانوا يِلعبوا بالفوتْبوْل، يَعِمْلوا فريق. دايماً كان في وَقت نْقضّيه سَوا، كان في تَواصُل بين هالوْلاد. هلّأ بالمرّة شي يَعْني بيخوِّف.

**Farah:** I remember when we were young, we'd go outside and play on our bikes, skateboards, or rollerskates. The boys would play football and form teams. We always spent time together, and there was communication between kids. Now, it's really scary.

**شرْبِل:** صحّ وكْتير بْتْذكّر كيف يَعْني كِنّا نِطْلع نِلْعب مع بعض ونْقضّي وَقت طَويل عم نِلْعب ونِرْكُض. وكِنّا نعِمْل كْتير أصْدِقاء جْداد يَعْني ونِتْعلّم كيف نِتْعامل مع بعضنا وهَيْدا الشّي يَعْني ساعدْنا مْناخُد مهارات إجْتماعية كْتير أساسية. وهَيْدا الشّي حتّى الوْلاد هلّأ عم بْيِفْتِقْدوا، يَعْني كْتير عم بيركّزوا على إنّو هيْك يِلعبوا على الشّاشات وهَيْدا الشّي عم بيأثّر إنّو ما كْتير يَعِمْلوا تفاعُل بين بعض.

**Charbel:** Right, and I remember how we used to go out and play together, spend a long time playing and running around. We made many new friends and learned how to interact with each other, which helped us develop essential social skills. Nowadays, kids are missing out on this because they are too focused on playing on screens, which affects their interaction with each other.

**فرح:** صحّ، اليوْم كِلّ الوْلاد عم بيقضّوا وَقِت كْتير طَويل على الشّاشات وهَيْدا الشّي عم بيخلّيُن يِفِقْدوا التّواصُل، التّواصُل الإجْتماعي الطّبيعي اللي نِحْنا عِنجدّ عايْشينو مِن قبل. بِتْشوف هالوْلاد هالإيّام بيفضّلوا يْضلُّن قاعْدين يِتْواصلوا مع بعْضُن على الأوْنْلاين بدل ما يِتْقابلوا أوْ يِتْحدّثوا مع بعضُن يَعْني وِجّ لَوِجّ.

**Farah:** True. These days, kids spend way too much time on screens, which is causing them to lose natural social interaction that we used to have. You see these kids today prefer to stay and communicate online rather than meeting or talking face-to-face.

**شَرْبِل:** وكمان يَعْني هَيْدا الإعْتِماد الكْبير على التّكْنُولُوْجْيا عم بيأَثِّر على صِحّتُن الجَسَدية. يَعْني الوْلاد اليوْم عم بيعانوا إذا بدِّك مِن مشاكِل بالـ.. إنّو بالنّظر، بالوَزِن الزّايِد يَعْني بيسبِّب قِلّةُ الحركة وإنّو بْيِقعْدوا كْتير فترات على هالْمُوبايْلات أوْ الآيْباد.

**Charbel:** Moreover, this heavy reliance on technology affects their physical health. Kids today are suffering from problems with their eyesight and weight gain due to lack of movement and sitting for long periods with their cell phones or iPads.

**فرح:** لازِم الأهالي يِنْتِبْهوا لهالنُّقْطة، ويْحاوْلوا يْشجْعوا وْلادُن إنّو يِخْتِلْطوا مع وْلاد تانْيين يِلْعبوا، يَعْملوا نشاطات مِتِل الرّياضة. بْتْذكّر أنا كْتير مْنيح مرّة كِنّا عم نِلْعب بالْبِسِكْليتات بهالشّارِع وصارِت معْنا هيْك مَواقِف بْتْضحِّك كْتير! كان دايْماً في روح الحماس بيْن هالوْلاد.

**Farah:** Parents really need to pay attention to this and try to encourage their kids to socialize with other children, to play and engage in activities like sports. I remember so well when we used to ride our bikes on the street, and we had such funny moments! There was always a spirit of enthusiasm among the kids.

**شَرْبِل:** مِيّة بالْمِيّة! وكمان لازِم يْكون في تَوازُن بيْن إسْتِخْدام التّكْنُولُوْجْيا والنّشاطات التّانْية. ليْكي التّكْنُولُوْجْيا جزء يَعْني ما فينا نِتْخلّى عنّو صار جزء أساسي وبِحَياتْنا اليَوْمية الكلّ بْيِعْتِمِد عْليْه. بسّ لازِم تْكون... مِش... ما لازِم يْكون كلّ حَياتْنا. الأطْفال هلّأ يَعْني لازِم يِتْعلّموا كيف يِسْتَخْدِموا أكيد المُوبايْلات وكلّ شي خصّو بالتّكْنُولُوْجْيا بسّ بْشكِل صحيح ويْكون في رقابة مِن الأهِل.

**Charbel:** Absolutely! There needs to be a balance between using technology and other activities. Look, technology is something we can't give up; it has become an essential part of our daily lives, and everyone relies on it. But it shouldn't take over our entire lives. Kids need to learn how to use phones and technology, but in a proper way, with supervision from parents.

**فرح:** مظْبوط. وَسائِل التّواصُل الإجْتِماعي فيا كْتير فَوايِد، بسّ لازِم عنْجدّ نَعْرِف كيف نِسْتَعْمِلا كْتير بْحذر. لازِم نِتْعلّم كيف نْحافِظ على خْصوصيّاتْنا، نِسْتَعْمِلا عنْجدّ بْشكِل يْكون كْتير إيجابي.

**Farah:** Exactly. Social media has a lot of benefits, but we need to learn how to use it cautiously. We need to learn how to maintain our privacy and use it positively.

**شَرْبِل:** وضَروري الأهِل يْكُونوا مِثال لِلوْلاد. إذا الوْلاد شافوا أهْلُن كمان كِلّ الوَقِت قاعْدين على هالتِّلِيفُونات لح يْقَلْدُون يَعْني. الأهِل لازِم يْكُونوا مِنْتَبْهين ويْخَصّصوا وَقِت لَوْلادُن بْعيد عن الشّاشات.

Charbel: And parents must set an example for their kids. If children see their parents always on their phones, they're going to imitate them. Parents need to be mindful and set aside time with their kids away from screens.

**فرح:** وبِالنِّهايِة، لازِم نِتْذكّر إنّو التَّوازُن هُوّ المِفْتاح. التِّكْنُولُوجْيا مُمْكِن تْكون وَسيلِة رائْعة إذا سْتَعْمِلْناها بِشكِل صحيح، بسّ لازِم نِتْأكّد إنّو وْلادْنا عم بيعيشوا طُفولِتُن بِشكِل طبيعي.

Farah: In the end, we have to remember that balance is key. Technology can be a great tool if we use it correctly, but we need to make sure our kids are living their childhoods in a natural way.

**شَرْبِل:** صحّ بْوافْقِك الرَّأي يا فرح، وهَيْدا بيطلّب جِهِد مِن الأهِل مِن الكِلّ مِن المدارِس مِن المُجْتمَّع. لازِم نِشْتِغِل مع بعْض لْنْساعِد هالْجيل الجْديد يْعيش حَياةْ مِتْوازْنِة وصُحّيّة، وخاصّةً هالوْلاد الصُّغار.

Charbel: I totally agree with you, Farah. And this requires effort from parents, schools, and the entire community. We all need to work together to help this new generation live a balanced and healthy life, especially young children.

**فرح:** شُكْراً إلك يا شرْبِل عَ هالْحديث الحِلو، وشُكْراً اللي عم بْيِسْمعونا. مْنِتْمنّى تْكونوا سْتفدْتوا. مْنِلْتِقي أكيد المرّة الجايِة بمَوْضوع وقُصص جْديدة مِن حَياتْنا بِلِبْنان.

Farah: Thank you, Charbel, for this lovely conversation, and thanks to everyone who's listening. We hope you've found this helpful. We'll definitely meet again next time with new topics and stories from our lives in Lebanon.

## Comprehension Questions

١. شو هُوّ مَوْضوع الحلْقة اللي حِكيوا عنّو شرْبِل وفرح؟

٢. كيف بِتْلاحِظ فرح تْغيرِّت عادات اللّعِب عِنْد الوِلاد بيِنْ قبل وهلّأً؟

٣. كيف بِتْأثِّر التِّكْنُولُوْجْيا على الصُّحّة العقْلية والجْسدية للأطْفال؟

٤. شو كان يَعْمُل شرْبِل وفرح لمّا كانوا صْغار بدل قعْدِة على الشاشات؟

٥. ليْش شرْبِل بْيِعْتِقِد إنّو الأطْفال اليوْم عم يِفْتِقْدوا المهارات الإجْتماعية؟

٦. شو هِيِّ المخاطِر الصُّحّية اللي بيواجْهُوا الأطْفال بِسبب القعْدِة الطَّويلِة على الشّاشات؟

٧. شو نصايح فرح للأهالي بِخْصوص تِشْجيع وْلادُن على اللّعِب والنّشاطات؟

٨. كيف بيوَضِّح شرْبِل أهمية التَّوازُن بين التِّكْنُوْلُوْجْيا والنّشاطات التّانْية؟

1. What is the topic of the episode discussed by Charbel and Farah?
2. How does Farah notice the change in children's play habits between the past and now?
3. How does technology affect the mental and physical health of children?
4. What did Charbel and Farah do when they were young instead of sitting on screens?
5. Why does Charbel believe that children today are missing out on social skills?
6. What are the health risks children face due to prolonged screen time?
7. What are Farah's suggestions for parents regarding encouraging their children to play and be active?
8. How does Charbel explain the importance of balancing technology with other activities?

## Discussion Questions

١. كيف بِتْأَثَّر وَسائِل التَّواصُل الإجْتِماعي على حَياتِك اليَوْمية؟

٢. شو هِيِّ الأنْشِطة اللي بِتْحِبّ تعْمِلا بْعيد عن الشّاشات؟

٣. كيف بِتْشوف الفرق بيْنْ طُفولْتك وطُفولةْ الجّيل الجْديد مِن ناحْيةْ اللّعِب والنّشاطات؟

٤. شو هِيِّ النّصايِح اللي بْتعْطيا للأهالي بِخْصوص إسْتِعْمال التِّكْنُولُوجْيا مِن قِبل وْلادُن؟

٥. كيف بِتْوازِن بيْن إسْتِخْدام التِّكْنُولُوجْيا والنّشاطات الجسدية والإجْتِماعية بِحَياتك؟

٦. هل بِتْشوف إنّو التَّواصُل الإجْتِماعي على الإنْترْنِت مُمْكِن يْعوِّض عن التَّواصُل الواقِعي؟ ليْش أوْ ليْش لأ؟

٧. شو هِيِّ المخاطِر الصُّحّية اللي بْتِعْتِقِد إنّو التِّكْنُولُوجْيا مُمْكِن تْسبِّبا؟ وكيف مُمْكِن نِتْجنّبا؟

٨. كيف بِتْشوف مُسْتقْبل الأطْفال بِظِل الإعْتِماد الكِبير على التِّكْنُولُوجْيا؟

1. How does social media affect your daily life?
2. What activities do you enjoy doing away from screens?
3. How do you see the difference between your childhood and the new generation's childhood in terms of play and activities?
4. What advice would you give to parents regarding their children's use of technology?
5. How do you balance technology use with physical and social activities in your life?
6. Do you think online social interaction can replace real-life interaction? Why or why not?
7. What health risks do you think technology might cause? How can we avoid them?
8. How do you see the future of children in light of the heavy reliance on technology?

# كُرةُ السّلّة والرّياضة بِلِبْنان

## Basketball and Sports in Lebanon

### In this episode...

Charbel and Omar dive into a topic close to the hearts of many Lebanese: basketball and sports in Lebanon. They talk about how basketball has become the country's most popular sport, with the national team and local clubs achieving impressive milestones. From the success of Lebanon's top teams like Al Riyadi to the incredible talents such as Wael Arakji, they highlight the impact these achievements have on the nation. The conversation also touches on the importance of developing young talent and the role sports play in promoting health, teamwork, and national pride in Lebanon.

## Vocabulary

| | |
|---|---|
| academy | أكاديمية |
| achievement | إنْجاز |
| championship | بُطولة |
| league | دَوْري |
| sportsmanship | روح رياضية |
| national | وَطني |
| sport | رِياضة |
| point guard | صانع الألْعاب |
| level | صعيد |
| by the way | على فِكْرة |
| teamwork | عمل جماعي |
| team | فريق (فِرق) |
| basketball | كُرِةْ السَّلِّة |
| to inspire | لهم (يِلْهُم) |
| outlet, escape [as in a way to relieve stress] | مُتنفّس |
| fan, supporter | مُشجِّع |
| court | ملْعب (ملاعِب) |
| national team | مُنْتخب |
| talent | مَوِهْبة (مَواهِب) |
| club | نادي (نَوادي) |

## Transcript

**شَرْبِل:** مَرحبا كيفْكُن؟ اليوْم رح نِحْكي عن مَوْضوع مْهمّ و أحبّ عَ قَلْب الشَّعْب اللُّبناني : كُرْة السَّلّة (الباسْكِتْبوْل) والرِّياضة بْلبْنان. أنا شرْبِل، ومعي اليوْم صديقي عُمر. كيفك يا عُمر؟

Charbel: Hello, how are you all? Today we're going to talk about an important topic that's dear to the hearts of the Lebanese people: basketball and sports in Lebanon. I'm Charbel, and with me today is my friend Omar. How are you, Omar?

**عُمر:** هاي شرْبِل! والله أنا كْتير مْنيح وصراحة كْتير كْتير كْتير مبْسوط إنّو رح نِحْكي عن الباسْكِتْبوْل لأنّو هِيِّ واحِدة مِن رياضاتي المُفضَّلِة.

Omar: Hi Charbel! I'm very good, and honestly, I'm really, really, really happy that we're going to talk about basketball because it's one of my favorite sports.

**شَرْبِل:** وأنا كمان! الباسْكِت بْلِبْنان مشهورة كْتير وهُوّ الدّوْر اللُّبْناني مِن الأفْضل بالمْنْطقة. عِنّا ثقافِةْ كُرْةْ السَّلّة كْتير قَوِيّة. وحتّى فريقْنا الوَطني حقّق إنْجازات كْبيرِة وخلّانا نِفْتِخِر فيه.

Charbel: Me too! Basketball is very popular in Lebanon, and the Lebanese league is one of the best in the region. We have a very strong basketball culture, and even our national team has achieved great things that have made us proud.

**عُمر:** صحّ مِيّة بالمِيّة. و أنا بْحِبّ زيد عْليْك وقِلك إنّو كُرْة السَّلّة بْلِبْنان هِيِّ اللّعْبة الشّعْبية الأولى. وأخدِت مِتِل ما بْقولوا شِهْرة وسرقِت قْلوب اللِّبْنانيِّين مِن وَرا mainly هَيْدوْل الإنْجازات يَلّي صارِت. أكيد شرْبِل يَلّي عم تْقولو كْتير مظْبوط وخاصّةً إنّو الفريق الوَطني اللُّبْناني أوْ المُنْتخب وُصِل لكاس العالم مرّتيْن ولدَوْلة بحجم لِبْنان يُعْتبر إنْجاز كْبير. وعلى فِكْرة حتّى صانِع الألْعاب عِنّا بالمُنْتخب وائِل عرقْجي طِلع أفْضل لاعِب بآسْيا! وهَيْدا بِدل على مُسْتَوى المَواهِب اللي عِنّا. وخاصّةً مِتِل ما قِلت إنّو نِحْنا بلد صْغير بسّ بِلعْبِة الباسْكِتْبوْل عم نْفرْجي قُدُرات كْتير كْبيرة.

Omar: Absolutely, one hundred percent! And I'd like to add that basketball in Lebanon is the number one most popular game. It has gained a lot of fame and has won the hearts of the Lebanese people mainly because of the achievements that have happened. Charbel, what you're saying is very true, especially since the Lebanese national team reached the World Cup twice, and for a country the size of Lebanon, that's a huge accomplishment. And by the way, our point guard, Wael Arakji, was named the best player in Asia! This shows the level of talent we have–especially as you said, for a small country like ours, we're showing great capabilities in basketball.

**شَرْبِل:** صحّ وبِالنِّسْبِة لِلْمَواهِب، الأنْدِية اللّبنانية كمان مِن الأفْضل بِالمِنْطقة. مثلاً هلّأ نادي الرِّياضي يَلّي فاز بِبُطولةْ لِبْنان رِبِح كذا مرّة بُطولةْ آسْيا ومُؤخّراً تَأهّل على بُطولةْ العالم لِلأنْدية. وكان وكمان إنّو هُوّ اللي عم تِحْكي عنّو كِنْت الـpoint guard، صانع الألْعاب وائِل عرقْجي بْيِلْعب مع هَيْدا الفريق الفريق "الرِّياضي".

Charbel: Right, and speaking of talent, Lebanese clubs are also some of the best in the region. For example, right now, the Riyadi Club, which won the Lebanese championship, has won the Asian championship several times and recently qualified for the Club World Cup. And as you mentioned, Wael Arakji, the point guard, plays for this team, the "Al Riyadi" team.

**عُمَر:** فِعْلاً نادي الرِّياضي بِآخِر كم مَوْسِم فرْجى إنّو هُوّ قُوّة ضارْبِة بِكُرَةْ السَّلِّة اللّبنانية حتّى بِالمِنْطقة كلّاً، و وُصولو لكأْس الأنْدية هَيْدا دليل على قدّيْش عِنْدُن مهارات قَوية وعم بْيِسْتثْمِروا بِلاعْبينُن وبِالخُبْرات اللي طالْعة جْديد وحتّى رح نْشوفُن عم يِتْنافسوا بِرأْيي على أعْلى المُسْتَوِيّات الدُّوَلية انْشالله.

Omar: Indeed, the Al Riyadi club has shown in the last few seasons that it is a formidable force in Lebanese basketball, even in the whole region. Their qualification for the Club World Championship is proof of how strong their skills are, and they're investing in their players and the new talents emerging. We'll see them competing, in my opinion, at the highest international levels, hopefully.

**شَرْبِل:** بْوافْقَك الرّأْي وهَيْدا الشّي بيكبِّر القلْب. مِش بسّ النّادي الرِّياضي في عِنْدك كذا نَوادي بِلِبْنان وُصْلوا قبل وإلُن تاريخ عريق يَعْني مِتِل الحِكْمة وغَيْرا وغَيْرا ما بدْنا نْسمّي الكلّ. وعنْجدّ يَعْني الباسْكِت بِلِبْنان تاريخا كْتير حِلو وبْتِضلّ الأفْضل وهَيْدي الرِّياضة بْتِعْطي كْتير هيك دعْم للشّعْب اللّبناني وعِنْدا كْتير جُمْهور. إن كان دَوْري محلّي وَلّا دُوَلي الحماس دايْماً عالي لِلباسْكِت.

Charbel: I agree with you, and this is heartwarming. Not only Al Riyadi but also several other clubs in Lebanon have reached high levels before and have a long history, like Hekmeh [Sagesse Sports Club] and others. Honestly, basketball in Lebanon has a beautiful history and remains the best. This sport provides a lot of support to the Lebanese people and has a huge fan base. Whether it's the local or international league, the enthusiasm for basketball is always high.

**عُمر:** صحّ صحّ شربِل. ومِتل ما قِلت يَعني نظراً للأوْضاع اللي بيمُرْق فيا لِبنان الباسكِتبوّل عم بِتكون مُتنفّس للشّعْب. كلّ حدا بيشجِّع فريقو وبيتْحمّس وهَيْدا الشّي عنْجد حِلو لأنّو مِن حَوّل الطّاقة لطاقة حِلوة ومْركّزة على الرّياضة والرّوح الرّياضية. وهَيْدا الشّي بيلْهِم كْتيرالأجيال الطّالْعة. وعلى فِكْرة المُشجّعين بلِبنان لفِرق الباسْكِتبوّل معروف عنُن إنّو كْتيرمُخلِصين و بيضلّوا مْتابعين فريقُن مِن أوّل المَوْسِم لآخْرو شو ما كانت النّتايج و كذا مرّة أنا حْضِرت مْتوشي بالْملعب و كان الجوّ، شربِل، بيعقِّد. بيِقْدروا يوْلّعوا و بِتْحسّ إنّو رح ينِزلوا يلِعبوا مع اللّاعْبين.

**Omar:** True, true, Charbel. And as you said, given the situations Lebanon is going through, basketball is becoming an outlet for the people. Everyone supports their team with enthusiasm, and it's really great because it turns energy into something positive and focused on sportsmanship. This is very inspiring for the younger generations. By the way, basketball fans in Lebanon are known for their loyalty— they follow their teams from the beginning of the season to the end, no matter the results. I've attended several games at the stadium, and the atmosphere, Charbel, is incredible. You feel like the fans are going to jump in and play with the players.

**شربِّل:** أكيد وما نِنْسى حتّى المَواهِب الجِّديدِة اللي عم تِطْلع في كْتير لاعْبين طموحين بلِبنان وبيحِبّوا يْحقِّقوا نجاح كْبير. الدّورات المحلّية والبرامج الشّبابية مْهمّة كْتير لتنمِيةْ المَواهِب، حتّى هلّأ صارِت بالْمدارِس وصار في كْتير أكاديميّات لَيطوّروا الباسكِتبوّل بلِبنان وهَيْدا شي كْتير بيشجِّع وعنْجدّ بيكبّر القلِب إنّو في هيْك شي بالْبلد! positive

**Charbel:** Absolutely, and let's not forget even the new talents that are emerging. There are many ambitious players in Lebanon who want to achieve great success. Local leagues and youth programs are very important for developing talents. Now, there are many academies to develop basketball in Lebanon, which is very encouraging and truly heartening to see something positive like this in the country!

**عُمر:** صحّ! وعلى فِكْرة شربِل نِحْنا محْظوظين إنّو بِهالْفترة عم نْشوف هالْبرامج عم بِتْساعِد اللّاعْبين الصِّغار مِن صِغرُن لَيطوّروا مهاراتُن. وهَيْدا الشّي كْتير مْهمّ لأنّو مِتل

ما مِنْشوف بِكِلّ أنْحاء العالَم بِتْبلِّش تُطْوير المَهارات عن عُمْر صْغير. لِأعْمار مِنّا كْتير كْبيرة بيبلْشوا يِنْخرطوا بالمُنْتخب وبالأنْدية الرِّياضية، وهَيْدا الشّي حلو لأنّو بيوَجِّه الشّباب والوْلاد عن عُمْر صْغير على مُمارسات صحّية وحِلْوة هيْك بْتِفْتحُلْن آفاق جْديدة.

Omar: Exactly! And by the way, Charbel, we're lucky to see these programs helping young players develop their skills from an early age. This is very important because, as we see around the world, developing skills starts at a young age. By the time they're not too old, they're already joining the national team and sports clubs. This is great because it guides youth from an early age toward healthy practices and opens up new opportunities for them.

شرْبِل: مِيّة بالْمِيّة. ومِش بسّ الباسْكِتْبْوْل. عِنّا... لِبْنان عِنْدو ثقافةٍ رياضية غنية بِشكِل عام يَعْني، مِن... حتّى الفوْليبوْل حتّى رياضات الفرْدية كالتِّنيس وألْعاب القِوى وفي كْتير عالم وُصْلت للأوْلمْبيكْس مِن... يَعْني بالرِّياضة يَعْني. لِيك الرِّياضة بْتِلْعب دوْر كْبير بِثقافتْنا وبِتْعزِّز اللِّياقة البدنية، العمل الجّماعي، وكِلّ شي خصّو بالسبوْر والرِّياضة عنْجدّ كْتير مُفيد للـ... إن كان على... على صعيد فرْدي ولّا على صعيد وَطني.

Charbel: Absolutely. And it's not just basketball; Lebanon has a rich sports culture in general, from... even volleyball, individual sports like tennis, and athletics. Many people have even reached the Olympics in... I mean, in sports. Sports play a big role in our culture, promoting physical fitness, teamwork, and everything related to sports. It's truly beneficial, whether on an individual level or on a national level.

عُمْر: أكيد وانْشالله يَعْني هَيْدي الترِنْد أوْ المجْهود اللي عم يِنْحطّ على الرِّياضة بِلِبْنان يِسْتمِرّ لأنّو أنا مِتْأكّد إنّو رح يْكون إلا تأْثير كْتير إيجابي على مُجْتمعاتْنا رح نْقْدُر نْشوف جيل جْديد طالِع بيروح كْتير رِياضية ومْوَجّه عَ أمورصحّية وبتْفيد المُجْتمّع ككِلّ.

Omar: Definitely, and hopefully, this trend or effort being put into sports in Lebanon will continue because I am sure it will have a very positive impact on our communities. We will be able to see a new generation growing up with a strong sports spirit, focusing on healthy activities that benefit society as a whole.

شرْبِل: ميرْسي يا عُمْر، وميرْسي لكِلّ اللي عم يِسْمعونا. رح نِلْتِقي مرّة تانْية بمَوْضوع جْديد. لَوَقْتا، انْشالله بِتْكونوا بِتْحِبّوا تابْعوا المُنْتخب وتابْعوا فريقْنا بالْباسْكِتْبْول وتِسْتِمتْعوا بالمُبارَيات!

**Charbel:** Thank you, Omar, and thank you to everyone who is listening. We will meet again with a new topic. Until then, we hope you follow our national team and our basketball team and enjoy the games!

**عُمر:** أكيد وأنا بْشجِّع كلّ اللي عم بْيِسْمعونا اليوْم إنّو يْكونوا داعْمين للرِّياضة بلِبْنان وللمُنْتخبات اللّبْنانية لأنّو هنّي بإمْكانات صْغيرِة عم يِقدْروا يوصلوا لمحلّات بْعيدِة. وأكيد أكيد بِحاجِة لكِلّ الدّعْم المُمْكِن نْأمّنْلُن ياه.

**Omar:** Absolutely, and I encourage everyone listening today to support sports in Lebanon and our national teams because they are achieving a lot with limited resources. They need all the support we can give them.

**شرْبِل:** يَلّا ميرْسي عُمر وانْشالله يْكون الكِلّ بْيِقْدر يَعْمُل رياضة لأنّو هَيْدا شي كمان صُحّي.

**Charbel:** Alright, thanks, Omar, and I hope everyone can get involved in sports because it's also healthy!

## Comprehension Questions

١. شو هُوِّ مَوْضوع الحلْقة اللي حِكْيوا عنّو شرْبِل وعُمر؟

٢. لَيْش عُمر مبْسوط إنّو رح يِحْكوا عن الباسْكِتْبوْل؟

٣. شو هِيِّ الإنْجازات اللي حققا الفريق الوَطني اللّبْناني بِكُرْة السِّلّة؟

٤. مين هُوِّ وائِل عرقْجي وشو إنْجازو؟

٥. أيّ نادي فاز بِبُطولة لِبْنان عِدّة مرّات وتْأهّل لبطولةْ العالمِ للأنْدية؟

٦. لَيْش الباسْكِتْبوْل مْهِمّ للشّعْب اللّبْناني، خْصوصاً بِظُلّ هالأوْضاع الحالية؟

٧. شو هِيِّ الأنْشِطة اللي عم تْساهِم بِتنْمية المَواهِب الشابّة بكُرْة السِّلّة بلِبْنان؟

٨. بأيّ رياضات تانْية عِنْدو لِبْنان ثقافة رياضية قَوية؟

1. What is the topic of the episode that Charbel and Omar discussed?
2. Why is Omar excited to talk about basketball?
3. What are the achievements of the Lebanese national basketball team?
4. Who is Wael Arakji and what is his accomplishment?
5. Which club has won the Lebanese Championship multiple times and qualified for the Club World Championship?
6. Why is basketball important to the Lebanese people, especially given the current circumstances?
7. What activities are contributing to the development of young basketball talents in Lebanon?
8. In what other sports does Lebanon have a strong sporting culture?

## Discussion Questions

١. بْتْحِبّ تِلْعب أَوْ تْشجِّع كُرَةْ السّلّة؟ لِيْش؟

٢. شو رأْيَك بمُسْتَوى كُرَةْ السّلّة بِبلدك مُقارنةً بِلِبْنان؟

٣. مين هُوّ اللاّعِب المُفضّل عِنْدك بِكُرَةْ السّلّة؟ لِيْش؟

٤. كيف بِتْشوف تأْثير الرّياضة على المُجْتْمّع بِلِبْنان؟

٥. شو هِيّ الرّياضة المُفضّلة عِنْدك؟ ولِيْش؟

٦. عِنْدك قُصص أَوْ ذِكْرَيات عن حُضور مُبارَيات كُرَةْ السّلّة؟ شارِكْنا.

٧. كيف بِتْشجِّع تَنْمية المَواهِب الرّياضية عِنْد الشّباب بِبلدك؟

٨. بْتِعْتِقِد إنّو الرّياضة بِتْساعِد بِتِطْوير القِيَم مِتِل العمل الجّماعي والإنْضِباط؟ لِيْش أَوْ لِيْش لأ؟

1. Do you like playing or watching basketball? Why?
2. What do you think of the level of basketball in your country compared to Lebanon?
3. Who is your favorite basketball player? Why?
4. How do you see the impact of sports on Lebanese society?
5. What is your favorite sport? Why?
6. Do you have any stories or memories of attending basketball games? Share them with us.
7. How do you encourage the development of young sports talents in your country?
8. Do you believe that sports help develop values like teamwork and discipline? Why or why not?

# العصْرالذّهبي للبْنان

## The Golden Age of Lebanon

## In this episode...

Charbel and Omar discuss Lebanon's golden age, spanning from the 1950s to the mid-1970s. During this period, Lebanon was known as the "Switzerland of the Middle East" and Beirut as the "Paris of the East." They explore the country's cultural and economic growth, highlighting Beirut's role as a financial hub and a center for the arts. Learn about Lebanon's thriving tourism, banking sector, and cultural icons like Fairouz and the Rahbani brothers. While the episode touches on the nostalgia of this era, it also reflects on the challenges that followed and the hope for a return to prosperity.

## Vocabulary

| | |
|---|---|
| prosperity, flourishing | إزْدِهار |
| investments | إسْتِثْمارات |
| stability | إسْتِقْرار |
| economic | إقْتِصادي |
| stock exchange | بورْصة |
| cultural | ثقافي |
| civil war | حرِب أهْلية |
| destruction | دمار |
| golden | ذهَبي/دهَبي |
| tourist | سَايِح (سِيّاح) |
| difficulty, challenge | صْعوبة |
| age, era | عصْر (عُصور) |
| currency | عِمْلة |
| period, era | فتْرة |
| hotel | فُنْدُق (فنادِق) |
| sector | قِطاع |
| institution | مُؤسّسِة |
| theater | مسْرح (مسارِح) |
| banking- (related to banks) | مصْرِفي |
| renaissance, revival | نهْضة |

# Transcript

**شَرْبِل:** مَرْحَبا، اليوْم رح نِحْكي عن فتْرة كْتير مْهِمَّة وهيْك فِيا حنين مِن تاريخ لِبْنان هُوِّ العصْر الذّهبي للِبْنان، يَلِّي مْتِدّ إذا بدّك من ١٩٥٠ لِسِنِةْ ١٩٧٥. معي رْفيقي عُمر رح يْشارِكْني اليوْم بِالْحديث وأنا شرْبِل. كيفك يا عُمر؟

Charbel: Hello, today we're going to talk about a very important and nostalgic period in Lebanon's history—the Golden Age of Lebanon, which spanned from 1950 to 1975. My friend Omar is here with me today, and I'm Charbel. How are you, Omar?

**عُمر:** أهْلا شرْبِل أهْلا، أنا مْنيح! هَيْدا المَوْضوع اللي رح نِحْكي عنّو اليوْم بيْخْلق فيِّي شُعور مُزْدوج يَعْني عِنْدي حنين وفخِر بِهَيْدي العصْر الذّهبي يَلِّي قطع في لِبْنان وتْلقّب بْسْويسْرا الشّرْق، بسّ بِذات الوَقت بيْخْلِق غصّة بِقلْبي لأِنّو لِلْأسف اليوْم عم نِقْطع بِصْعوبات بسّ عَ أمل إنّو نِرْجع لِهَيْدي الفتْرة الذّهبية.

Omar: Hello Charbel, hello! I'm good! The topic we're discussing today brings about mixed feelings for me. I feel both nostalgia and pride for that golden era that Lebanon went through, when it was known as the Switzerland of the East, but at the same time, it makes me sad because unfortunately, today we're facing challenges. But I'm hopeful that we can return to that golden period.

**شرْبِل:** أكيد عُمر، وياريْت نِحْنا كِنّا إذا بدّك عَ هَيْدا العصْر كمان. ليْك العصْر الذّهبي بِلِبْنان يُعْتبر فتْرة إزْدِهار نْمو ثقافي وإقْتِصادي. كان وَقْتا بَيْروت معْروفة بِإسِم باريس الشّرْق الأوْسط ولِبْنان كان مِتِل ما قِلِت سْويسْرا الشّرْق.

Charbel: Absolutely, Omar. I wish we had lived during that era as well. The Golden Age in Lebanon is considered a period of cultural and economic prosperity. Back then, Beirut was known as the Paris of the Middle East, and as you said, Lebanon was like the Switzerland of the East.

**عُمر:** صحيح، بِهالْفتْرة لِبْنان كان مركز للِفنّ الموسيقى والأدب، وحتّى كان يِجْذُب السّيّاح مِن كِلّ أنْواع... أنْحاء العالم لَيِتْمتّعوا بِالْحَياةْ اللّيْلية يَلِّي كانِت شْتهرِت بِهالْفتْرة. شْواطِئ الجّميلِة، الطّبيعة، تُراث، ثقافة، كِلّ شي حِلو.

Omar: True, during that time, Lebanon was a center for art, music, and literature. It even attracted tourists from all over the world who came to enjoy the nightlife that was famous during that period. The beautiful beaches, nature, heritage, culture—everything was wonderful.

**شَرْبِل:** لِيْك واحْدِة مِن العَوامِل الرَّئيسية اللي إذا بِدّك نِحْكي شْوَيّ هيْك عَ هالْفتْرة، واحْدِة مِن هالْعَوامِل الرَّئيسية إنّو ساهمِت بِهَيْدا العصْر الذَّهبي هُوّ أكيد الإسْتِقْرار، الإقْتِصاد اللي كان مفْتوح بِلِبْنان، القِطاع المصْرِفي كْتير زْدهر وَقْتا وصارِت بَيْروت مركز مالي بالْمِنْطقة شي مُخيف! وهَيْدا شي جذب كْتير إسْتِثْمارات وخلق بيئة كْتير مِزْدِهْرة للأعْمال.

Charbel: One of the main factors—if we talk a bit about that time—that contributed to this golden age was definitely stability. Lebanon had an open economy, and the banking sector thrived during that period, making Beirut a financial hub in the region, which was incredible! This attracted a lot of investments and created a very prosperous environment for businesses.

**عُمر:** مِيّة بالْمِيّة، وبِهَيْدي الفترة صارِت اللّيرة اللُّبْنانية يَلّي هِيّ العمْلة الوَطنية، عِمْلة كْتير قَوية بِتْنافِس أهمّ العِمْلات العالمية. صارِت مطْلوبة بِكِلّ أنْحاء العالم يَعْني حتّى بورْصة نْيويورْك وفرَنْسا كانوا يطِلْبوا العِمْلة اللُّبْنانية للإدّخار لأنّو كانت عِمْلة كْتير قَوية وفيا ثِقة. بسّ بغضّ النّظر اليوْم على هَيْدا الشِّق مِن العصْر الذَّهبي بِلِبْنان نْخلق إذا بِدّك بِمَوازاة هالنّهْضة الإقْتِصادية نهْضة ثقافية صارِت وخلّت كْتير مِن الفنّانين الموسيقِيّين الكِتّاب يْحقّقوا شِهْرة عالمية. مِتِل ما ذكرْنا بِحلْقات سابْقة عن فَيْروز والأخْوان رِحْباني مثلاً على... صاروا أسْماء كْتير معْروفة مِش بسّ بِلِبْنان بِكِلّ العالم وطْلعوا على كِلّ مسارِح العالمية ونشروا الثّقافة اللُّبْنانية.

Omar: Absolutely, and during this period, the Lebanese lira, which is the national currency, became very strong, competing with the world's top currencies. It was in demand worldwide—even the New York Stock Exchange and France sought the Lebanese currency for savings because it was very strong and trusted. But beyond the economic aspect, the golden age of Lebanon also saw a cultural renaissance, with many artists, musicians, and writers achieving international fame. As we mentioned in previous episodes, artists like Fairouz and the Rahbani brothers became well-known not just in Lebanon, but all over the world, performing on international stages and spreading Lebanese culture.

**شَرْبِل:** صحّ حْكينا كْتير عن هَيْدا المَوْضوع عنْجدّ وَقْتا المسْرح اللّبْناني. ما كان... بهالْفتْرة ما كان بْيِتْقدّر بتمن. كانِت مسْرحِيّات وأغاني الأخَوان رِحْباني كانِت جَوْهر الثّقافة اللّبْنانية ولمست قْلوب الكلّ.

Charbel: We've talked a lot about this topic. Back then, Lebanese theater was invaluable. The plays and songs of the Rahbani brothers were the essence of Lebanese culture and touched everyone's hearts.

**عُمر:** مظْبوط! وزْيادة كمان يَعْني إذا بِتْشوف هَيْدي الفتْرة عنْجدّ كانِت فتْرة ذهبية للِبْنان، لأنّو مِتل ما حْكينا إقْتصادِيّاً ثقافِيّاً وفنِّيّاً كانِت فتْرة مُزْدهرة. وهَيْدا الشّي جذب عدد كْبير مِن سُوّاح العالم مِن جنْسِيّات مِن كلّ أقْطار العالم لَيجوا يْزوروا لِبْنان ويْشوفوا بعْيونُن شو هَيْدي العاصْمة يَلّي عم بْينْحكى فيا وين ما كان. وأكيد بَيْروت وجميع المناطِق اللّبْنانية صارت مِلْيانة بالسُوّاح العرب والأجانِب. وهَيْدا شي خلّى إذا بدّك قِطاع الفنادِق والضّيافة بلِبْنان تِزْدهِر كمان وساهم كمان بالنّهْضة الإقْتصادية.

Omar: Exactly! And if you look at that period, it truly was a golden era for Lebanon. As we mentioned, economically, culturally, and artistically, it was a thriving period. This attracted a large number of tourists from all over the world who came to visit Lebanon and see for themselves the capital that everyone was talking about. And of course, Beirut and all the Lebanese regions were filled with Arab and foreign tourists, which also contributed to the booming hospitality and hotel industry in Lebanon, further fueling the economic renaissance.

**شَرْبِل:** اللي عم تِحْكي صحّ، وكِنْت بِتْمنّى عيش هالْفتْرة يا عُمر وأنا بِسْمع خبْرِيّات مِن جدّي وأصْحاب جِدّي إنّو كيف كانِت بَيْروت مِلْيانة بالحَياة وكان فيا حركِة بهالْفتْرة. دايْماً بْيِحْكوا عن سان جوْرْج أوْتيْل السّان جوْرْج وكازينو لِبْنان اللي كانوا إذا بدّك مركز وicon بهَيْدا الوَقِت.

Charbel: What you're saying is true, and I wish I could have lived during that time, Omar. I hear stories from my grandfather and his friends about how Beirut was full of life and vibrant during that period. They always talk about Saint George and Casino du Liban, which were the icons of that time.

**عُمر:** صحيح صحيح! وبْحِبّ ضيف على فِكْرة إيّام بْينْسُوا بسّ يذكِّروا هَيْدي الفتْرة الدّهبية، هِيِّ الجانِب التّعْليمي. يَعْني بهَيْدي الفتْرة زْدهر القِطاع التّعْليمِ بلِبْنان،

وصار معروف بمؤسّساتو التّعْليمية المِمْتازة يَلّي جذبِت طُلّاب مِن وَيْن ما كان. وأهمّ مؤسّسات التّعْليمية بهالْفتْرة كانت الجّامْعة اللِّبْنانية كانوا الأساتْذة يَلّي يْحاضْروا فيا كانوا مِن أهمّ الدّكاتْرا المَوْجودين بالْمِنْطقة، وكمان ما فينا نِنْسى الجّامْعة الأميركية بْبَيْروت يَلّي بعْدا لليَوْم مُعْترف فيا دوليّاً وبِتْخَرِّج طُلّاب ذو كفاءة عالْية.

**Omar:** Absolutely! And I'd like to add something that people often forget when they talk about this golden age, which is the educational aspect. During that time, Lebanon's educational sector flourished, becoming known for its excellent institutions that attracted students from all over the world. Some of the most important educational institutions during that time were the Lebanese University, where the professors were among the best in the region. We can't forget the American University of Beirut, which is still internationally recognized today and produces highly qualified graduates.

**شرْبِل:** لَيْك للأسف يا عُمر هَيْدا... هالْفتْرة أوهَيْدا العصْر الذّهْبي، هيْك فجْأة خطفوا مِن لبْنان إذا بدّك نْقول يَعْني نْخطف بعْد ما صار في حرْب أهْلية بلِبْنان سنةْ ١٩٧٥. ومنعِت هَيْدا الإزْدِهار ومِتِل كأنّو بدّن يْفشْلوا لهالْبلد. الحرْب سبّبِت كْتير مِتِل ما مْنعْرِف بدمار وخسايِر كْبيرة. وبعِدْنا لهلّأ بلد عم يِتْعافى يَعْني وبيضَلّ في خْبار بهالْبلد مِن وَرا هالْحرْب اللي قطعْنا فيا.

**Charbel:** Look, unfortunately, Omar, that... that golden era was suddenly snatched away from Lebanon, if we can say so, it was taken away after the civil war started in Lebanon in 1975. This prosperity was halted, and it was like they wanted to bring down this country. The war caused a lot of destruction and huge losses, as we know. And until now, the country is still recovering, and there are always issues in this country because of the war we went through.

**عُمر:** أيْه مظْبوط، يَعْني كانت تحدّيّات صعْبة، بسّ بذات الوَقِت الشّي اللي بْيَعْطي أمل للّبْنانية وللبْنان هُوّ هَيْدي الفتْرة الذّهبية يَلّي حْكينا عنّا، لأنّو مِتِل ما بيقولوا إذا في بلد وشعْب قِدِر يوصل لهَيْدا الشّي بْيِقْدر يوصل عْليه مرّة تانْية وتالْتة ورابْعة. على أمل بالْمُسْتقْبل القْريب يقْدُر... نِقْدر نِحْنا كلبْنانية نْرجِّع لبْنان لهالْفتْرة الذّهبية.

**Omar:** Yes, that's true. I mean, there were difficult challenges, but at the same time, what gives hope to the Lebanese people and to Lebanon is that golden era we talked about. Because, as they say, if a country and its people are able to reach that level once, they can reach it a second, third, and fourth time. Hopefully, in the near future, we can... as Lebanese, bring Lebanon back to that golden era.

**شَرْبِل:** عم تِحْكي دهب يا عُمر. ميرْسي لإلك عَ هالْمُشاركِة الحِلْوِة هيْك اللي فيا فرْحة وغصّة مِتِل ما قِلِت بِذات الوَقِت. ميرْسي للْمُسْتمِعين. بِتْمنّى تْكونوا سْتمْتعْتوا، بِتْمنّى لِبْنان يِرْجع يِزْدِهِر ويْصير مِش بسّ فتْرة ذهبية فتْرة مألْمْزة كمان. مْنِلْتِقي بِمَوْضوع تاني خبْرْية جْديدِة عن لِبْنان. لَوَقْتا نْتِبْهوا عَ حالْكُن وميرْسي لإلك مرّة تانْية يا عُمر.

Charbel: You're speaking gold, Omar. Thank you for this wonderful participation, which brings both joy and sorrow at the same time, as you said. Thanks to the listeners. I hope you enjoyed it, and I hope Lebanon not only returns to a golden era but to a diamond era as well. We'll meet again with another topic and a new story about Lebanon. Until then, take care of yourselves, and thank you again, Omar.

## Comprehension Questions

١. شو هِيِّ الفَتْرة اللي بْتِسمُّوا العصْر الذّهبي بِلِبْنان، وأيْمتى كانِت؟

٢. كيف بيحِسّ عُمر لِلْعصْر الذّهبي للِبْنان؟

٣. ليْش كانِت بَيْروت تُلقّب بباريس الشّرْق الأوْسط خِلال العصْر الذّهبي؟

٤. شو العَوامِل الرّئيسية اللي ساهمِت بإزْدِهار الإقْتِصاد اللِّبناني بِهَيْدا العصْر؟

٥. كيف أثّرِت اللّيرة اللِّبْنانية بِهَيْدا العصْر، وشو كان وَضعا بالنِّسْبة لِلْعِمْلات العالمية؟

٦. مين مِن الفنّانين اللِّبْنانيّين حقّقوا شِهْرة عالمية وَقْت العصْر الذّهبي؟

٧. ليْش كانِت بَيْروت تِجْذُب السِّياح مِن جميع أنْحاء العالم بِهالْفتْرة؟

٨. شو الحدث اللي أدّى لِنِهايِةْ العصْر الذّهبي للِبْنان، وكيف أثّر على البلد؟

1. What is the period known as the golden era of Lebanon, and when did it take place?
2. How does Omar feel about the golden age of Lebanon?
3. Why was Beirut called the Paris of the Middle East during the golden age?
4. What were the main factors that contributed to the economic prosperity of Lebanon during this era?
5. How did the Lebanese pound fare during this era, and what was its status compared to global currencies?
6. Which Lebanese artists gained international fame during the golden age?
7. Why was Beirut attracting tourists from all over the world during this period?
8. What event led to the end of the golden age of Lebanon, and how did it affect the country?

## Discussion Questions

١.  كيف بِتْشوف إنّو الإسْتِقْرار والإزْدِهار الإقْتِصادي ساهموا بِتكْوين العصْر الذّهبي للبْنان؟

٢.  وِيْن بِتْشوف أمل للبْنان اليوْم لَيرْجع يْحقِّق إزْدِهار مُشابِهْ للْعصْر الذّهبي؟

٣.  كيف برأْيَك الإسْتِقْرار والإزْدِهار الإقْتِصادي بِبلدك أثّروا على تطَوُّروا مُقارنةً بِالْعصْر الذّهبي اللي مرق على لبْنان؟

٤.  شو هُوَّ الدّوْر اللي بْيِلْعبوا بلدك بالْمشْهد الثّقافي والفنّي العالمي اليوْم؟

٥.  إذا فيك تِخْتار فترْة ذهبية بِتاريخ بلدك، أيْمتى بِتْكون وليْش؟

٦.  كيف برأْيَك الموسيقى والفنّ شكّلوا الهَوية الوَطنية بِبلدك؟

٧.  شو هنّي الأحْداث التّاريخية الكِبيرة بِبلدك اللي تركِت أثر طَويل، مِتِل تأْثير الحرب الأهْلية اللّبْنانية على العصْر الذّهبي بِلبْنان؟

٨.  وِيْن بِتْشوف فُرص لنهْضة ثقافية أوْ إقْتِصادية بِبلدك اللي مُمْكِن تْقود لعصْر ذهبي جْديد؟

1. How do you see the role of stability and economic prosperity in shaping the golden age of Lebanon?
2. Where do you see hope for Lebanon today to achieve a resurgence similar to the golden age?
3. How do you think stability and economic prosperity in your country have influenced its development compared to Lebanon's golden age?
4. What role does your country play in the global cultural and artistic scene today?
5. If you could choose a golden age in your country's history, when would it be, and why?
6. How has music and art shaped the national identity in your country?
7. What major historical events in your country have had a lasting impact, similar to the Lebanese Civil War's effect on Lebanon's golden age?
8. Where do you see opportunities for cultural or economic revival in your country that could lead to a new golden age?

# الزَّواج وتِكْوين العَيْلة
## Marriage and Starting a Family

### In this episode...

Charbel and Farah discuss the essential topic of marriage and starting a family. They reflect on the joys and challenges of building a life together, from balancing work and family responsibilities to raising children. You'll hear about the cultural importance of family in Lebanon, including the support from extended families, and how they help make the journey a little easier. Charbel and Farah also share their personal experiences, offering insight into the rewards of marriage and parenthood, and how love, patience, and support are key to making it all worthwhile.

## Vocabulary

| | |
|---|---|
| belonging | إنْتِماء |
| married life | الحَياةْ الزَّوْجية |
| baby | بايْبي |
| preparations | تِحْضيرات |
| raising children | تَرْبيةْ الأطْفال |
| cooperation | تعاوُن |
| understanding | تفاهُم |
| starting a family | تكْوين العَيْلة |
| time management | تِنْظيم الوَقِت |
| balanced life | حَياةْ مِتْوازْنة |
| long working hours | دَوام طَويل |
| routine | روتين |
| marriage | زَواج |
| partner, spouse | شْريك |
| patience | صبِر |
| wedding | عِرس (أعْراس) |
| extended family | عَيْلة مِمْتدّة |
| the institution of the family | مُؤسّسةْ العَيْلة |
| stages | مراحِل |
| responsibility | مسْؤولية |

## Transcript

**شربِل:** مرحبا، كيفْكُن؟ تمام؟ اليوْم رح نِحْكي عن مَوْضوع أساسي إذا بدُكُن: الزَّواج وتِكْوين العَيْلة. معكُن شرْبِل ومعي اليوْم صديقْتي فرح كيفِك يا فرح؟

**Charbel:** Hello, how are you all? Doing well? Today, we're going to talk about an essential topic, if you will: marriage and starting a family. I'm Charbel, and today my friend Farah is with me. How are you, Farah?

**فرح:** أهْلا يا شرْبِل! الحمْدِلله، إنْتَ كيفك؟

**Farah:** Hi, Charbel! Thank God, I'm good. How are you?

**شرْبِل:** كْتير مْنيح، اليوْم مَوْضوع هيْك شْوَيّ حِلو. الزَّواج شي مْقدّس وشي كْتير رائع إنّو تْكوِّن عَيْلة وتحْقِّق نفس الأهْداف مع شْريك الحَياةْ عنْجدّ شي رائع. كمان بذات الوَقِت منّو هيّن أبداً إنّو إنْتي تْعيشي هيْك مع شخص واحد طول حَياتِك وكِلّ شي في مسؤولِيّات وكِلّ القِصص اللي بْتِجي معا. يَعْني فرح كمان إنْتي مْجوّزة وبْتعِرْفي هَيْدا المَوْضوع.

**Charbel:** I'm doing great. Today's topic is quite lovely. Marriage is something sacred and really wonderful. Starting a family and achieving the same goals with your life partner is truly amazing. But at the same time, it's not easy at all to live with one person for the rest of your life, with all the responsibilities and everything that comes with it. Farah, you're married too, so you understand this topic.

**فرح:** صحّ يا شرْبِل، الزَّواج بْيِطلّب كْتير مِن التّفاهُم وكْتير مِن التّعاوُن، بسّ بالنِّهاية هُوّ رِحْلة بِتعلّمْنا كْتير أشْيا وبِتْخلّينا نِكْبر مع بعِض. إذا بدّك خبِّرْنا شْوَيّ عن تجْرِبْتِك بالزَّواج وبْتِكْوين العَيْلة.

**Farah:** That's right, Charbel. Marriage requires a lot of understanding and cooperation, but in the end, it's a journey that teaches us a lot and helps us grow together. If you'd like, tell us a bit about your experience with marriage and starting a family.

**شرْبِل:** أكيد، صراحة أنا مْجوّز وعِنْدي بايبي. ولخبِّرُك شْوَيّ، هيْك رِحْلةْ الزَّواج حِلوة يَعْني تِتْجوّزي الشّخِص اللي بِتحِبّيه وهيْك بْكون مِحمّسة تْكفّي حَياتِك معو بْقلْب بيْت وبيْت واحد تْكوْني عَيْلة ويصير عِنْدِك بايبي مِن هالشّخِص اللي بْتحِبّي يَعْني شي أكْتر

مِن رائِع. بسّ الفِكرة ويْن إنّو بدِّك تعرْفي إنّو في مسؤوليّات يَعني هَيدا مِش لِعْبة. بدّك تِتْجوّزي، بدِّك تْكوِّني عَيْلة، في مسؤولية كبيرة عنْدك حَيصير عنْدك وْلاد إن ألله راد بدّك تِهتمّي بالوَلد، بدّك عنْدك خْبار الوَلد بدِّك تضلّك منتْبها عْليه، تْأمْنيلو المينيموم، بين أكِل، كِلّ اللّوازِم. وحتّى بتْصير القِصص أصْعب يَعني، بيصير بدّك تْشوفي كيف تْدبْري حالِك وتْدبْري حال شْريك حَياتِك بين شِغْلو وشغْلِك وكيف بدّك تِهتمّي بالْبايْبي. يَعْني روتين شْوَيّ بتْتفاجْئي يَعْني بكِلّ القُصص، بسّ كِلّو حِلو وكِلّو هيْك بيفرّح القلْب، يَعْني عنْجدّ الحمْدِلله على كِلّ شي.

**Charbel:** Sure. truth be told, I'm married, and I have a baby. To tell you a bit, this journey of marriage is beautiful—marrying the person you love and being excited to continue your life with them, building a home and family together, and having a baby with the person you love is truly amazing. But the idea is that you need to understand there are responsibilities; this isn't a game. You're getting married, starting a family, and there's a big responsibility. You'll have children, God willing, and you'll need to care for them and provide them with the essentials like food and all their needs. And things can get more challenging; you'll have to figure out how to manage yourself and your life partner between work and taking care of the baby. The routine can be surprising, that is, with all these things coming together, but it's all beautiful and really heartwarming. Thank God for everything.

**فرح:** صحّ يا شرْبِل، معك حقّ. مؤسّسةِ العَيْلة والزّواج كْتير مْهمّين بحَياتِنا specially بلِبْنان بسّ مسؤولية كْتير كبيرة كمان لأنّا نِحْنا بلِبْنان. لتْأسّس عَيْلة وتِتْجوّز بدّك تِقطع بمراحِل قبْلا كْتير طَويلة مِن التّجْهيزات، مِن تحْضيرات البيْت، مِن تحْضيرات العِرس تْعيش عنْجدّ مع الشّخص اللي إنْتَ بتْحبّو بتْتّفِق إنْتَ ويّا. ومِن بعْدا لمّا يْصير في وَلد بتْكبر أكْتر المسؤولية. يَعْني عم بِحْكي أنا عن تجرِبْتي كإمْرأة عايْشة بلِبْنان بتْشتِغل، تْجوّزِت وصار عِنْدي بايْبي كانِت مسؤولية كْتير كْتير كبيرة، لتْأمْنلو لكِلّ شي بدّو يا الوَلد بدّك تِتْعب. وعنّا شي حِلو وبِشِع بلِبْنان إنّو المرة بقانون العمل ما عنْدا ساعات مْعيّنة تِشْتِغلو بدّا تِشْتِغل دَوام طَويل وهَيدا الشّي بيأثّر شْوَيّ على الوَقت تْقْضيّ مع العَيْلة. بسّ بالآخِر بِتْلاقي هيْك كِلّ شي عم بيصير لمّا تِرْجع على البيْت آخِر نْهار وتْشوف إنّك عم بِتْضحّكِك ومِشتْقْلك وكيف بْيِرْكُض لعنْدك. هَيدا الشّي عنْجدّ كْتير حِلو.

**Farah:** True, Charbel; you're right. Starting a family and marriage are very important in our lives, especially in Lebanon, but they are also a big responsibility because we're in Lebanon. To start a family and get married, you have to go through long phases of preparations, from getting the house ready to preparing for the wedding, to finally living with the person you love and agreeing on everything together. And after that, when you have a child, the responsibility grows even more. Speaking from my experience as a woman living in Lebanon, working, getting married, and having a baby, it was a huge responsibility to provide everything my child needed, and you have to work very hard. In Lebanon, there's something both good and bad—the labor law doesn't set specific working hours, so you have to work long hours, which affects the time you spend with your family. But in the end, you realize that everything is worth it when you come home at the end of the day and see your child smiling at you, missing you, and running toward you. That's truly a beautiful thing.

**شَرْبِل:** عم تِحْكي مِيّة بِالمِيّة. يَعْني إنْتي مْجوّزة وعِنْدك بايبي وأنا كمان ذات الشّي وبِفْهم هَيْدا الشّعور اللي عم تِحْكي. لَيْكي بِلِبْنان هَيْدا الشّي صعب خاصّةً إنّو الوَضِع كْتير عم بيكون سئيل واللي ما عم بيكون مِرْتاح مادّيّاً إذا بدّك. عم يِتْعذّب لَيْلاقي وَقِت لعَيْلْتو أكْتر. بفْهم هَيْدا الشّي، بسّ في شغْلي عِنّا بِلِبْنان وإذا بدّك ثقافتْنا ثقافةْ العَيْلة وبعاداتْنا إنّو في عِنْدك extended family متِل ما بيقولولا أَوْ العَيْلِة المِمْتدّة. يَعْني هَيْدي الثّقافة إنّو نِحْنا مِش بسّ family صْغيرة كْتير في عِنّا قْرايْبين نِعْتِمِد عْلَيْن وهَيْدا الشّي بيساعِد إنّو مثلاً الوَلد بْيِبْقى عِنْد سِتّو ...عِنْد سِتّو وجدّو يَعْني في هَيْدي الـ part مِن ثقافتْنا بِلِبْنان إنّو بيساعِد شْوَيّ بيساعِد المرة بِلِبْنان.

**Charbel:** You're absolutely right. You're married, you have a baby, and I'm in the same situation, so I understand the feeling you're talking about. You see, in Lebanon, it's difficult, especially since the situation is tough and not everyone is financially comfortable. It's hard to find enough time for your family. I understand that, but one thing we have in Lebanon, and if you will, part of our culture, is the extended family. This culture isn't just about a small family; we have relatives we rely on, and this helps, like when the child stays with their grandmother and grandfather. This aspect of our culture in Lebanon helps the woman a bit.

**فرح:** مظْبوط، العَيْلِة المِمْتدّة كْتير مُهِمّة لأنّو بيساعْدوك خُصوصاً لمّا يْكونوا قاعْدين حدّك. يَعْني أنا عن تجْرِبْتي أنا إمّي هِيِّ بْتِضِلّ مِنْتِبْها عَ إبْني كِلّ نْهار خِلال أنا بْكون بِالشّغِل. أيّام وَقِت أنا بِدّي إرْتاح أَوْ مثلاً بِدّي إضْهر ضهْرة مع أصْحابي أَوْ even بِدّي

إضْهر مع جَوْزي إمّي بْتاخْدو للْوَلد وبْتِهْتمّ في وبْيِبْقى عِنْدو. يَعْني ما بِعْتل همّ إنّو مثلاً ما عِنْدي حدا حدّي أوْ أنا مِضْطرّة جيب حدا غريب قعْدو بِبَيْتي وما بعْرف شو مُمْكِن يْصير بالْبَيْت.

**Farah:** That's true. The extended family is very important because they help, especially when they live nearby. Speaking from my experience, my mother takes care of my son every day while I'm at work. Sometimes, when I need to rest or go out with my friends or even go out with my husband, my mother takes care of the child. So, I don't have to worry about not having someone close by or needing to bring a stranger into my home.

**شرْبِل:** صحّ وهَيْدا شي شْوَيّ بيخفِّف عَ الـ family يَعْني عَ أهِل وليْك الوَلد بيصير كمان يِتْعلّق بِسِتّو وجدّو، هَيْدا شي حِلو يَعْني. بيصير في عِنْدو هَيْدا الجَوّ الإنْتِماء للعَيْلِة الكِبيرِة. صراحة هيْك عَ بالي إسألِك سُؤال شو بِتْحِسّي أصْعب part إنْتي كإمّ؟

**Charbel:** Exactly, and this eases the burden on the family, on the parents, and it also strengthens the bond between the child and their grandparents, which is a beautiful thing. The child starts to feel a sense of belonging to the extended family. Honestly, I'd like to ask you a question: What do you think is the hardest part of being a mother?

**فرح:** أصْعب part كَوْني إمّ إنّي أنا مسؤولِة عن إبْني ومسؤولِة عن بَيْتي وأنا بدّي لحّق أعْمُل كلّ شي، وأعْمُل مِتِل تِنْظيم لَوَقْتي بيْن بَيْتي، بيْن وَقِت أعْطي لإبْني، بيْن شِغْلي، بيْن حَياتي الخاصّة مع أصْحابي. هَيْدا شْوَيّ بالْبِدايات كان كْتير صعْب عْلَيّ.

**Farah:** The hardest part of being a mother is that I'm responsible for my child and my home, and I have to manage everything—organizing my time between home, giving time to my son, my job, and my personal life with my friends. This was quite difficult for me at the beginning.

**شرْبِل:** أيْه! بِقْدر... بِقْدر أتْخيّل هَيْدا الشّي. ليْكي بالنِّسْبة لألي أنا بْحِسّ إنّو تْضلّك هيْك إنّو في عِنْدك وَلد وإنْتي مسؤولِة عنّو، يَعْني بدِّك تْكوني مِثالية قدّامو تْعلّمي الصّحّ مِن الغلط وخاصّةً بهيْك مُجْتمّع بلِبْنان. صراحة هيْك شُعور غريب بيْخوّف على مُتْعِب على... بِذات الوَقِت كْتير بْيبْسُط.

*Lebanese Arabic Dardashi · 126*

**Charbel:** Yes, I can imagine. For me, the hardest part is knowing that you're responsible for a child, and you have to be a role model for them, teaching them right from wrong, especially in a society like ours in Lebanon. It's a strange feeling—both scary and exhausting, but at the same time, very rewarding.

**فرح:** أكيد بفْهم هَيدا الشّي هِيِّ مسؤولية كْتير كْبيرِة بسّ كمان فرْحة كْتير حِلْوة. الزَّواج والعَيْلِة كْتير شي حِلو. بِتْكون مليانِة بالطِّلْعات والنِّزْلات بسّ الحُبّ والدّعْم بيخلّوا كِلّ شي بْيِسْتاهل.

**Farah:** Absolutely, I understand that. It's a big responsibility but also a great joy. Marriage and family are wonderful, filled with ups and downs, but love and support make it all worthwhile.

**شرْبِل:** عنْجدّ مِيِّة بالْمِيِّة. رِحْلِة بتْعلْمِك كْتير عن الحُبّ، الصّبِر، التّضْحية، شي كْتير حِلو! ميرْسي لألِك يا فرح والله يْخلّيلِك عَيْلْتِك وميرْسي للْمُسْتمِعين وبتْمنّى يْكونوا هيْك سْتفادوا لنّو شْوَيّ. وانْشالله مْنِلْتِقي بمَوْضوع جْديد وقِصص حِلْوة.

**Charbel:** Absolutely, 100%. It's a journey that teaches you a lot about love, patience, and sacrifice—truly a wonderful thing! Thank you, Farah, and may God bless your family. Thanks to our listeners, and I hope they benefited from this even if just a bit. Hopefully, we'll meet again with a new topic and beautiful stories.

**فرح:** ميرْسي يا شرْبِل. ويْخلّيلِك عَيْلْتِك عَ اللّبْناني وميرْسي للْمُسْتمِعين. وبْحِبّ هيْك زيد شغْلِة نِحْنا بِلِبْنان كصبايا وشباب مِن جيلْنا نِحْنا أبْطال.

**Farah:** Thank you, Charbel, and may God bless your family too. Thank you to our listeners. I'd like to add that we, the young generation in Lebanon, are heroes.

**شرْبِل:** عنْجدّ. Thank you so much .

**Charbel:** Absolutely. Thank you so much.

## Comprehension Questions

1. شو هُوّ مَوْضوع الحلْقة اللي حِكْيوا عنّو شرْبِل وفرح؟

2. كيف وَصف شرْبِل تجرْبِةْ الزَّواج وتِكْوين العَيْلة؟

3. شو هِيِّ التحدِّيّات اللي بِتْواجِهْ فرح كإمّ بِلِبْنان؟

4. كيف بِتْساعِد العَيْلِة المِمْتدِّة بِتخْفيف المسْؤوليّات عن الأهِل بِلِبْنان؟

5. لِيْش بِتْشوف فرح إنّو الزَّواج مسْؤولية كْبيرة؟

6. شو هِيِّ أهميةْ دعْم الأهْل لبعْضُن البعِض حسب شرْبِل؟

7. كيف بِتْساعِد إمّ فرح بِرِعايةْ إبْنا؟

8. شو هُوّ الشُّعور اللي بيحِسّ في شرْبِل بِكَوْنو مسْؤول عن وَلدو؟

1. What is the topic of the episode that Charbel and Farah discussed?
2. How did Charbel describe the experience of marriage and starting a family?
3. What are the challenges Farah faces as a mother in Lebanon?
4. How does the extended family help relieve the responsibilities of parents in Lebanon?
5. Why does Farah see marriage as a big responsibility?
6. What is the importance of family support according to Charbel?
7. How does Farah's mother help take care of her son?
8. What feeling does Charbel experience being responsible for his child?

## Discussion Questions

1. كيف بِتْشوف الزَّواج وتكْوين العَيْلة بِبلدك؟

2. شو هِيِّ التحدِّيّات اللي بِتْواجِها كأَبّ أَوْ إمّ بِتِرْبايةْ الوْلاد؟

3. كيف بِتْساعِد العَيْلة المِمْتدِّة بِتخْفيف الأَعْباء اليَوْمية؟

4. شو هِيِّ النّصايِح اللي بْتعْطيا للأَزْواج الِجْداد بِخْصوص الزَّواج وتِكْوين العَيْلة؟

5. كيف بِتْوازِن بينْ الحَياةْ العملية والعائِلية؟

6. كيف بِتْشوف دوْر الأَهْل بِدعْم وْلادُن بالزَّواج وتِكْوين العَيْلة؟

7. شو هِيِّ القِيَم اللي بِتْحِبّ تِزْرعا بِوْلادك؟

8. كيف بِتْشوف الفرْق بينْ تَرْبيةْ الوْلاد اليوْم وتَرْبيتُنْ بوَقِت أَهْلك؟

1. How do you see marriage and starting a family in your country?
2. What challenges do you face as a parent in raising children?
3. How does the extended family help relieve your daily burdens?
4. What advice do you give to new couples about marriage and starting a family?
5. How do you balance work and family life?
6. How do you see the role of parents in supporting their children in marriage and starting a family?
7. What values do you want to instill in your children?
8. How do you see the difference between raising children today and raising them in your parents' time?

# إتِّجاه الطّاقة الشَّمْسية والتّنقُّل الكهْرُبائي بِلِبْنان

## The Shift Towards Solar Energy and Electric Transportation in Lebanon

### In this episode...

Charbel and Omar explore the rise of solar energy and electric vehicles in Lebanon. They discuss how the country's energy crisis has led many to adopt solar power as a practical solution, reducing reliance on unreliable electricity. They also touch on the growing popularity of electric cars, which offer both cost savings and environmental benefits. Learn how these innovations are beginning to reshape daily life in Lebanon.

## *Vocabulary*

| | |
|---|---|
| crisis | أزْمِة |
| solar panels | ألْواح شمْسية |
| import | إسْتيراد |
| gasoline | بنْزين |
| environment | بيئة |
| rationing | تقْنين |
| cost | تكْلِفة |
| electric transportation | تنقُّل كهْرُبائي |
| customs duties | جُمْرُك |
| neighborhood | حيّ (أحْيا) |
| oil | زيْت (زْيوت) |
| electric car | سيّارة كهْرُبائية |
| winter | شِتي |
| maintenance | صِيانِة |
| solar energy | طاقة شمْسية |
| electricity | كهْربا |
| trend | موْضة |
| generator | مُوَلِّد |
| expenses | نفقات |
| means of transportation | وَسائِل النّقِل |

**Transcript**

**شَربِل:** هاي، كيفْكُن اليوْم؟ مَوْضوعُنا اليوْم رح نِحْكي فيه عن شي جْديد، شي فجْأة هيْك طُلع بلِبْنان وحَيّفاجِئْكُن: الطّاقة الشّمْسية والتّنَقُّل الكهْرُبائي. معكُن شَربِل ومعي رْفيقي عُمر. كيف عُمر؟

Charbel: Hi, how are you all today? Our topic today is about something new, something that suddenly emerged in Lebanon and might surprise you—solar energy and electric mobility. I'm Charbel, and with me is my friend Omar. How are you, Omar?

**عُمر:** هاي شرْبِل، أنا مْنيح، إنْتَ كيف؟

Omar: Hi, Charbel! I'm good. How are you?

**شرْبِل:** كْتير مْنيح! خبِّرْنا شْوَيّ هيْك يا عُمر عن هالمَوْضوع. كيف فجْأة هيْك ظهر بلِبْنان وكيف إنّو هالْبلد اللي تعْبان إقْتِصادياً فجْأة صار عِنْدو هالحُبّ للْبيئة وهالطّاقة الشّمْسية؟

Charbel: I'm doing great! So, Omar, tell us a bit about this topic. How did it suddenly emerge in Lebanon, and how did this country, which is struggling economically, suddenly develop this love for the environment and solar energy?

**عُمر:** لكون صريح معك ولكون صريح مع المُسْتمعين، ما بعْتقِد هَيْدا التّحوُّل نحْوَ الطّاقة المُتجدِّدة أوْ الطّاقة الشّمْسية كان ناتج عن رغْبة بسّ للْحِفاظ على البيئة. للأسف بلِبْنان ومِن سْنين لوَرا مِنْعاني مِن أزْمةْ طاقة. يَعْني بعد إذا هلّأ عم يسْمعونا المُسْتمعين يمكِن يِسْتغرْبوا إنّو بلِبْنان بعْدا لهلّأ الطّاقة الكهْرُبائية مِنّا مِتْوَفّرة ٢٤ على ٢٤. فا بالْماضي وبالسّنين الأخيرة لجأوا العالم للْمُوَلِّدات الكهْرُبائية. اليوْم مِنْشوف بكِلّ الأحْيا بْبيْروت وبالْمناطق اللُّبْنانية كِلّا، في... مِنْسمّي موتور الحيّ أوْ مُوَلِّد الحيّ يَلّي بغياب الكهْربا بكهْرَبْةْ الدَّوْلة صاحب المُوَلِّد بيوَزِّع كهْربا على المُواطِنين. للأسف بعد ما بلّشِت الأزْمة الإقْتِصادية بلِبْنان وصارِت تدهْوُر بالْعمْلة اللُّبْنانية، صار الحُصول على دوْلارات لإسْتيراد النّفْط لَيْغزّي معامِل الكهْربا وحتّى يْغزّي هوْلي المُوَلِّدات الخاصّة صار شي صعِب. وقطعْنا بفِتْرة وَجيزة إنّو صار في تِقْنين قاسي فا

*Lebanese Arabic Dardashi · 132*

ضْطرَّت العالم لتقدُر تُكمِّل حَياتا تْنبِّش على وَسائِل طاقة جْديدِة، ووَقْتا كان أَكْثر حَلّ مُجْدي إقْتِصاديّاً وكان حَلّ هيِّن ويقْدُر يِتْطبّق بِسِرْعة كانت الطّاقة الشّمْسية.

**Omar:** To be honest with you and with our listeners, I don't think this shift towards renewable energy or solar energy was purely out of a desire to protect the environment. Unfortunately, in Lebanon, we've been suffering from an energy crisis for years. Even now, our listeners might be surprised to learn that electricity in Lebanon isn't available 24/7. In the past, and especially in recent years, people relied on generators. Today, you can see in every neighborhood in Beirut and across Lebanon what we call the "neighborhood motor" or "neighborhood generator," where, when there are state power outages, the generator owner distributes electricity to the residents. Unfortunately, after the economic crisis started in Lebanon and the Lebanese currency deteriorated, it became difficult to obtain dollars to import fuel to power the electricity plants and even to fuel these private generators. We went through a brief period of severe rationing, and people had to find new energy solutions to continue their lives. The most economically viable and quickly implementable solution at that time was solar energy.

**شرْبِل:** واو عُمر يَعْني عطيْتُن للمُسْتمِعين مُلخَّص واضِح وشامِل كيف نْتقلْنا بِلبْنان. ليْك صراحة أنا كِنت شخْصيّاً قرّرت ركّب أَلْواح شمْسية وخاصّةً بهالْفتْرة اللي حْكيت عنّا. وكِنت مِترَدِّد بِالْبِداية بسّ لأنّو إذا بدّك هالْتكْلِفة الأوّلية بسّ بعد هالْفتْرة القصيرِة حسِبت إنّو لَأ حكون رِبْحان يَعْني، وبطّلِت عم عاني مِن قطْعِت كهْربا وبطّلِت عِتْلان همّ إنّو في كهْربا أَوْ لَأ. وصار فيني شغِّل كِلّ شي بِالْبيْت بدون ما أَعْمُل حْساب، بدون ما حتّى إعْتِل همّ، بيدور ما بيدور في كهْربا هلّأ... يَعْني إذا بدّك تخبِّر المُسْتمِعين شوَيِّ إنّو نِحْنا بِلبْنان عنّا ثقافِة بِتْقول إنّو يَعْني "راحِت الدّوْلة إجت الدّوْلة" اللي هيِّ هيِّ عم نِحْكي عن الكهْربا وَقْتا كيف بْيِفْصُل مِتِل ما قِلِت بيْن الكهْربا اللي بْتعطيا الدّوْلة وبيْن الكهْربا اللي بْيَعْطيا مُولِّد الحيِّ.

**Charbel:** Wow, Omar, you've given our listeners a clear and comprehensive summary of how we transitioned in Lebanon. Honestly, I personally decided to install solar panels, especially during the period you mentioned. I was hesitant at first because of the initial cost, but after a short while, I realized that I was actually saving money. I no longer suffered from power outages or worried about whether the electricity would be on or not. I can now run everything in my house without any concerns. You could explain to the listeners that in Lebanon, we have a saying that goes, "the state comes, the state goes," which refers to the power cuts and how people switch between state electricity and generator electricity.

**عُمَر:** صحيح شرْبِل وعَ فِكْرة الطَّاقة الشَّمْسية بِلبْنان لاقت إِزْدِهار غِيْر إنّو إِجِت لَتْحِلّ مشاكِل الكهْربا والطَّاقة. كانِت فعّالة لأنّو لِبْنان بلد مِشْمِس يَعْني حتَّى بْفِصْل الشِّتي الشَّمِس بْتِطْلع وبِمعدّل يَعْني ٥٠ أَوْ ٤٠ نْهار بالسِّنة بسّ مْنِشْهد عَواصِف قاسْية وغْياب للشَّمِس. فا إجا هَيْدا الحلّ pratique وسْتعْملوا الكلّ بِفعالية كْتير عالْية.

Omar: That's right, Charbel. And by the way, solar energy in Lebanon has seen a boom not only because it solves electricity and energy problems but also because it's effective due to Lebanon being a sunny country. Even in winter, the sun shines, and we only experience about 50 to 40 days a year of severe storms and cloudy weather. So, this was a practical solution that everyone used very effectively.

**شرْبِل:** مظْبوط! يَعْني العالم بلّشِت تْوفِّر عَ حالا ولحِسْن الحظّ هَيْدا الشّي كْتير إنّو صديق لَلبِيئة. ولِيْك شو اللي بِفاجِئْني هلّأ lately إنّو كمان صارِت موْضة إنّو السِّيارات الكهْرُبائية والتّنقّل بالسِّيارات الكهْرُبائية بِلبْنان عم يِزْدِهِر. يَعْني عم بيصير خِيار كْتير مْتوفِّر، اللِّبْناني عم يِتْقبّلو واللي عِنْدو طاقة شمْسية بالبِيْت عم بيقول إنّو أنا إذا جِبت سِيّارة كمان عَ الطّاقة الشَّمْسية بْكون عم بْوفِّر بِنْزين وبِذات الوَقِت بْكون عم حافِظ عَ البِيئة، وخاصّةً عم نْشوف هالسِّيارات اللي عم يْكون شكْلا حِلو تِشْتري أَوْ تِقْني عِنْدك بالبِيْت.

Charbel: Exactly! People started saving money, and luckily, it's also very eco-friendly. What surprises me lately is that electric cars and electric mobility are also booming in Lebanon. It's becoming a widely accepted option, and those with solar energy at home are saying, "If I get an electric car powered by solar energy, I'll save on fuel and also help protect the environment." especially since we're seeing these cars that not only look great but are also practical to own at home.

**عُمَر:** صحيح والسِّيارات الكهْرُبائية أَوْ بِشكِل إجْمالي، وَسائِل النّقِل الكهْرُبائية أَثْبتت فعالِيّتا ومِش بسّ بِلبْنان، بالْعالم ككُلّ. والحِلو أَوْ الميِّزة تبع هَيْدا السِّيارات إنّو هِيّ عم بِتْواجِهْ مشاكِل تِقْنية أَقلّ مِن السِّيارات التّقْليدية. يَعْني بالنِّهاية اليوْم تكْلِفْة الصِّيانة يَلّي بتُحْطّا على الزُّيوت تبع سِيّارْتك التّقْليدية، على كلّ القُصص اللي مِعْقول

*Lebanese Arabic Dardashi · 134*

تِتْخرْبط مع الوَقِت هَيْدا ما عم تِتْواجَهْ... ما عم بِتْواجِهْ العالم يَلّي عِنْدُن سِيّارات كهْرْبائية.

**Omar:** True, and electric cars—or electric transportation in general—have proven to be effective not just in Lebanon but worldwide. The nice thing about these cars is that they face fewer technical issues than traditional cars. Today, the maintenance costs for oil and all the parts that can break down over time are not something that electric car owners have to deal with.

**شرْبِل:** مظْبوط وليْك الشّي اللي بيفاجِئْني وحتّى لَوْ إنّو minimal إنّو من الدَّوْلة إنّو هيِّ عم بِتْساعِد عَ إسْتيراد هالسِّيارات الكهْرُبائية، وعم بِتْخفِّف شْوَيّ مِن الجُمْرُك عْلَيْن وهَيْدي خُطْوة كْتير حِلْوة ومُمْتازة. انْشالله لبْنان بْيِزْدِهِر أكْتر ومنْشوف هيْك حُلول بغيْر قِطاعات. عُمر thank you لإلك عَ هالْمُحادثة الحِلْوة والمليئة بالْمعْلومات وميرْسي للْمُسْتمعين. انْشالله نْكون خبرّْناهُن فِكْرة ويْن رايح لِبْنان. نْتِبْهوا عَ حالْكُن ومِنْشوفْكُن بمَوْضوع تاني ومِن خبْرية مِن لِبْنان.

**Charbel:** That's right! And what surprises me, even though it's minimal, is that the government is helping by reducing the customs duties on these electric cars. This is a great and promising step. Hopefully, Lebanon will continue to prosper, and we'll see similar solutions in other sectors. Omar, thank you for this great conversation full of information, and thanks to the listeners. We hope we've given you an idea of where Lebanon is headed. Take care, and we'll see you next time with another topic and another story from Lebanon.

## Comprehension Questions

١. لَيْش لجأ العالم بِلِبْنان للطَّاقة الشَّمْسية؟

٢. كيف ساهمِت الطَّاقة الشَّمْسية بحلّ مِشْكْلةْ الكهْربا بِلِبْنان؟

٣. شو كانِت الصُّعوبات الإقْتِصادية اللي واجها لِبْنان وتْسبّبِت باللُّجوء للطَّاقة الشَّمْسية؟

٤. شو هِيِّ العلاقة بيْن الطَّاقة الشَّمْسية والبيئة بِلِبْنان؟

٥. لَيْش صارِت السَّيارات الكهْرُبائية مِنْتِشْرة أكْتر بِلِبْنان؟

٦. كيف ساعدِت الدَّوْلة اللِّبْنانية على تِسْهيل إسْتيراد السَّيارات الكهْرُبائية؟

٧. شو كانِت فَوايِد السَّيارات الكهْرُبائية مُقارنةً بِالسَّيارات التِّقْليدية حسب عُمر؟

٨. كيف كانِت تجْرُبِةْ شرْبِل الشَّخْصية مع ترْكيب الألْواح الشَّمْسية بِبَيْتو؟

1. Why did people in Lebanon turn to solar energy?
2. How did solar energy help solve the electricity problem in Lebanon?
3. What were the economic challenges that Lebanon faced that led to the adoption of solar energy?
4. What is the relationship between solar energy and the environment in Lebanon?
5. Why have electric cars become more widespread in Lebanon?
6. How did the Lebanese government help facilitate the import of electric cars?
7. What were the benefits of electric cars compared to traditional cars according to Omar?
8. How was Charbels's personal experience with installing solar panels at his home?

## Discussion Questions

١. كيف بلدك بْيِعْتِمْدوا على مصادِرِ الطّاقة المُتَجَدِّدة؟ في شي إسْتِخْدام للطّاقة الشّمْسية؟

٢. شو هِيِّ الوَسائِل اللي بْتِسْتعْمِلا بِحَياتك اليَوْمية لتَوْفير الطّاقة؟ بْتِعْتِقِد إنّا كافْية؟

٣. شو هِيِّ المشاكِل البيئية اللي بْتْواجِها بِبلدك وكيف عم تِتْعامل معا؟

٤. كيف بِتْشوف المُسْتَقْبل للسَّيارات الكهْرُبائية بِبلدك؟ بْتِعْتِقِد رح تِقْدر تْحِلّ مشاكِل النّقِل التّقْليدي؟

٥. هل بِتْفكِّر إنّو بِبلدك مُمْكِن يْصير إعْتِماد أكْبر على السَّيارات الكهْرُبائية بِالْمُسْتقْبل؟ لِيْش أَوْ لِيْش لأ؟

٦. كيف تِتْعامل مع مِشْكْلِةْ إنْقِطاع الكهْربا بِمنْطقْتك؟ بِتْفكِّر في إسْتِخْدام طاقة بديلة؟

٧. بْتِعْتِقِد إنّو في وَعي كافي لأهمية إسْتِعْمال الطّاقة المُتَجَدِّدة بين أفْراد مُجْتَمّعك؟

٨. كيف بِتْشوف دوْر الدَّوْلةِ بِدعْم المُبادرات البيئية بِبلدك؟ في دعْم كافي؟

1. How does your country rely on renewable energy sources? Is solar energy used?
2. What methods do you use in your daily life to save energy? Do you think they are enough?
3. What are the environmental problems facing your country and how are they being dealt with?
4. How do you see the future of electric cars in your country? Do you think they could solve traditional transportation problems?
5. Do you think your country might rely more on electric cars in the future? Why or why not?
6. How do you deal with power outages in your area? Are you considering using alternative energy?
7. Do you think there is enough awareness about the importance of using renewable energy among the people in your community?
8. How do you view the role of the government in supporting environmental initiatives in your country? Is there enough support?

# الإشيا اللي بْتِسْتفِزّنا
## Pet Peeves

## In this episode...

Charbel and Farah dive into the everyday annoyances that get under our skin, commonly known as "pet peeves." From traffic violations like running red lights to inconsiderate behaviors in public spaces, they discuss the little things that frustrate them and many others in Lebanon. They share personal stories of people being loud on their phones, cutting in line, and playing music too loudly. It's a light-hearted conversation about the challenges of dealing with these irritations and how to stay calm despite them.

## Vocabulary

| | |
|---|---|
| meeting | إِجْتِماع |
| red light (traffic signal) | إشارة حمْرا |
| inside the bus | بِقلْب الباص |
| accident | حادِث (حَوادِث) |
| to speak loudly | حِكِي (يِحْكِي) بِصوْت عالي |
| garbage, trash | زْبالة |
| to bother | زعج (يُزْعِج) |
| to honk | زمّر (يِزمِّر) |
| to annoy, provoke | سْتفزّ (يِسْتفِزّ) |
| to distract | شتّت (يْشتِّت) الإنْتِباهْ |
| to spoil the view | شوّهْ (يْشوّهْ) المنْظر |
| patient | صبور |
| to harm the environment | ضرّ (يْضُرّ) بِالْبيئة |
| chaos | فَوْضى |
| lack of respect | قِلّة إحْتِرام |
| rude | قليل أخْلاق |
| motorcycle | موْتوْ (موْتوْيات) |
| appointment | مَوْعد (مْواعيد) |
| to annoy, get on one's nerves | نرْفز (يْنرْفِز) |
| to stand in line | وِقِف (يوقف) بِالدّوْر |

## Transcript

**شرْبِل:** هاي جميعاً، اليوْم رح نِحْكي عن مَوْضوع شْوَيّ هيْك بِيِخْتِلِف وعن القُصص اللي بِتِزْعِجْنا، مِنْسمّيا pet peeves وهِيِّ قِصص بْتِسْتِفِزْنا. معْكُن شرْبِل ومعي رِفْيِقْتي فرح.

Charbel: Hi, everyone! Today we're going to talk about a topic that's a bit different—about the things that annoy us, what we call "pet peeves," those little things that get under our skin. I'm Charbel, and with me is my friend Farah.

**فرح:** أهْلا شرْبِل كيفك؟

Farah: Hi, Charbel. How are you?

**شرْبِل:** أنا كْتير مْنيح. خلّينا نْبلِّش شْوَيّ بِشرح شو يَعْني أوْ شو القِصص أوْ شو يَعْني بْتِزْعِجْنا وبْتِسْتِفِزْنا بِحَياتْنا اليَوْمية. بالنِّسْبة لألِك فرح، شو هيْك قِصص معْقول تِسْتِفِزّك؟

Charbel: I'm doing great. Let's start by explaining what "pet peeves" are, or in other words, the things that bother us and annoy us in our daily lives. So, Farah, what are some things that really get on your nerves?

**فرح:** والله يا شرْبِل في كْتير شغْلات بتِسْتِفِزْني وشغْلة مِنُّن لمّا عنْجدّ العالم بْيِقْطعوا الإشارة الحمْرا. هيْدا الشّي عنْجدّ بيخوّف، بيسبِّب حَوادِث، شي مِش مقْبول بالنِّسْبة لإلي. وكْتير هيْدا الشّي بْيِسْتِفِزْني لمّا يْصير قِدّامي. وإنْتَ يا شرْبِل؟ شو أكْتر شي بْيِسْتِفِزّك؟

Farah: Oh, Charbel, there are many things that annoy me. One of them is when people run red lights. It's really scary and can cause accidents; it's totally unacceptable to me. And it really bothers me when I see it happening in front of me. What about you, Charbel? What bothers you the most?

**شرْبِل:** أنا مِن القِصص اللي بْتِسْتِفِزْني وخاصّةً هوْن بِلِبْنان في كْتير قُصص هيْك شَواز عن... قُصص بْيِسْتِفِزّوكي مِتِل ما حْكيتي عن الإشارة الحمْرا في كمان يَلّي ضِغْري بيزمِّر بسّ تِمْشي بسّ تْصير الإشارة خضْرا. وفي كمان شي بْيِسْتِفِزْني هوِّ لمّا النّاس بْيِحْكوا بِصوْت عالي على التِّليفوْن ويقلْب الباص أوْ بِالتّاكْسي وبْحِسّ إنّو ما عِنْدُن إحْتِرام للآخرين.

*Lebanese Arabic Dardashi · 140*

**Charbel:** Well, one of the things that really annoys me, especially here in Lebanon, is when people honk the second the light turns green. And another thing that bothers me is when people talk loudly on the phone in the bus or taxi, with no consideration for others around them.

**فرح:** مظبوط، في كمان شغلة بْتِسْتِفِزّني كْتير هِيِّ لمّا العالم يْكِبّوا زْبالة على الأرض بدل ما يْحُطُّوا بالسِّلّة المْخصّصة للزُّبالة. هَيدا الشّي بيشوِّه المنْظر وبيضُرّ بالبيئة. يَعْني أنا كمان هَيدوْل بْشوفُن كْتير يَعْني بْنِبِهْلُن يَعْني هوْل القِصص عنْجدّ بْيِسْتِفِزّوني فا بْصير إنْتَبِه أكْتر لهلإشْيا. إنْتَ كمان شو بِتْخبِّرْنا في قُصص بْتِسْتِفِزّك؟

**Farah:** Absolutely, another thing that really gets on my nerves is when people throw garbage on the ground instead of putting it in the trash can. It ruins the scenery and harms the environment. I see this happening a lot, and it really frustrates me, so I pay extra attention to these things. Are there other things that annoy you too?

**شرْبِل:** يَعْني فرح هلّأ عم نِحْكي وعم برْجع هيْك إسْتجْمع أفْكاري، صراحة في كْتير قِصص هيْك بْيِستفِزّوكي بالحَياة اليَوْمية وبيعصْبوكي. مثلاً العالم يَلّي بْتِترُك الـcart تبع السّوبرِمارْكِت أوْ الـchariot مِتل ما مِنْقِلّا نِحْنا، بنُصّ الطّريق وبيروحوا لَيْجيبوا غْراضُن وبيكون مثلاً مْسكّرا المحلّ يَلّي بدّك تِقْطعي فيه. يَعْني هَيدا الشّي كمان بْيَعْمُل فوْضى وبيخلّيكي هَيكي تِسْتصِعْبي تِمِرْقي.

**Charbel:** Well, now that we're talking, I'm starting to remember more things that annoy me in daily life. For example, when people leave their supermarket carts (or 'chariots,' as we call them) in the middle of the aisle and then walk away to get something, blocking the way for others. It creates chaos and makes it difficult to get through.

**فرح:** صح هَيدي شغْلة عنْجدّ مزِعْجة. في كمان شغْلة أنا كْتير صراحةً بِتْضايقْني وكْتير مرّات بْواجها خْصوصة بْشِغْلي هِيِّ لمّا عنْجدّ لمّا العالم يِتْأخّروا على الإجْتِماعات أوْ المواعيد مِن غير ما يِعْطوك خبر. بِتْحِسّ عنْجدّ إنّو وَقْتك مِش مْهِمّ بالنِّسْبة لإلُن.

**Farah:** Right, that's really annoying. Another thing that really bothers me, especially at work, is when people are late to meetings or appointments without letting you know. It makes you feel like your time isn't important to them.

**شَرْبِل:** مِيّة بِالْمِيّة هَيْدي شَغْلِة كْتير قِلِّة إحْتِرام كمان. يَعْني ما بْحِبّ أبداً أنا إتْأخَّر على مَوْعِد أوْ نِطّر حدا يَعْني. وْفي شَغْلِة كمان فينا نِحْكي عنّا هِيِّ لمّا النّاس بيخلّوا صَوْت الـ... تِليفوْناتُن عالْية بِالْمَطْعم بمحلّات public وأوْقات كمان بِالـlibraries يَعْني محلّات واحد رايِح هَيْكي يِقْرا عَ رَواق، بْتْلاقي عالم بيدِقّ تِليفوْنا أوْ عم بـ... بِيحْكوا عَ صَوْت عالي كمان هَيْدا شي ما بْيَعْطي خُصوصية وكمان قِلِّة إحْتِرام لَلْآخرين.

Charbel: Exactly, it's a sign of disrespect, too. I hate being late for an appointment or making someone wait. Another thing we can talk about is when people leave their phone volume high in restaurants or public places, or even in libraries—places where people go to read quietly. Then, someone's phone rings loudly, or they start talking loudly, which disrupts the peace and shows a lack of respect for others.

**فرح:** في كمان شَغْلِة تانْية وهيِّ لمّا النّاس بْيِسْتعِمْلوا تِليفوْناتُن بِالْمَسْرح أوْ بِالسّينِما، الضّوّ تبع التِّليفوْن بِشِتّت الإنْتِباه يَعْني ما بيخلّيك تْرِكِّز.

Farah: Another thing that annoys me is when people use their phones in the theater or cinema. The light from the phone is distracting and makes it hard to focus.

**شَرْبِل:** صحّ وصايْرة معي. يَعْني هَيْدا شي هَيْك سئيل تْكوني عم تِحْضري movie وتْلاقي واحد ضوّى ضوّ أوْ دقّ تِليفوْنو عَ صَوْت عالي وبْصير تْبطّلي مْركّزة على الـmovie. وْفي شَغْلِة فينا نِحْكي عنّا هِيِّ كمان لمّا النّاس ما بْيوقفوا بِالدّوْر وبيصيروا بدُّن يْقرّبوا لَقِدّام أوْ ياخْدوا محلّ غَيْرُن. هَيْدا شي كْتير عنّا بِلِبْنان مَوْجودة، ويا ريت مثلاً بيحِسّوا عَ دمُّن هَيْدي العالم وهَيْك شْوَيّ بيبِلْشوا ويوقفوا بِنْظام أكْتر، بْتِحسّي إنّو كْتير ما في نِظام بخاصّةً بمحلّات shopping ومحلّات كلّ شي في waiting. بدّك تْنُطْري تاخِدي مثلاً coffee بْتْلاقي بلّش واحد يِدْفِّش، بدّك تْروحي على سوبِرْماركِت مثلاً لتِدْفعي الفاتورة بْتْلاقي واحد سبقِك بلّش يِدْفِّش قطع عنّك، هَيْدا الشّي سوبّر سوبّر سوبّر مِزْعِج وسوبّر قليل أخْلاق.

Charbel: Yes, that's happened to me too. It's really annoying when you're watching a movie, and someone's phone lights up or they receive a loud call, making it impossible to stay focused on the movie. Another thing is when people don't wait their turn and try to push ahead in line. This is very common in Lebanon, especially in shopping places or anywhere you have to wait in line.

You're waiting for your coffee, and someone starts pushing in front of you. You go to the supermarket to pay your bill, and someone cuts in front of you. It's incredibly frustrating and shows a lack of manners.

**فرح:** صحّ، هَيْدي الشّغْلِة كْتير مزعْجِة. كمان في شغْلِة تانْيِة هيِّ لمّا عنجدّ العالم بيحِطّوا هالْموسيقى العالْيِة بهالسّيارات وهنّي واقْفين عِنْد الإشارة. هَيْدي الشّغْلِة بِتْضايق كِلّ العالم كِلّ السّيارات especially لمّا يْكونوا حاطّين نوْع موسيقى مُسْتَفِزّ يَعْني بِتْحِسّوا الأرض عم بِتْرِجّ. يَعْني كِلّ السّيارات بيصيروا يِتْطلّعوا إنّو شو في شو صايِر يَعْني.

Farah: Absolutely, that's very irritating. Another thing that bothers me is when people blast loud music in their cars while stopped at a red light. It disturbs everyone around, especially when it's an obnoxious kind of music that makes the ground shake. All the cars around start looking around like, "What's going on?"

**شربيل:** مِيّة بالْميّة! وما بدّنا نِنْسى المَوْتوْيّات الصّوْتا عالي كمان يَعْني بْيِقْطع قصْداً وبيصير يْقوّي بهالْموتوْ كِرمال يِزْعُج حَوالَيْه. لَيْكي فرح القِصص صْغيرة وبتْصير معْنا on daily basis يَوْمية بسّ عنجدّ بِتْخلّيكي تِتْنَرْفزي وتعْصبي وإنْتي بِغنّي عن كِلّ هالstress. هُوّ أهمّ مِن كِلّ هالْقِصص إنّو نْجرّب نْكون أكْتر شْوَيّ صبورين ونْجرّب نِتْعامل معا برَواء هيْك كِرمال بسّ ما نْضلّ مْعصّبين ونِحْنا عم نْقضّي نْهارْنا. فرح بِدّي قِلّك thank you ومِيرْسي عَ هالْمُشاركة ومِيرْسي للْمُسْتمِعين أكيد رح نِلْتِقي مرّة تانْيِة بمَوْضوع جْديد وخبْرْية جْديدة مِن حَياتْنا بِلِبْنان.

Charbel: Exactly! And we can't forget the motorcycles with loud engines that purposely rev up to annoy everyone around. Farah, these are small things that happen to us on a daily basis, but they really make you nervous and upset, and you could do without that stress. The most important thing is to try to be a bit more patient and handle these situations calmly so we don't stay upset all day. Farah, thank you for sharing, and thanks to our listeners. We'll definitely meet again with a new topic and another story from our lives in Lebanon.

**فرح:** شُكْراً إلك يا شرْبِل، وشُكْراً لكِلّ المُسْتمِعين.

Farah: Thank you, Charbel, and thanks to all the listeners.

## Comprehension Questions

١. شو يَعْني "pet peeves" أَوْ الإشْيا اللي بْتِسْتفِزْنا بِحسب شرْبِل وفرح؟

٢. شو هِيِّ الإشْيا اللي بْتِسْتفِزّ فرح لمّا تْكون عم تْسوق؟

٣. شو الإشْيا اللي بْتِزْعِج شرْبِل بالْمُواصلات العامِّة؟

٤. لَيْش بْتِعْتبِر فرح كبّ الزِّبالة على الأَرْض شي بْيِسْتفِزّا؟

٥. شو هِيِّ المَواقِف اللي بْتِسْتفِزّ شرْبِل بالسّوبِرْماركِت؟

٦. كيف بِيأَثِّر التَّأْخير على المَواعيد والإجْتِماعات على فرح؟

٧. شو هِيِّ المِشِكْلة اللي بِتْواجِها فرح بالْمسْرح أَوْ السّينما؟

٨. شو رأْي شرْبِل بِخْصوص النّاس اللي ما بْيوقفوا بالدّوْر وبيجرّبوا يقْطعوا عن غَيْرُن؟

1. What does "pet peeves" or things that annoy us mean according to Charbel and Farah?
2. What are the things that annoy Farah when she's driving?
3. What things bother Charbel in public transportation?
4. Why does Farah find littering on the ground annoying?
5. What situations in the supermarket annoy Charbel?
6. How does being late for meetings or appointments affect Farah?
7. What problem does Farah face in the theater or cinema?
8. What is Charbel's opinion about people who don't wait in line and try to skip ahead?

## Discussion Questions

١. شو هِيِّ الإشْيا اللي بْتِسْتِفزّك بِحَياتك اليَوْمية؟

٢. كيف بْتِتْعامل مع المَواقِف اللي بْتِزِعْجك أَوْ بْتِسْتِفزّك؟

٣. شو رأيَك بِتَصرُّف النّاس يَلّي ما بْيِحْترِموا إشارات المُرور؟

٤. كيف بِتْشوف أهمية الإحْترِام المُتْبادل بِالْمُواصلات العامّة؟

٥. بِتْواجِهْ مَواقِف مِتْلا بِالأَسْواق أَوْ السّوبِرْماركِت بِبلدك؟ كيف بْتِتْعامل معا؟

٦. كيف بِتْشوف تأْثير التّأْخير على المَواعيد على إنْتاجيةْ اليوْم؟

٧. شو هِيِّ الطّريقة الأنْسب للتّعامُل مع النّاس اللي بْيِزِعْجوا غَيْرُن بِالضَّوْضاء بِالأَماكِن العامّة؟

٨. كيف مُمْكِن نْزيد مِن الوَعي عِنْد النّاس لَيْكونوا أكْتر إحْترِاماً للآخرين بِالأَماكِن العامّة؟

1. What are the things that annoy you in your daily life?
2. How do you handle situations that annoy or frustrate you?
3. What do you think about people who don't respect traffic signals?
4. How important do you think mutual respect is in public transportation?
5. Do you encounter similar situations in markets or supermarkets in your country? How do you handle them?
6. How do you think being late for appointments affects the productivity of the day?
7. What is the best way to deal with people who disturb others with noise in public places?
8. How can we raise awareness among people to be more respectful of others in public places?

# أوّل وَظيفة

## First Jobs

## In this episode...

Charbel and Omar share funny and memorable stories from their first jobs. They reminisce about the awkward and sometimes embarrassing moments that come with entering the workforce for the first time. From Charbel's mishaps at a fastfood chain to Omar's experience selling electronics, they reflect on how these early jobs taught them valuable lessons. Tune in for some laughs as they talk about the challenges and surprises of starting a first job and how those experiences shape us for the future.

## Vocabulary

| experience | تِجْرِبة (تجارِب) |
|---|---|
| closing [as in closing time of a store] | تِسْكير |
| to learn | تْعَلَّم (يِتْعَلَّم) |
| experience [in the context of work] | خِبْرة |
| (work) shift | دَوام |
| customer | زْبون (زَباين) |
| young man/person | شابّ (شِبّان) |
| work, job | شِغِل (أَشْغال) |
| branch [of a store or company] | فَرِع (فْروع) |
| size, measurement | قْياس |
| value | قيمِة |
| society, community | مُجْتَمع |
| embarrassing | مُحْرِج |
| manager | مُدير (مُدرا) |
| adolescence | مُراهقة |
| money | مصاري |
| (clothing) size | مقاس |
| situation, position | مَوْقِف (مَواقِف) |
| it seems like/that... | هَيّئتو |
| job, position | وَظيفِة (وَظايِف) |

## Transcript

**شَرْبِل:** مَرْحبا! اليوْم رح نِحْكي عن أوّل وَظيفة وكِلّ القُصص اللي بِتْضحِّك اللي بْتيجي معا. أنا شرْبِل، وهَيْدا صديقّي عُمر. كيفك يا عُمر اليوْم؟

Charbel: Hello! Today we're going to talk about our first jobs and all the funny stories that come with them. I'm Charbel, and this is my friend Omar. How are you, Omar, today?

**عُمر:** هاي شرْبِل، الحمْدِلله، إنْتَ كيفك؟

Omar: Hi Charbel, I'm good, thank God. How are you?

**شَرْبِل:** الحمْدِلله، الحمْدِلله، تمام. أوّل وَظيفة بِتْكون هيْك دايْماً يَعْني تجْرِبِة فريدِة نَوْعاً ما، إنّو أوّل مرّة رايح إنْتَ لتِشْتِغِل، مِش عارِف شو ناطْرك. وكِلّ حدا عِنْدو ذِكْرَيات وقُصص بِتْضحِّك من أوّل شِغِل لإلو. شو كانِت أوّل وَظيفة لإلك يا عُمر؟

Charbel: Thank God, thank God, I'm good. The first job is always a unique experience; it's the first time you go to work, not knowing what to expect. Everyone has memories and funny stories from their first job. What was your first job, Omar?

**عُمر:** والله يا شرْبِل ردّيْتْني كْتير لَوَرا هلّأ، بسّ بِتْذكّر إنّو أوّل وَظيفة إلي كانِت مُساعِد بِسوبِرْماركِت. كِنت بِشْتِغِل لجيب شْوَيِّة مصاري، وبعْديْن كْتشفت إنّو فِعْلاً كانِت تجْرِبِة كْتير حِلْوِة. إنْتَ خبِّرْني شو كانِت أوّل وَظيفة لإلك؟

Omar: Honestly, Charbel, you've taken me way back. But I remember that my first job was as an assistant in a supermarket. I worked to make some money, and then I realized it was a really great experience. Tell me, what was your first job?

**شَرْبِل:** أوّل شِغِل لإلي بِتْذكّر كان بالماكْدو يَعْني نِحْنا هوْن ميكدونالْدز، مِنْسمّي عنّا بِلبْنان ماكْدو هيْك على... عَ الفرنْسي. كِنت حابِب إشْتِغِل بسّ لأعْمُل خِبْرة وطلِّع شْوَيِّة مصْروف لإلي بالصَّيْفية. بِتْذكّر لمّا رِحت أنا ورْفيقي لجيب الـuniform أوْ الكوسْتوم تبع الشِّغِل، ما كِنت عارِف قْياس البنْطلوْن. كان عُمْري بِتْذكّر كان عُمْري ١٦ سِنة يَعْني، فا أخدِت قْياس أصْغر أوْ عِطْيوني قْياس أصْغر. ولمّا لبِسْتو وقِت الشِّغِل (كان عِنْدي دوام يَعْني ضُغْري تاني نْهار حتّى ما قيّست فوْق، لبِسْتو ورِحِت على الدّوام) كان شكْلي سوبِّر بيضحِّك، كان قصير وضيِّق عْليِّ الـpants يَعْني. وحتّى المُدير... يَعْني

كان شكلي سوبرّ غريب، حتّى المُدير وَقْتا طلبْلي قْياس تاني. وكان الوَضِع سوبرّ مُحْرِج لِأنّو كِنِت كِلّ مرّة بدّي إتْحرّك حِسّ البنْطلوْن لح يِنْخِزِق.

**Charbel:** I remember my first job was at McDonald's. Here in Lebanon, we call it "Macdo" like in French. I wanted to work just to gain experience and earn some spending money for the summer. I remember when my friend and I went to get the uniform, I didn't know my pants size. I was, I think, 16 years old, so I took a smaller size or they gave me a smaller size. When I wore it to work–I had a shift the next day, and without trying it on beforehand, I went to work–I looked super funny because the pants were short and tight on me. Even the manager... my appearance was so odd that the manager ordered a new size for me. It was super embarrassing because every time I moved, I felt like the pants would rip.

**عُمر:** والله يا شرْبِل هالْخبْرية بِتْضحّك. عم جرّب إتْخايَلك هلّأ بْراسي وإتْخيّل شكلك كيف كان. بسّ أكيد إذا اليوْم بْتِرْجع بِتْفكّر فِيا، هالتّجرِبة خلّتك تِتْعلّم إنّو دايْماً لازِم تعْرِف مقاسك، مظْبوط؟

**Omar:** Charbel, that's a funny story. I'm trying to imagine how you looked then. But if you think about it again today, that experience taught you always to know your size, right?

**شرْبِل:** مظْبوط مظْبوط! مرّة كمان الفرْع كان... هُوّ الفرْع الماكدو اللي شْتغِلِت فيه كان قريب على بيْت أهْلي. فا مرّة ساقبِت تأْخّرْنا كْتير للتّسْكير بالمطْعم، سوْ صارِت شي ساعة تْلاتة الصّبْح. فا ما بْلاقي إلّا الـmanager عم يْعيّطْلي هُوّ ومعصّب. شو طْلعِت الخبْرية يا عُمر؟ وَقْتا إجا بيّي على الفرِع وصار يْدقّ عَالشّباك للـmanager ويْعيّط عْليه إنّو كيف مُخلّ هالشّباب عم تِشْتِغِل لهيْدا الوَقت. كان الموْقف سوبرّ بيضحّك على مُحْرِج على مِش معْروف إنّو برْكي إنّو شو عم يَعْمُل بيّي هوْن عم بِحرّجْني أوّل شِغِل لألي؟ فا ضْطرّ الـmanager وَقْتا يْفلّلْنا أنا وكذا حدا مِن الـteam على البيْت بكّير. صراحة الموْقف كان مُحْرِج وفاجأني، بسّ الشّباب اللي كانوا معي بالشّغِل صار بيّي مِتِل البطل تبعُن إنّو خلّاهُن يْفِلّوا بكّير وزمّطُن مِن هالْمِهمّة.

**Charbel:** Right, right! Another time, the branch... the McDonald's branch I worked at was close to my parents' house. So, one time, we were really late closing the restaurant, and it was around 3 in the morning. Then, suddenly, the manager starts yelling at me, all upset. What was the story, Omar? It turned out my dad had come to the branch and was knocking on the manager's window, yelling at him about how he was letting these kids work so late. The situation was super funny, awkward, and confusing, like, what is my dad even doing here, embarrassing me at my first job? So, the manager had to send me and a few others from the team home early. Honestly, the situation was embarrassing and surprised me, but the guys who were with me at work started seeing my dad as a hero because he got them to leave early and escape from that task.

**عُمر:** والله يا شربِل هَيْئتو قُصصك بالوَظايف ما بتُخْلص. ليْك لصَراحة أنا بعْتبِر إنّو أوّل وَظايف ع طول بتْكون مِلْيانة مَواقِف بتْضحّك وبتْعلِّمْنا كْتير، خاصّةً لأنّو هَيْدا الشّي بيكون أوّل مرّة يَعْني مِن كون عم نُضْهر مِن جوّ المدْرسة وجوّا العيْلة لنِلْتقى بمُجْتمَّع غريب عنّا. بتْعرِف يا شربِل إنّو بلبْنان عادةً النّاس بتْبلّش شِغل على بعُمْر المُراهقة وخاصّةً بالصّيْف بيكون part time job. الشّابّ أوْ الصّبية بيكونوا حابّين يطّلّعوا شْويّةً مصاري يصرْفُون مع أصْحابْن بالصّيْفية، وهيْك بذات الوَقِت بيكونوا عم يِتْعلّموا قيمةْ العمل. والشّغِل هَيْكي بتْكون تجرِبة حِلْوة ولذيذة.

Omar: Honestly, Charbel, it seems like your job stories never end. To be honest, I think that first jobs are always full of funny situations and teach us a lot, especially because it's the first time we're stepping out of the school and family environment to meet a society that's unfamiliar to us. You know, Charbel, in Lebanon, it's common for people to start working during their teenage years, especially in the summer, with a part-time job. The young guys or girls usually want to make some money to spend with their friends during the summer, and at the same time, they're learning the value of work. It ends up being a really nice and enjoyable experience.

**شربِل:** ليْك صحّ صحّ يا عُمر! وعادةً أوّل الأشْغال يَعْني هيْك متِل ما عم بتْقول بتْكون بسوبِرمارْكِت، مطْعم أوْ حتّى بالـ bookshop، بالْمكاتِب. النّاس بيبلّشوا بشِغل بسيط لَيِتْعلّموا كيف يِتْعاملوا مع النّاس ويكْتِسْبوا مهارات جْديدة. كْتير مِن الشّباب بْيِشْتِغْلوا كمان بِالـ club، بنَوادي صَيْفية، بْيِشْتِغْلوا كـ maitre nageur أوْ إذا بدّك أوْ الشّخِص اللي بيراقِب بالْمسْبح وبْيِشْتِغْلوا كمان مُدرِّبين رياضيِّين.

Charbel: Hey, you're right, right, Omar! And usually, the first jobs, like you're saying, are in a supermarket, a restaurant, or even in a bookshop. People start with simple jobs to learn how to deal with others and gain new skills. A lot of young people also work in clubs, summer camps, as lifeguards or, if you will, the person who watches over the swimming pool, and they also work as sports coaches.

**عُمَر:** هلّأ يا شَربِل، صار وَقِت خبّرَك أنا عن قُصّة كْتير بِتْضحّك كمان، صارِت معي بِأوّل الأشْغال اللي شْتغلْتا. مرّة مِن زمان كْتير وبعْد السّوپِرماركِت قرّرِت طوّر حالي قِلِت بِشْتغِل كمان بِمحلّ حدّ البيْت بيبيع electronics، يَعْني قُصص للبيْت التّيڤي، بُرّاد، غسّالة. وكِنِت مبْسوط لأنّو كانِت هَيْدي القُصص بِتْهِمْني بوَقْتا. فا هونِيك نْهار بيفوت لعِنّا زْبون هُوّ ومرْتو لذيذين وحبّوبين وكْتير مْهذّبين، طلبوا مِنّي فرجيْن شو عِنّا تيڤيّات جْديدة بالْمحلّ، ووَقْتا كان نازِل تيليڤيزيوْن كْتير جْديد ووَقْتا كان... نْسمّيه Smart TV. كِنِت أنا كْتير مْحمّس إنّو بيع أوّل Smart TV بالْمحلّ. فا خبّرْتو عنّو للمُسْيو ومدامْتو وخبّرْتُن إنّو هَيْدا بِيْلْقط إنْترْنِت وكْتير مْتطوّر وتْحمّسوا وفِعْلاً شْتروا التّيڤي بوَقْتا وأنا كِنِت كْتير مبْسوط. بسّ تاني نْهار أنا وقاعِد بالشِّغِل بيفوت ذات المُسْيو يَلّي شْترى التّيڤي مْعصّب وعم بيْطْلُب يحْكي مع الـmanager وعم بيقول إنّو إنْتو غشّيتوني وعم بْنبِّش عْلَيِّ شخْصيّاً لَيْلومْني. وَقْتا مْنِرْكُض لعِنْدو ومْنِسْألو: "مُسْيو شو المِشْكْلة؟ خبّرْنا، برْكي نِحْنا مْنِقْدُر نْساعْدك." قالْنا: "هَيْدا التّيڤي اللي بِعْتوني يا ما في WiFi!" قِلْنالو: "مُسْيو نِحْنا أكيدين إنّو في WiFi." ولمّا طوّل السّيرة كْتير، بعِد فترْة يَعْني بعِد وَقِت مِن ما أخد وعطا كْتشفْنا إنّو الزّلمِة ما عِنْدو إنْترْنِت بالْبيْت.

**Omar:** Now, Charbel, it's time for me to tell you about a really funny story that happened to me during one of the first jobs I ever had. A long time ago, after working at the supermarket, I decided to develop myself, so I thought I'd work at a shop near my house that sells electronics, you know, things for the house like TVs, refrigerators, and washing machines. I was excited because I was interested in those things at the time. So, one day, this really nice and polite customer and his wife come into the store. They asked me to show them what new TVs we had in stock, and at that time, a brand new TV had just come out—we called it a Smart TV. I was really excited about selling the first Smart TV in the store. So, I told the gentleman and his wife all about it, explaining how it could connect to the internet and how advanced it was. They got really excited and actually bought the TV on the spot, and I was thrilled. But the next day, as I was sitting at work, the same gentleman who had bought the TV comes in, upset and asking to speak to the manager, saying, "You cheated me," and he was specifically looking for me to blame. So, we ran over to him and asked, "Sir, what's the problem? Tell us, maybe we can help." He said, "This TV you sold me doesn't have WiFi!" We told him, "Sir, we're sure it has WiFi." After a lot of back-and-forth discussion, we eventually discovered that the man didn't have internet at home!

**شُرْبِل:** يَعْني عَنْجِدّ هاي القْصَص ما بْتِنْتْسا وبِتْضِحِّك. لِيْك عُمر عَنْجِدّ اللي ما جرّب يِشْتِغِل مِن قبِل أَوْ هيْك كْتير قُصَص بيروّحا مِن الشّخْصِية تبعو. ميرْسي كْتير على هالْحديث الحِلو والـsharing تبع الـexperience تبعك. وأكيد يا ريْت كِلّ واحد مِنّا بْيِقْدر يْكون عِنْدو هيْك ذِكْرَيات حِلْوة يْشارِكا بْأوّل أشْغال مِنّو. لَوَقْتا خلّوا بالْكُن مِن حالْكُن وسْتِمتْعوا بْحَياتْكُن.

**Charbel:** These stories are unforgettable and funny. Omar, those who haven't worked before miss out on these personality-building experiences. Thank you for this great conversation and for sharing your experiences. I hope everyone has such wonderful memories to share from their first jobs. Until then, take care and enjoy your lives.

## Comprehension Questions

١. شو كان مَوْضوع الحلْقة يَلّي حِكْيوا عنّا شرْبِل وعُمر؟

٢. شو كانِت أوّل وَظيفة لعُمر؟

٣. شو كانِت أوّل وَظيفة لشرْبِل وشو صار معو بِالْمَوْقف المُحْرِج؟

٤. كيف تْصرّف والِد شرْبِل بخْصوص تأخُّر شرْبِل بِالشِّغِل؟

٥. شو بِتْعلِّم أوّل وَظيفة للشّباب بِلِبْنان حسب عُمر؟

٦. وَيْن عادةً الشّباب بِلِبْنان بْيِشْتِغْلوا بأوّل وَظيفة؟

٧. شو الشِّغِل يَلّي جرّبو عُمر بعْد السّوبِرْماركِت وشو صار معو؟

٨. شو كانِت المِشْكْلِة مع الزّبون والـSmart TV؟

1. What was the topic of the episode that Charbel and Omar talked about?
2. What was Omar's first job?
3. What was Charbel's first job and what happened to him in the embarrassing situation?
4. How did Charbel's father react to Charbel working late?
5. What does a first job teach young people in Lebanon according to Omar?
6. Where do young people in Lebanon typically work in their first job?
7. What job did Omar try after the supermarket and what happened to him?
8. What was the issue with the customer and the "Smart TV"?

## Discussion Questions

١. شو كانِت أوّل وَظيفة إلك؟ خبّرْنا عنّا.

٢. عِنْدك شي قُصص بِتْضحِّك مِن أوّل وَظيفة شْتغلْتا؟

٣. شو هيّ المهارات اللي كْتسبْتا مِن أوّل وَظيفة؟

٤. برأْيَك، ليْش مْهِمّ للشّباب يِشْتغْلوا بوَقِت مُبْكر؟

٥. كيف بْيِخْتِلِف التّعامُل مع الزّباين بيْن وظيفْتك الأولى ووَظيفْتك الحالية؟

٦. شو النّصيحة اللي بْتعْطيا لشخِص عم يْبلِّش بأوّل وَظيفة إلو؟

٧. بِتْفضِّل الشِّغِل بأماكِن مِتل المطاعِم أَوْ المحلّات التِّجارية؟ ليْش؟

٨. كيف بْتِتْعامل مع المواقِف المُحْرِجْة أَوْ الصّعْبة بالشِّغِل؟ شاركْنا بتِجْرِبة.

1. What was your first job? Tell us about it.
2. Do you have any funny stories from your first job?
3. What skills did you gain from your first job?
4. In your opinion, why is it important for young people to work early?
5. How does dealing with customers differ between your first job and your current job?
6. What advice would you give to someone starting their first job?
7. Do you prefer working in places like restaurants or retail stores? Why?
8. How do you handle embarrassing or difficult situations at work? Share an experience.

# جِبْران خليل جِبْران وكْتابو النّبي

## Gibran Khalil Gibran and

## His Book "The Prophet"

### In this episode...

Charbel and Farah discuss the legendary Lebanese author and philosopher Gibran Khalil Gibran and his famous book, The Prophet. They explore Gibran's life, from his roots in Lebanon to his literary success in America, and the profound impact his work has had on readers worldwide. They reflect on the timeless themes of The Prophet, including love, work, and freedom, and share their favorite passages from the book. Whether you're already familiar with Gibran or discovering him for the first time, this episode offers an inspiring look into his wisdom and legacy.

## Vocabulary

| | |
|---|---|
| literature | أدب |
| legacy, heritage | إرْث |
| Pen League (a group of writers, including Gibran) | الرّابْطة القلمية |
| The Prophet (title of Gibran's book) | النّبي |
| freedom | حُرّية |
| dialogue, conversation | حِوار |
| drawing, painting | رسِم (رُسوم) |
| personality, figure | شخْصية |
| poetry | شِعِر |
| giving, contribution | عطاء |
| to think | فكّر (يْفكِّر) |
| philosophy | فلْسفة |
| philosopher | فَيْلسوف (فلاسْفة) |
| book | كْتاب (كُتُب) |
| painting, artwork | لَوْحة |
| collection, group | مجْموعة |
| correspondence, letters | مُراسلات |
| feelings, emotions | مشاعِر |
| talented | مَوْهوب |
| text, passage | نصّ (نُصوص) |

*Transcript*

**شرْبِل:** هاي كيفكُن اليوْم؟ رح نِحْكي اليوْم عن شخْصية عظيمة كْتير بالأدب اللّبْناني وبالْعالمي، جبْران خليل جِبْران وكْتابو الشّهير النّبّي. أنا شرْبِل ومعي رُفيقْتي فرح، كيفِك فرح اليوْم؟

**Charbel:** How are you all today? Today, we're going to talk about a very great figure in Lebanese and world literature, Gibran Khalil Gibran, and his famous book "The Prophet." I'm Charbel, and with me is my friend Farah. How are you today, Farah?

**فرح:** هاي شرْبِل، الحمْدِلله أنا مْنيحة، إنْتَ كيف؟

**Farah:** Hi Charbel, thank God, I'm good. How are you?

**شرْبِل:** أنا الحمْدِلله مْنيح! جبْران خليل جِبْران، واو! شو هالْإسِم؟ واحد مِن أعْظم الأدبا والفلاسْفة اللي طلّعُن لِبْنان، كْتابو النّبّي بْيُعْتبر مِن أهمّ الكُتُب الأدبية والفلْسفية بالْعصْر الحديث. شو بْتعرْفي عن جبْران يا فرح؟

**Charbel:** Thank God, I'm good! Gibran Khalil Gibran, wow! What a name! One of the greatest writers and philosophers Lebanon has produced. His book The Prophet is considered one of the most important literary and philosophical works of the modern era. What do you know about Gibran, Farah?

**فرح:** مِتل ما قلِت، واو! جبْران خليل جِبْران خِلِق بِبْشرّي لِبْنان سِنةْ ١٨٨٣، هاجر مع عَيْلْتو عَ أميرْكا هُوّ وصْغير، وكمّل درْسو هوْنيك، كتب بالإنْكْليزي وبالْعربي، وأشْهر كُتْبو هُوّ النّبّي اللي نشرو سِنةْ ١٩٢٣.

**Farah:** As you said, wow! Gibran Khalil Gibran was born in Bsharri, Lebanon, in 1883. He emigrated with his family to America when he was young and continued his studies there. He wrote in both English and Arabic, and his most famous book is The Prophet, which he published in 1923.

**شرْبِل:** مظْبوط، النّبّي عِبارة عن مجْموعة مِن النّصوص الشِّعْرية الفلْسفية اللي بْتِحْكي عن مَواضيع الحَياة المخْتلِفة مِتل الحُبّ، الزّواج، الشِّغِل، الحُرّية. الكِتاب عِبارة عن حِوار بيْن النّبّي اللي إسْمو المُصْطفى وأهْل مدينةْ أورْفِلِس قبِل ما يْغادِر المدينة بعِد ١٢ سِنةٍ مِن العَيْش فيا.

*Lebanese Arabic Dardashi · 157*

**Charbel:** That's right. "The Prophet" is a collection of philosophical poetic essays that talk about different aspects of life, such as love, marriage, work, and freedom. The book is a dialogue between the prophet, whose name is Al Mustafa, and the people of the city of Orphalese before he leaves the city after living there for 12 years.

**فرح:** الكِتاب بْيِتْميّز بِلِغّتو الحِلْوة والعميقة وأفْكارو الفلْسفية اللي عنْجد بْتِلْمُس قُلوب العالم. جبْران كان عِنْدو قِدْرة فريدِة على التّعْبير عن المشاعِر والأفْكار بِطريقة بسيطة وعميقة بِنفْس الوَقِت.

**Farah:** The book is distinguished by its beautiful, deep language and its philosophical ideas that truly touch people's hearts. Gibran had a unique ability to express emotions and ideas in a way that's both simple and profound at the same time.

**شربِل:** عنْجدّ، الكِتاب تُرْجِم لأكْتر مِن خمْسين لِغّة عم تِتْخايَلي؟ وبعْدو لهلّأ بْيِقْرا النّاس بِكِلّ أنْحاء العالم. بْتعِرْفي يا فرح في كْتير مِن النّصوص بهيْدا الكِتاب هيْك بْتِلمِسْني شخْصيّاً مِتِل النّصّ اللي بْيِحْكي عن الحُبّ بيقول: "إذا أحْببْتُ فلا تْقُل الله في قلْبي ولكِن قُل أنا في قلْب الله." عنْجدّ يَعْني عم تِتْخايَلي؟

**Charbel:** Indeed, the book has been translated into more than fifty languages—can you imagine? And it's still being read by people all over the world. You know, Farah, there are many passages in this book that really touch me personally, like the one about love where he says, "When you love, you should not say, 'God is in my heart,' but rather, 'I am in the heart of God.'" Can you imagine?

**فرح:** مِيّة بالْميّة، كلامو بيخلّينا نْفكّر بعُمْق. كمان النّصّ اللي بْيِحْكي عن العمل بيقول: "العمل هُوَ الحُبّ الذي يُترجم إلى أفْعال." هالْكلام بيخلّينا نْشوف العمل بِطريقة مِخْتِلْفة كجُزْء مِن الحُبّ والعطاء.

**Farah:** Absolutely, his words make us think deeply. Another passage about work says, "Work is love made visible." These words make us see work in a different way, as part of love and giving.

**شربِل:** ومِن الإشْيا اللي بِتْميّز النّبي إنّو بيمِسّ مَواضيع حَياتية بسيطة بسّ بِنظْرة هيْك فلْسفية عميقة يَعْني بيخلّي اللي عم بْيِقْرا يْعيد النّظر بِكيف إنّو كيف بدّو يِتْعامل مع الحَياةْ والنّاس اللي حْواليْه.

**Charbel:** One of the things that distinguishes The Prophet is that it touches on simple aspects of life but with a deep philosophical perspective. It makes the reader reconsider how they want to approach life and the people around them.

**فرح:** جِبْران كان فِنّان مَوْهوب، رسم كْتير لَوْحات حِلْوة، اللي رافِقِت كُتْبو، فَنّو كان بيمثّل رؤْيْتو الفلْسفية والأدبية، كان قادِر يْعبّر عن مشاعْرو وأفْكارو بالرُّسوم بْنفس الجمال اللي عبّر في بالْكلمات.

**Farah:** Gibran was a talented artist too; he painted many beautiful paintings that accompanied his books. His art represented his philosophical and literary vision. He was able to express his feelings and thoughts through drawings with the same beauty he did with words.

**شرْبِل:** فِعْلا! يَعْني جِبْران كان عِنْدو هيْك تأْثير كْبير على الأدب العربي والأميرْكيحتّى. كان جزء مِن الرّابِطة القلمية وهِيِّ جماعة مِن الكِتّاب والشُّعرا العرب اللي كانوا بْيِكْتِبوا بأميرْكا وبيحاوْلوا يِدمْجوا بيْن الثّقافتيْن العربية والغرْبية.

**Charbel:** Exactly! Gibran had a significant influence on Arabic and even American literature. He was part of the Pen League, a group of Arab writers and poets who wrote in America and tried to blend Arabic and Western cultures.

**فرح:** ميّة بالْميّة! وما نِنْسى كان عِنْدو علاقة كْتير مُميّزة مع ماي زْيادة الكاتْبة والأدبية المصْرية، لبْنانية، المُراسلات بيْناتُن كانِت مليانة بالْفِكِر والفلْسفة والحُبّ الرّوحي هالْعلاقة أثّرِت على أعْمالُن الأدبية بشكْل كْبير.

**Farah:** Absolutely! And we shouldn't forget that he had a very special relationship with May Ziadeh, the Egyptian-Lebanese writer and intellectual. Their correspondence was full of thought, philosophy, and spiritual love. This relationship greatly influenced their literary works.

**شرْبِل:** عنْجدّ! جِبْران خليل جِبْران ترك قِرْث كْبير بالْأدب والفن والفلْسفة وكْتابو النّبي بيضلّ واحد مِن أهمّ الكُتْب اللي مُمْكِن نِقْراها ونِسْتفيد مِنّا بْحَياتْنا اليَوْمية.

**Charbel:** Indeed! Gibran Khalil Gibran left a great legacy in literature, art, and philosophy, and his book The Prophet remains one of the most important books we can read and benefit from in our daily lives.

**فرح:** إذا ما قْريتوا النّبي، لهلّأ بْنِصحْكُن تِقْروا! كْتاب رح يِلْمُس قْلوبْكُن ويْغيِّر نظْرِتْكُن للْحَياة.

**Farah:** If you haven't read The Prophet yet, I recommend you do! It's a book that will touch your hearts and change your outlook on life.

**شرْبِل:** thank you إلِك فرح، وميرْسي لكِلّ اللي عم بْيِسْمعْنا! رح نِلْتِقي المرّة الجايِة بمَوْضوع جْديد وحْكايات جْديدة مِن حَياتْنا بِلِبْنان لَوَقْتا، نْتِبْهوا عَ حالْكُن وسْتمتْعوا بِحَياتْكُن!

**Charbel:** Thank you, Farah, and thank you to everyone who is listening! We'll meet again next time with a new topic and new stories from our lives in Lebanon. Until then, take care of yourselves and enjoy life!

**فرح:** ميرْسي شرْبِل ميرْسي!

**Farah:** Thank you, Charbel, thank you!

## Comprehension Questions

١. مين هُوّ جِبْران خليل جِبْران، وشو أهميةْ كْتابو النّبي؟

٢. كيف وَصفِت فرح أُسْلوب جِبْران بالْكِتابِة بِكْتاب النّبي؟

٣. شو هُوّ مَوْضوع كْتاب النّبي وشو المَواضيع اللي بْيِحْكي عنّا؟

٤. كيف أثّرِت نُصوص كْتاب النّبي على شرْبِل وفرح شخْصيّاً؟ عْطي أمْثِلِة.

٥. شو هِيِّ العلاقة بيْن جِبْران خليل جِبْران والكاتْبِة ماي زْيادة؟

٦. كيف أثّرِت أعْمال جِبْران خليل جِبْران على الأدب العربي والأميركي؟

٧. شو الدّوْر اللي لِعْبو جِبْران خليل جِبْران بالرّابْطة القلمية؟

٨. ليْش بِتْشوف فرح إنّو قْرايةْ كْتاب النّبي مْهِمّ ومُمْكِن يْغيّر نظِرْتك للْحَياةْ؟

1. Who is Gibran Khalil Gibran, and what is the significance of his book "The Prophet"?
2. How did Farah describe Gibran's writing style in "The Prophet"?
3. What is the theme of the book "The Prophet," and what topics does it address?
4. How did the texts from "The Prophet" impact Charbel and Farah personally? Give examples.
5. What is the relationship between Gibran Khalil Gibran and the writer May Ziadeh?
6. How did Gibran Khalil Gibran's works influence both Arabic and American literature?
7. What role did Gibran Khalil Gibran play in the Pen League?
8. Why does Farah think reading "The Prophet" is important and can change your perspective on life?

## Discussion Questions

١. شو هُوّ رأيَك بِأُسْلوب جبْران خليل جبْران بالْكِتابة؟ بِتْحِسّ إنو بيأثِّر عْلَيْك؟

٢. في شي كْتاب قْريتو غَيّر نظِرْتك للْحَياةْ؟ خبِّرْنا عنّو.

٣. كيف بِتْشوف دوْر الأدب بالْفِكِر والفلْسفة بِحَياتْنا اليَوْمية؟

٤. شو هِيّ المَواضيع اللي بِتْحِبّ تِقْرا عنّا بالْأدب؟ ولَيْش؟

٥. إذا بدّك تِنْصح حدا بِكْتاب مْعيّن، شو بِتْختار ولَيْش؟

٦. كيف بِتْشوف دوْر الفَنّ والأدب بِتعْزيز ثقافِتْنا وهَويِّتْنا؟

٧. شو هُوّ أكْتر نصّ شِعْري أوْ فلْسفي لمسك وخلّاك تِفكِّر بِعِمِق؟

٨. إذا كان عِنْدك الفُرْصة تِكْتِب كْتاب، عن شو بِتْحِبّ تِكْتِب؟

1. What do you think of Gibran Khalil Gibran's writing style? Do you feel it has an impact on you?
2. Is there a book you've read that changed your perspective on life? Tell us about it.
3. How do you see the role of literature in shaping thoughts and philosophy in our daily lives?
4. What are the topics you enjoy reading about in literature, and why?
5. If you were to recommend a book to someone, which one would you choose and why?
6. How do you view the role of art and literature in enhancing our culture and identity?
7. What is the most touching or thought-provoking poem or philosophical text you've come across?
8. If you had the opportunity to write a book, what would you like to write about?

# الأكْل اللّبْناني

## *Lebanese Cuisine*

### In this episode...

Charbel and Omar talk about the delicious world of Lebanese food. From mezze to shawarma, they discuss the wide variety of dishes that make Lebanese cuisine so special. They share funny personal stories, including how guests new to the cuisine often underestimate the sheer amount of food served at Lebanese meals. The episode highlights not only the flavors of traditional dishes like hummus, tabbouleh, and grilled meats but also how Lebanon's hospitality industry is rooted in its culture. Whether you're familiar with Lebanese food or new to it, this conversation will definitely leave you craving a bite!

## Vocabulary

| | |
|---|---|
| tabbouleh (a fresh, herby salad made from finely chopped parsley, tomatoes, onions, mint, and bulgur, dressed with olive oil and lemon juice) | تبّولِة |
| preparation (of food) | تُحْضير |
| breakfast | تِرْويقة |
| hungry | جوعان |
| hummus (a creamy dip made from blended chickpeas, tahini, olive oil, lemon juice, and garlic) | حُمُّص |
| to taste | داق (يْدوق) |
| to savor | سْتطْعِم (يِسْتطْعِم) |
| sandwich | سنْدْويش |
| shawarma (a dish consisting of marinated meat, usually beef, lamb, or chicken, that is slow-cooked on a vertical rotisserie and typically served in a wrap or pita bread) | شاوَرْما |
| to make one's mouth water | شهّى (يْشهّي) |
| dessert table | طاوْلِةْ الحِلو |
| fattoush (a salad made with mixed greens, vegetables, and crispy pieces of fried or toasted pita bread, often seasoned with sumac) | فتّوش |
| unique | فريد |
| relatives | قرايب |
| kibbeh (a traditional dish made from bulgur wheat, minced onions, and ground meat, typically lamb or beef, shaped into fried croquettes filled with spiced meat and pine nuts) | كِبّة |
| mezze (a variety of small dishes served as appetizers) | مزات |
| grilled meats | مشاوي |
| cuisine; kitchen | مطْبخ (مطابِخ) |
| appetizers | مقبِّلات |
| stuffed grape leaves (grape leaves filled with a mixture of rice, spices, and sometimes meat) | وَرق عِنب |

## Transcript

**شربِل:** هاي كيفكُن؟ اليوْم مَوْضوعْنا بيشهّي: مَوْضوع عن الأكْل اللّبْناني. معكُن شربِل ومعي رْفيقي عُمر. كيفك عُمر؟

**Charbel:** Hi, how are you all? Today our topic is mouthwatering. A topic about Lebanese food. I'm Charbel, and with me is my friend Omar. How are you, Omar?

**عُمر:** أهْلا شرْبِل، أنا كْتير مْنيح وهلّأ صِرْت أحْسن بعد ما خبّرْتِني وخبّرْت المُسْتمعين عن المَوْضوع اللي بدّنا نِحْكي عنّو. الأكِل هَيْدا شي بْيِجمعْنا أنا ويّاك مِن إيّام الطّفولةِ يِمْكِن، صحّ؟

**Omar:** Hello Charbel, I'm doing great, and now I feel even better after you told me and our listeners about the topic we're going to discuss. Food is something that has brought us together since our childhood, isn't that right?

**شربِل:** مِيّة بالْمِيّة يا عُمر. ذكْرَيات مليئة بِتعْبايةٍ بطن إذا بدّك مِتِل ما مِنْقول عَ اللّبْناني. ليْك عُمر مِش الكِلّ بلاحِظا بسّ الأكِل أوْ إذا بدّك الشّغْلة الوَحيدة اللي بْيَعْمْلا الإنْسان وهِيِّ تْلات مرّات بالنّهار وكلّ مرّة بْيِسْتلزّ فيا كأنّو أوّل مرّة بْيَعْمِلا هِيِّ الأكِل وإنّو تِسْتطْعِم الأكِل.

**Charbel:** Absolutely, Omar. We have so many memories filled with belly-stuffing, as we Lebanese like to say. Look, Omar, not everyone notices this, but food—or if you will, the one thing that people do three times a day, and each time they enjoy it as if it were the first time—is eating and savoring food.

**عُمر:** مِيّة بالْمِيّة! عالم الأكِل عالم واسِع وكيف إذا عم نِحْكي عن المطْبخ اللّبْناني. المطْبخ اللّبْناني مطْبخ غني كْتير. مْنِسْتعْمِل مَوادّ كْتير واسْعة والحِلو بالْمطْعم اللّبْناني كمان شرْبِل إنّو عَ طول بتِجدّد دايم. بلِبْنان بْتِقْدر تْشوف المطاعِم الصّغيرةِ مِنْسمّيا سْناكات أوْ السّتْريت فود. مْنِقْدر نْشوف المطاعِم القديمة يَلّي صارْلا سْنين مَوْجودةِ بالْبلد وعم تِتْوارث مِن جيل لجيل. وعم نِقْدر نْشوف المطاعِم الجْديدة اللي عم يِخْلْقوا concept جْديد بالْمطْبخ اللّبْناني أوْ مِتِل ما مِنْسمّيه twist، بيدخْلوا twist على Lebanese menu وهَيْدا شي عنْجدّ مُدْهِش.

**Omar:** Exactly! The world of food is vast, especially when we're talking about Lebanese cuisine. The Lebanese kitchen is very rich. We use a wide variety of ingredients, and the great thing about Lebanese cuisine, Charbel, is that it's always evolving. In Lebanon, you can find small eateries, which we call "snacks" or street food. We can also see the old restaurants that have been around for years, passed down from generation to generation. And we're also seeing new restaurants that are creating new concepts in Lebanese cuisine, or as we call it, a twist—adding a twist to the Lebanese menu, and that's truly amazing.

**شَرْبِل:** لَيْك اللي عم تِحْكي مَظْبوط وخاصّةً إنّو بِتْلاقي بِهالْوَضع البلد يَعْني المُقلْقِز وهيْك، بِتْلاقي مِش مَعْقول كيف عم تِفْتح هالمحلّات كلّا. قُبول للأكل، قُبول للمطاعم. إنّتَ عُمر ما بْتعْرف اللي يمْكِن المُسْتمعين مِش كلّ بْيَعِرْفوا إنّو بلدْنا هالْقد صغير وهالْقدّ غني بالأكل. وعنْجدّ اللي بيْجي مِن برّا وبيدوق أكل اللِّبْناني بيْنْغُرِم بالأكل اللِّبْناني. عم نِحْكي إذا بدّك شاوِرْما، عم نِحْكي عن الحُمُّص، عم نِحْكي عن التَّبولة، عم نِحْكي عن اللِّبْنة البلدية. يَعْني في أطْيَب مِنّا تِرْويقة لِبْنة بلدية، زيْت زيْتون، راس بنْدورة، خْيار؟ عنْجدّ وَلا أطْيَب.

Charbel: Look, what you're saying is absolutely right, especially considering the current situation in the country with all the uncertainty. You wouldn't believe how these restaurants are still opening up everywhere. There's a demand for food, a demand for restaurants. Omar, you might not know this, and maybe not all the listeners are aware, but our country is so small and yet so rich in food. Honestly, people who come from abroad and taste Lebanese food fall in love with Lebanese food. We're talking arbout shawarma, hummus, tabbouleh, homemade labneh—can you think of a tastier breakfast than homemade labneh, olive oil, a tomato, and cucumber? Honestly, nothing tastes better.

**عُمر:** يَعْني يا شرْبِل إذا واحد بدّو يُبلِّش يْعِد الأطْباق اللِّبْنانية يمْكِن بدّنا أكْتر مِن حلْقة أو تْنيْن أو تْلاتة. لأعْطي شْويّ هيْك المُسْتمعين فِكْرة عن التّجارُب بِتجْرِبِة المطْعم اللِّبْناني تجْرِبِة فريدة مِن نَوْعاً وما بْتِشْبه غيْر تجارب لأنّو مِتل ما مَعْروف بالْعالم بسّ تْفوت على مطْعم تُطْلُب الـentree أو المُقبّلات بعْديْن تُطْلُب الطّبق الرّئيسي وإذا بْتْحِبّ تخْتُم بالـdessert. نحْنا بِلبْنان عنّا تجْرِبِة كْتير مخْتِلْفة لأنّو بسّ توصل على المطْعم اللِّبْناني بدّك تْبلِّش بالمزّات الباردة يَلّي هيّ الحُمُّص، التّبولة، الفتّوش، اللّحْمة النيّة، الكِبّة، كِلّ المُقبّلات المُسقّعة مِتل ما مِنْقِلّا. وهيْدي في كْتير إيّام عالم بْتِتفاجأوا بيفكّروا إنّو هيْدا هُوّ ها هيّ التّجرِبة، بسّ بعْديْن بتْنِزل المُقبّلات السّاخْنة

مِتِل المقانق القصبِة الدّجاج والرُّقِقات والمعجّنات. بعْدِيْن بيْنزِلوا الطّبق الرّئيسي يَلِّي هوِّ عِبارة عَن المشاوي، طووق، الكفْتة، اللّحْمة وأكيد غَيْرا كْتير. وما بْتخْلص المايْدِة اللّبْنانية إلّا بطاوْلِةْ الحِلو مِتِل القِشْطة بْعسل مِتِل الحلاوِة والدِّبس الخرّوب وأكيد الفْواكِه البلدية.

**Omar:** I mean, Charbel, if someone were to start listing Lebanese dishes, we might need more than one, two, or even three episodes. To give our listeners an idea, the experience of a Lebanese restaurant is unique and unlike other experiences. As it's known worldwide when you go to a restaurant, you order the entrée or appetizers, then the main course, and if you'd like, you finish with dessert. In Lebanon, we have a very different experience because when you arrive at a Lebanese restaurant, you start with the cold mezze, which includes hummus, tabbouleh, fattoush, raw meat, kibbeh, and all the cold appetizers we call "mse2a'a." Many times, people are surprised, thinking that's the whole experience, but then the hot appetizers arrive, like sausages, chicken wings, rolls, and pastries. Then, the main course comes, which consists of grilled meats—shish tawook, kafta, lamb, and much more. And the Lebanese table isn't complete without a dessert spread, like ashta with honey, halawa, carob molasses, and of course, local fruits.

**شرْبِل:** يَعْني عُمر خبّرْتْنا brief حِلو عن الأكل! خلّيني خبّرك خبْرية بتْضحّك شْوَيّ مِن وَرا هَيْدا المَوْضوع اللي قلْتِلّي عنّو. إنّو في مرّة كان عنّا قْرايِبْنا مْجوّز حدا مِن برّا وقرّر يِجي لعنّا عَ لِبْنان هوِّ وكذا حدا مِن قرايْبو، وساقِبت بْتقرِّر الوالِدة تعِمْلو عزيمة عنّا على الغدا. أوّل ما إجوا لعنّا أكيد عَ تحْضير مِن عشية للصّبح الوالِدة مع إخْواتا عمر يْحضّروا أكِل، فا بيبلّشوا يْنزِّلوا الأكِل البارِد كان عنّا، وَرق عِنب وحُمّص وكِلّ هالْمُقبِّلات اللي حْكيت عنّا. فا بسّ خلّص حدا مِن الأشْخاص الأكِل قام ليْغسِّل إيدَيْه وقعد غَيْر محلّ فا تْفاجأْنا كلّنا إنّو ليْش قام عن الطّاوْلة فكّرْنا إنّو قلِّل إحْتِرام أوْ شي، عْرِفْنا بعْدِيْن إنّو هوِّ فكّر إنّو هَيْدا هوِّ الأكِل، وناسي إنّو في بعد كْمالِة الأكِل اللي هِيّ كِلّ القِصص السُّخْنة اللي عِمْلِتا الطّبق الرّئيسي اللي كان هوِّ رِزّ عَ دْجاج غَيْر الكِبّة بالصّيْنية وأكيد كان في الحِلو، فا كانوا مِتْفاجْئين وفلّوا مِن عنّا مفْزورين مِن الأكِل بسّ أكيد كانوا مبْسوطين.

**Charbel:** Omar, you've given us a nice brief about the food! Let me tell you a funny story related to this topic. You mentioned that once, we had some relatives who married someone from abroad, and they decided to come to Lebanon with some of their relatives. My mother decided to host a lunch for them. The preparations started the night before and continued until morning. My mother and her sisters were preparing food, and they started serving the cold dishes like grape leaves, hummus, and all the appetizers we talked about. After one of the guests finished eating, he got up to wash his hands and sat somewhere else, which surprised us all. We thought it was a sign of disrespect or something. We later found out that he thought that was all the food and didn't realize there was more to come, including the hot main course, which was rice with chicken besides kibbeh in the tray, and of course, there was dessert. They were so surprised and left completely stuffed, but they were happy.

**عُمَر:** أيْه والله يا شرْبِل تجْرِبة فريدة، بسّ المطاعِم بلِبْنان هيْك بسّ بسّ تنْخبِّر المُسْتمعين إنّو ما بْتِقْتْصِر بسّ على المطْعم اللّبْناني. نحْنا اللّبْنانية كمان سْتوْردْنا إذا بدّك المطاعِم مِن كلّ أنْحاء العالم المطاعِم الإيطالية اليابانية الصّينية الكورية وشو ما بدّك بْتِقْدر تْلاقي بلِبْنان. والحلو بالْموْضوع إنّو طبّقوا أعْلى معايير هيْدوْل المطابِخ اللي حْكينا عنّا. يَعْني اليوْم إذا بِتْفوت لتاكُل بمطْعم ياباني بِتْحسّ حالك عنْجدّ إنْتَ بِطوْكْيو وعم بِتْعيش التّجْرِبة مِتِل ما بيعيشوَا اليابانية.

Omar: Indeed, Charbel, that was a unique experience! But to let our listeners know, restaurants in Lebanon are not limited to just Lebanese cuisine. We Lebanese have also imported restaurants from all over the world—Italian, Japanese, Chinese, Korean—you name it, you can find it in Lebanon. The great thing is that they've adopted the highest standards of these cuisines. Today, if you go to eat in a Japanese restaurant, you feel like you're really in Tokyo, living the experience just as the Japanese do.

**شرْبِل:** مِيّة بالْمِيّة واللي عم تِحْكي مظْبوط! وبسّ نِحْكي عن الأكِل اللّبْناني والمطاعِم عم نِحْكي مِن الأهمّ الأشْخاص اللي بيقدّموا hospitality. نحْنا معْروفين بِحسْن الضّيافة وهيْدا الشّي دُرّس ودرسْناه وعلّمْناه إذا بدّك. لمّا بِتْشوف هلّأ بالدُّوَل الخليج كِلّا بِتْلاقي تْلات رُباع العالم اللي مِسْتِلْمي أهمّ المطاعِم هِيّ لِبْنانية. تْلات رُباع العالم اللي مِسْتِلْمي الأوْتيْلات هِنّي لِبْنانية، وهيْدا الشّي مِن ثقافِتْنا ومِن تُراثْنا ومِنْفِتْخِر بهيْدا الشّي.

Charbel: Absolutely, you're right! And when we talk about Lebanese food and restaurants, we're talking about some of the most important people in the hospitality industry. We are known for our hospitality, and this is something we've learned and perfected. When you look now in the Gulf countries, you'll find that three-quarters of the people managing the top restaurants are Lebanese. Three-quarters of those managing the hotels are Lebanese, and this is something from our culture and heritage that we are proud of.

**عُمر:** بْحِبّ إِشْكُر المُسْتَمِعين لِأَنّو رافقونا اليوْم بِهَيْدي الحلْقة وشربِل يَعْني هَيْدا المَوْضوع جوّعْني، فا أنا طالِع هلّأ ضُغْري يَعْني بِدّي أُطْلُب دِليفِري سَنْدْويش شاوَرْما مع توم. إنْتَ بِتْحِبّ تاكُل شي؟

**Omar:** I'd like to thank the listeners for joining us in this episode. Charbel, this topic made me hungry, so I'm going to order a shawarma sandwich with garlic sauce. Do you want anything?

**شرْبِل:** عنْجَدّ عُمر شهَّيْتْنا! ميرْسي لإلك وميرْسي للمُسْتَمِعين وانْشالله نِلْتِقي مرّة تانْية بمَوْضوع جْديد وخبْرْية جْديدِة مِن لِبْنان. لَوَقْتا نْتْبِهوا على حالْكُن وما تْضَلّكُن جوعانين.

**Charbel:** Honestly, Omar, you've made us all hungry! Thank you, and thank you to our listeners. Hopefully, we'll meet again with a new topic and story from Lebanon. Until then, take care of yourselves and don't stay hungry!

## Comprehension Questions

١. لَيْش بِيشوفوا شِرْبِل وعُمر إنّو الأكِل مْهِمّ بِلِبْنان؟

٢. كيف بْيوصُف عُمر التّنوُّع بالْمطاعِم بِلِبْنان، سِواء كانِت تِقْليدية أوْ جْديدِة؟

٣. شو هِيِّ التّجْرِبِة اللي خبّرا شِرْبِل عن قْرايِبُن اللي زاروا لِبْنان لأوّل مرّة؟

٤. كيف بْيوصُف عُمر تأْثير المطاعِم اللِّبْنانية على الأجانِب اللي بيزوروا البلد؟

٥. شو هِيِّ الأطْباق اللِّبْنانية اللي ذكرُوَا شِرْبِل وعُمر بالْحلْقة؟

٦. كيف بيناقْشوا شِرْبِل وعُمر أهميةْ "الضِّيافة" بالثّقافة اللِّبْنانية؟

٧. شو بْيوصُف عُمر عن التّنوُّع بالْمطابخ العالمية المَوْجودِة بِلِبْنان؟

٨. لَيْش عُمر قرّر يِطْلُب سنْدْويش شاوَرْما بعِد النِّقاش؟

1. Why do Charbel and Omar think food is important in Lebanon?
2. How does Omar describe the diversity of restaurants in Lebanon, whether traditional or new?
3. What is the story Charbel shared about their relatives who visited Lebanon for the first time?
4. How does Omar describe the impact of Lebanese restaurants on foreigners visiting the country?
5. What are the Lebanese dishes mentioned by Charbel and Omar during the episode?
6. How do Charbel and Omar discuss the importance of "hospitality" in Lebanese culture?
7. What does Omar describe about the variety of international cuisines available in Lebanon?
8. Why did Omar decide to order a shawarma sandwich after the discussion?

## Discussion Questions

١. شو هيِّ الأطْباق اللّبْنانية المُفَضّلِة عِنْدك؟ وليْش بِتْحِبّا؟

٢. كيف بِتْشوف تجْرِبِةْ الأكِل بالْمطاعِم اللّبْنانية مُقارنةً مع المطاعِم بِبِلْدان تانْية؟

٣. جرّبِت شي مرّة الأكِل اللّبْناني بِبلدك أوْ بِلد تاني؟ كيف كانِت تجْرِبْتك؟

٤. شو رأْيَك بِتأْثير الضِّيافة اللّبْنانية على سِمْعةْ البلد؟

٥. كيف بِتْشوف التّنوُّع بالْمطاعِم بِبلدِك؟ بِتْجرِّب أكِل مِن ثقافات مِخْتِلْفة؟

٦. شو هُوِّ المطْعم اللّبْناني المُفَضّل عِنْدك؟ شو أكْتر طبق بِتْحِبّو فيه؟

٧. كيف بِتْشوف أهميةْ الحِفاظ على التُّراث الغِذائي اللّبْناني بْوجّ التِّغْيرات الحديثة؟

٨. عِنْدك شي قُصص مُضْحِكِة أَوْ مُفاجْئِة عن تجارْبك مع الأكِل أَوْ المطاعِم؟

1. What are your favorite Lebanese dishes? Why do you like them?
2. How do you compare the dining experience in Lebanese restaurants with restaurants in other countries?
3. Have you ever tried Lebanese food in your country or another country? How was your experience?
4. What do you think about the impact of Lebanese hospitality on the country's reputation?
5. How do you see the diversity of restaurants in your country? Do you try foods from different cultures?
6. What is your favorite Lebanese restaurant? What is your favorite dish there?
7. How important do you think it is to preserve the Lebanese culinary heritage in the face of modern changes?
8. Do you have any funny or surprising stories about your experiences with food or restaurants?

# بِناء المُسْتقْبل والتَّعْليم الجامِعي

## Building a Future and
## University Education

## In this episode...

Charbel and Farah discuss the importance of building a successful future through education and career development. They highlight how discovering one's passion early on can guide students in choosing the right academic and career paths. Parents, schools, and hands-on experience play a key role in shaping these decisions. They also emphasize that university education is not only about academics but personal growth and gaining practical skills through internships or part-time jobs, all of which are crucial for long-term success.

## Vocabulary

| | |
|---|---|
| choice | إخْتِيار |
| career guidance | إرْشاد مِهني |
| continuity | إسْتِمْرارية |
| lifelong learning | التّعلُّم على مدى الحَياةْ |
| critical thinking | التِّفْكير النّقْدي |
| personal growth | النُّمو الشّخْصي |
| program | بِرْنامِج (برامِج) |
| building the future | بِناء المُسْتقْبل |
| major, specialization | تخصُّص |
| training | تِدْريب |
| volunteering | تطوُّع |
| university education | تِعْليم جامِعي |
| practical experience | خِبْرة عملية |
| job market | سوق العمل |
| passion | شغف |
| perseverance | مُثابرة |
| focused | مْركّز |
| career path | مسار مِهني |
| success | نجاح |
| goal | هدف (أهْداف) |

## Transcript

**شَرْبِل:** مَرْحَبا، كيفْكُن؟ اليوْم رح نِحْكي عن بِناء المُسْتَقْبَل، شْوَيّ عن الشّغِل وأكيد عن التّعْليم الجامِعي. أنا شَرْبِل ومعي اليوْم رْفيقْتي فرح. كيفِك اليوْم يا فرح؟

Charbel: Hi, how are you all? Today, we're going to talk about building a future, a bit about work, and, of course, about university education. I'm Charbel, and with me today is my friend Farah. How are you today, Farah?

**فرح:** أهْلا شَرْبِل! أنا مْنيحة، شُكْراً. مِتْحَمّسة كْتير نِحْكي عن هالْمَوْضوع المْهِمّ.

Farah: Hi Charbel! I'm good, thanks. I'm really excited to talk about this important topic.

**شَرْبِل:** وأنا كمان! خلّينا شْوَيّ نْبلّش كيف إنّو الواحد مْهِمّ يَعْرِف شو بيحِبّ، و بآخِر يَعْني بآخِر سنوات المدْرسة. وبعْتِقِد إنّو إكْتِشاف الشّغف والـ passion عِنْد الواحد بوَقِت مُبْكِر بيِقْدر إذا بدّك يْساعِد إنّو الواحد يْشكّل المُسْتَقْبل تبعو بِشكِل أكْبر.

Charbel: Me too! Let's start by talking about how important it is to know what you love, especially in the last years of school. I believe that discovering one's passion early on helps shape one's future more effectively.

**فرح:** أكيد، كْتير ضروري تْلاقي شي بِتْحِبّو لِأنّو رح تِتْفوّق فيه ورح تِسْتمْتِع بالشّغِل عْليْه. اليوْم مع كِلّ هالصّعوبات، كْتير صعِب للطّلّاب يَعِرْفوا شو بدّن، الأهِل لازِم يْوَجْهوا كِلّ وْلادُن مِن هِنّي وصْغار.

Farah: Absolutely, it's very important to find something you love because you'll excel in it and enjoy working on it. Today, with all these challenges, it's really hard for students to know what they want. Parents need to guide their children from a young age.

**شَرْبِل:** مِيّة بالْمِيّة، الأهْل دَوْرُن كْتير رئيسي إنّو يْساعْدوا الوْلاد يَعِرْفوا إذا بدّك يِكْتِشْفوا إهْتِماماتْن ونِقاط القُوّة تبعُن. وحتّى المدارس كمان ضروري يْكون عِنْدا مسْؤولية كْبيرة إنّو تِدْعم وتْوَعّي هالطّلّاب وتْفرْجيُن إذا بدّك عِدّة مسارات مِهنية مِخْتِلْفة ويْكون عِنْدا هالْإمْكانِيّات.

Charbel: One hundred percent. Parents play a key role in helping their kids discover their interests and strengths. Schools also have a big responsibility to support and raise awareness among students, showing them various career paths and providing the resources.

**فرح:** صحّ، المَدارِس لازِم تْقَدِّم إرْشاد مِهَنِي أكْتَر. الطُّلّاب لازِم يِفْهَموا الخِيارات المُخْتَلِفة المَتاحة إلْن والخُطُوات اللّازِمة لِتَحْقيق أهْدافُن. المَوْضوع مِش بسّ أكاديمي، هُوِّ عن تَطْبيقات الحَياة الواقِعية والمِهَن المِسْتَقْبِلية.

**Farah:** True. schools need to offer more career guidance. Students need to understand the various options available to them and the steps necessary to achieve their goals. It's not just about academics; it's about real-life applications and future careers.

**شَرْبِل:** مْهِمّ تاخُد الأُمور خُطْوة بخُطْوة لتوصل لأهْدافك. اليوْم الكِلّ بدّو كِلّ شي بْسِرْعة بِدون ما يْجَرُّبوا يِشْتِغْلوا عنْجَدّ، بسّ النّجاح الحقيقي بْيِتْطَلّب صبِر ومُثابَرة وواحِد بِشْتِغِل أكْتَر ويِتْعَب.

**Charbel:** It's important to take things step by step to reach your goals. Today, everyone wants everything quickly without putting in the effort, but true success requires patience, perseverance, and hard work.

**فرح:** هَيْدا صحيح. تَحْقيق أحْلامك بْياخُد وَقِت وجُهِدّ، هُوِّ رِحْلِة فيا كْتير خُطْوات. ولازِم تْكون مِلْتزِم تِتْشَتِغِل بجِدّ وتْضَلّ مْرَكِّز. وَقِت تْلاقي المجال اللي بِتْحِبّي هالرِّحْلِة كْتير تْكون مُمْتِعة.

**Farah:** That's right. Achieving your dreams takes time and effort—it's a journey with many steps. You have to be committed to working hard and staying focused. When you find the field you love, the journey becomes much more enjoyable.

**شَرْبِل:** مَظْبوط، ولمّا تْلاقي هالـpassion هالشّغف، التَّعْليم الجامِعي بيصير خُطْوة أساسية لتِبْني مُسْتقْبَلك، بْيَعْطيك المَعْرِفة، المهارات اللّازِمة حتّى لمسيرْتك المِهَنية، بسّ كمان هُوِّ عن النّمو الشّخْصي وإنّو تِتْعَلّم التّفْكير النّقْدي.

**Charbel:** Exactly, and once you find that passion, university education becomes a crucial step in building your future. It provides you with the knowledge and skills you need for your career, but it's also about personal growth and learning critical thinking.

**فرح:** صحّ، الجامعة فترة مْهِمّة لتِطْوير الشّخْصي والمِهني. هُوّ وَقِت تِسْتكْشِف أفْكار جْديدِة، تْتعرّف على عالم جْديد، وتِبْني معارِف معْقول يْساعْدوك بمسيرْتك. بس الأهمّ هُوّ إخْتِيار الجّامْعة المُناسْبِة والتّخصُّص المُناسِب كْتير أساسي.

**Farah:** Right, university is an important time for both personal and professional development. It's a time to explore new ideas, meet new people, and build connections that could help you in your career. But the most important thing is choosing the right university and major—it's a very critical decision.

**شرْبِل:** أكيد اللي عم تِحْكي صحّ، إنّو تْنقّي وتِنْبُشي عَ الجامْعات وبرامِجا كْتير مْهِمّ، تْشوفي شو بِيقدّموا، سِمْعِتْن، وكيف بْيِتْناسبوا مع الأهْداف أوْ الـ goals تبعِك، هُوّ قرار كْتير كْبير ولازِم تْكوني على كْتير مِن الإطّلاع يَعْني.

**Charbel:** Absolutely, what you're saying is correct. It's really important to research and explore universities and their programs, see what they offer, their reputation, and how they align with your goals. It's a big decision, and you need to be well-informed.

**فرح:** مع إنّو التِّعْليم الجّامِعي مْهِمّ، بس ضروري تاخُد خِبْرة بنفْس الوَقِت، مِتِل إنّو تعْمُل training، part-time jobs، وحتّى فيك تِتْطوّع. كلّ هَيْدا بيخلّيك تِقْوى وتعْمُل خِبْرة بالشّغِل وكيف تِتْصرّف مع العالم، بعْتِقِد إنّو ما رح تْلاقِيُن بالكُتُب.

**Farah:** While a university education is important, gaining experience at the same time is essential, like doing internships and part-time jobs, and you can even volunteer. All these experiences strengthen you and provide work experience and interpersonal skills that you won't find in books.

**شرْبِل:** صحّ، الخِبْرة العملية ما بْتِتْقدّر بتمن. بِتْساعْدك تْطبّقي اللي تْعلّمْتي بالصّفّ على الحَياةْ الواقِعية، وبِتْخلّيكي أكْتر تْنافسي بسوق العمل.

**Charbel:** That's right, practical experience is invaluable. It helps you apply what you've learned in class to real life and makes you more competitive in the job market.

**فرح:** لمّا الواحد يْبلّش يِشْتِغِل بشِركات، رح يْضلّ في إسْتِمْرارية بالتّعْليم، الشّغِل دايْماً بْيِتْغيّر، والواحد ضروري يْضلّ يِتْطلّع على تطوُّرات والقُصص الجّْديدِة بمجال شِغْلو حتّى يِتْطوّر ويتْقدّم.

**Farah:** When you start working for companies, learning doesn't stop. Work is always changing, and it's essential to stay updated with new developments and trends in your field so that you can grow and advance.

**شرْبِل:** مِيّة بالْمِيّة، لَيْكي التّعلُّم على مدى الحَياةْ هُوّ مِفْتاح لكْتير قُصص. مِن خِلال الواحد ياخُد شْهادة رسْمية، أوْ حتّى دَوْرات عَ الإنْترْنِت، trainings online، trainings بالشِّغِل، ياخُد certificates، كلّو هَيْدا بيْساعد الشّخِص لَيْضل يِتْطوّر ويبْني المُسْتقْبل وهيّ عملية مُسْتمرّة مِتِل ما قِلْتي للْواحد يْحقِّق نجاح تبعو.

**Charbel:** Absolutely! Lifelong learning is key to many things. Whether through formal degrees, online courses, on-the-job training, or certifications, all of this helps a person to continually develop and build their future. It's a continuous process to achieve success.

**فرح:** شُكْراً على هالنِّقاش الرّائِع، شرْبِل. وشُكْراً لكلّ المُسْتمِعين. بتْمنّى تْكونوا سْتفدْتوا مِن حديثْنا.

**Farah:** Thanks for this great discussion, Charbel. And thanks to all the listeners. I hope you found our talk beneficial.

**شرْبِل:** وميرْسي لإلِك فرح عنْجدّ، وشُكْراً للْمُسْتمِعين. رح نِلْتِقي مرّة تانْية بمَوْضوع تاني. لَوقْتا انْشالله تْكونوا عارْفين كيف تْحقّقوا أهْدافْكُن وتِسْتمِتْعوا بهالرِّحْلة، رِحْلةْ الحَياةْ والعمل والتّعْليم.

**Charbel:** Thank you, Farah, really, and thanks to the listeners. We'll meet again with another topic. Until then, I hope you all know how to achieve your goals and enjoy this journey–the journey of life, work, and education.

## Comprehension Questions

١. شو هُوِّ مَوْضوع الحلْقة اللي حِكْيوا عنّو شرْبِل وفرح؟

٢. ليْش مْهمّ يَعْرِف الشّخِص شو بيحِبّ بآخِر سنَوات المدْرسة؟

٣. كيف بيِلْعب الأهِل دوْر رئيسي بمُساعدِةْ وْلادُن يِكْتِشْفوا إهْتماماتُن؟

٤. شو هِيِّ المسْؤولية اللي لازِم المدارِس تِتْحمّلا تِجاهْ الطُّلّاب؟

٥. ليْش النّجاح الحقيقي بيِتْطلّب صبِر ومُثابرة حسب شرْبِل؟

٦. شو هِيِّ الفَوايِد اللي بيِحْصل عْلَيا الطّالِب مِن التّعْليم الجامِعي حسب فرح؟

٧. ليْش إخْتِيار الجامْعة والتّخصُّص المْناسِبين مْهمّ؟

٨. كيف بتِسْاعِد الخِبرْة العملية الطّالِب حسب النِّقاش بينْ شرْبِل وفرح؟

1. What is the topic of the episode that Charbel and Farah discussed?
2. Why is it important for a person to know what they love in their last years of school?
3. How do parents play a key role in helping their children discover their interests?
4. What responsibility should schools take towards students?
5. Why does true success require patience and perseverance according to Charbel?
6. What are the benefits students gain from higher education according to Farah?
7. Why is choosing the right university and major important?
8. How does practical experience help students according to the discussion between Charbel and Farah?

## Discussion Questions

1. شو هِيِّ إهْتِماماتك الأكاديمية والمِهنية؟ كيف كْتشفْتا؟

2. كيف كان دوْر أهْلك بِعملية إخْتِيار مجالك الأكاديمي أوْ المِهني؟

3. شو هُوِّ أهمية الإرْشاد المِهني بِالْمدارِس بِوِجْهِةْ نظرك؟

4. شو رأيَك بِأهميةْ الصّبرِ والمُثابرة لتحْقيق النّجاح؟

5. كيف ساعدك التّعْليم الجامِعي بِتنْميةْ شخْصيتك ومهاراتك؟

6. شو هُوِّ التّخصُّص اللي خْترْتو أوْ ناوي تِخْتارو؟ وليْش؟

7. كيف ساعدتك الخبرات العملية مِتِل التّدْريب أوْ الوَظايِف الجِزْئِية بِتطْوير مهاراتك؟

8. شو هِيِّ خُططك للتّعلُّم المُسْتمِر بعِد التّخرُّج مِن الجامْعة؟

1. What are your academic and professional interests? How did you discover them?
2. How did your parents play a role in choosing your academic or career path?
3. What is your opinion on the importance of career guidance in schools?
4. What do you think about the importance of patience and perseverance in achieving success?
5. How has higher education helped in developing your personality and skills?
6. What major did you choose or plan to choose? Why?
7. How have practical experiences like internships or part-time jobs helped in developing your skills?
8. What are your plans for continuous learning after graduating from university?

# التَّزلُّج بِلِبْنان

## *Skiing in Lebanon*

## In this episode...

Charbel and Omar dive into the exciting winter activity of skiing in Lebanon. They explore how Lebanon, known for its beaches and rich history, is also a prime destination for skiing in the Middle East. From the popular slopes of Faraya Mzaar to the scenic Cedars resort, they share personal stories and highlight the unique experience of skiing in the country. Whether you're a beginner or an expert, skiing in Lebanon offers breathtaking views, from snowy mountains to the Mediterranean Sea. Tune in to discover why Lebanon is a hidden gem for winter sports enthusiasts!

## Vocabulary

| | |
|---|---|
| skiing | تزلُّج |
| to swim | تْسبّح (يِتْسبّح) |
| snow | تلْج |
| mountainous | جبلي |
| geography | جِغْرافْية |
| danger | خُطورة |
| dangerous | خطير |
| coast | ساحِل |
| chalet | شاليْه |
| winter- | شَتَوي |
| lunch | غدا |
| close, nearby | قريب |
| cup | كاس |
| coach, trainer, instructor | كوْتْش (كوْتْشية) |
| equipment | معدّات |
| climate | مناخ |
| resort | مُنْتجع |
| slope | مُنْحدر |
| region | مِنْطْقة |
| activity | نشاط |

## Transcript

**شرْبِل:** هاي كيفْكُن؟ اليوْم رح نِحْكي عن نشاط وسْبوْر مَعْقول تْفاجِئْكُن إنّو في مِنّا بلِبْنان هيِّ التّزلُّج. أنا شرْبِل ومعي رْفيقي عُمر. كيفك يا عُمر؟

**Charbel:** Hi, how are you all? Today, we're going to talk about an activity and sport that might surprise you exists in Lebanon—skiing. I'm Charbel, and with me today is my friend Omar. How are you, Omar?

**عُمر:** هاي شرْبِل، أنا مْنيح، إنْتَ كيف؟ كْتير مِتْحمّس نِحْكي عن التّزلُّج بلِبْنان. هيْدي واحْدِة مْن الهوايات ونشاطات الشّتَوية المُفضّلِة عِنْدي.

**Omar:** Hi, Charbel. I'm good. How about you? I'm really excited to talk about skiing in Lebanon. It's one of my favorite winter activities.

**شرْبِلِ:** عنْجدّ، هَيْدا النّشاط رائع. كْتير ناس يمْكِن ما بْيَعِرْفوا إنّو لِبْنان هُوّ وِجْهة أساسية ومْهِمّة للتّزلُّج بالمِنْطقة. نحْنا عادةً مِنرُبْط لِبْنان بالشّواطِئ الحِلْوة، بالأكل، بالْمطاعِم، بالسّهر، حتّى تاريخو الغني، بسّ الـ ski أَوْ التّزلُّج هُوّ جِزءٍ كْبير مِن ثقافِتْنا.

**Charbel:** Really, this is an amazing activity. Many people might not know that Lebanon is actually a major and important skiing destination in the region. We usually associate Lebanon with beautiful beaches, food, restaurants, nightlife, and its rich history, but skiing is a big part of our culture as well.

**عُمر:** مظْبوط، اللي عم تْقولو ميّة بالْميّة صحيح. ويمْكِن هَيْدي الفِكْرة إجت مِن وَرا إنّو لِبْنان بلد عربي، يمْكِن ما كان عِنْدو المناخ المُناسِب للتّزلُّج. بسّ عَ فِكْرة، لِبْنان عِنْدو مِن أفْضل مُنْتجعات التّزلُّج بالشّرْق الأَوْسط. الجْبال عنّا بْتِتْغطّى بالتّلْج كْتير بالشِّتي وهَيْدا بيخلّيا مثالية للتّزلُّج. وهيِّ واحْدِة مِن أشْهر المُنْتجعات بالْمِنْطقة، وفينا أهمّ نِذْكُر فارَيا المْزار.

**Omar:** Exactly, what you're saying is 100% true. Maybe this idea comes from the fact that Lebanon is an Arab country, so people might think it doesn't have the right climate for skiing. But actually, Lebanon has some of the best ski resorts in the Middle East. Our mountains get heavily covered with snow in the winter, making them ideal for skiing. One of the most famous resorts in the region is Faraya Mzaar.

**شَرْبِل:** صحّ، فارَيا مُزار destination أوْ محلّ للـ ski والتَّزَلُّج مُمتاز، عِنْدو إذا بدّك أكْتَر مِن ٨٠ كم مِن المُنْحدرات يَعْني عم تِتْخايَل وبيناسِب كلّ المُسْتَوِيّات مِن المُبْتَدِئين للمُحْتَرِفين يَعْني. والحِلو بهَيْدا... بْفارَيا إنّو إذا كان الطَّقِس كْتير صافي فيك إنْتَ وعم تِتْزَلَّج تْشوف البْحِر، يَعْني عم تِتْخايَل هَيْدا المنْظر إنْتَ عم تعْمُل ski.

**Charbel:** That's right. Faraya Mzaar is an excellent ski destination with more than 80 kilometers of slopes, catering to all levels from beginners to professionals. The great thing about Mzaar is that if the weather is really clear, you can see the sea while you're skiing. Just imagine that view while you're skiing.

**عُمَر:** مظْبوط، وكمان في... ما فينا ما نِنْسى مُنْتجع التَّزَلُّج بالأَرْز. للأَشْخاص اللي بيحِبّوا المناظِر الجبلية أكْتَر، مُنْتجع الأَرْز مَوْجود بشْمال لِبْنان. هُوّ عَ فِكْرة أقْدم مُنْتجعات التَّزَلُّج بالبلد، وبيقدِّم تجْرِبة فريدِة. المناظِر فوْق كْتير حِلْوة، خِلّابة مِتِل ما بيقولوا، خُصوصاً إذا عم تِتْزَلَّج وعم تِتْفرّج على أشْجار الأَرْز المُعمِّرة والقديمة.

**Omar:** Exactly! And we can't forget the Cedars ski resort. For those who love more mountainous landscapes, the Cedars resort is located in northern Lebanon. It's actually the oldest ski resort in the country and offers a unique experience. The views up there are stunning, especially when you're skiing and looking at the ancient cedar trees.

**شَرْبِل:** لِيْك عُمَر إنّو تِجْمع بين التَّزَلُّج والأهمية التّاريخية للأَشْجار الأَرْز، يَلّي هُوّ رمْز لِبْنان ومَوْجود على العلم، بيخلّي كمان هَيْدا المحلّ كْتير مُميّز. خبِّرْنا شْوَيّ، عِنْدك شْوَيّ ذِكْرَيات مْعيّنة بالـ ski ولِبْنان؟

**Charbel:** Omar, combining skiing with the historical significance of the cedar trees, which are a symbol of Lebanon and are on our flag, makes this place even more special. Tell us, do you have any specific skiing memories from Lebanon?

**عُمَر:** أوْه! أكيد عِنْدي ذِكْرَيات. مرّة رِحِت تأعْمُل ski بْفارَيا مع مجْموعة مِن الأَصْحاب. قرّرْنا نِتْحدّى حالْنا ونْجرِّب بعْض المُنْحدرات اللي كانِت تُعْتبر كْتير صعْبِة. بِتْذكّر واحد مِن رِفْقاتي فقد السَّيْطرة، وعلى شْوَيّ كان قلْب بالْوادي.

**Omar:** Oh, for sure! I have a lot of memories. One time I went skiing in Faraya with a group of friends. We decided to challenge ourselves and try some of the more difficult slopes. I remember one of my friends lost control and almost fell into the valley.

**شِرْبِل:** لَيْك يَعْني كانِت... وشي بيضحِّك يَعْني وشي خَطير كمان. ما بدّنا نِنْكُر إنّو هَيْدا الـski قدّي سْبوْر حِلْوة وفِيا كْتير جهِد بدني بسّ كمان بِتْشكِّل خُطورة. بِتْذكّر أنا أوّل مرّة بلّشِت الـski كانِت بالأَرْز، وكِنْت شْوَيّ مِتْوَتِّر لأنّو كانِت أوّل مرّة باخُد ski وبِعْمُل. ووَقعِت كذا مرّة بسّ كانوا ...كان معي كوْتْشية (مْدرّبين) كانوا كْتير عم يْساعْدوني، وقْدِرِت هيْك إتْعلّم ويِمْشي حالي.

**Charbel:** Wow, that sounds both funny and dangerous! We can't deny that skiing is a great and physically demanding sport, but it also comes with risks. I remember the first time I started skiing was in the Cedars. I was a bit nervous because it was my first time skiing. I fell several times, but there were coaches (trainers) with me who were very helpful, and I managed to learn and get the hang of it.

**عُمر:** مظْبوط! وهَيْدا شي مُميّز عنّا بالمُنْتجعات السِّياحية تبع الـski بلِبْنان لأنّو عنّا نخْبة مِن المُدرّبين يَلّي إجْمالاً بيكونوا كِلُّن سكّان المناطِق الجبلية وتْربّوا على هَيْدي الرِّياضة. وهِنّي أشْخاص كْتير عِنْدُن خِبْرة وبْينْقْلُوَا للشّخِص اللي ع بالو يِتْعلّم بطريقة كْتير حِلْوة. وهِنّي أشْخاص هيْك شاطْرين ووَدودين بذات الوَقْت. بيخلّوا عملِيّة التّعلُّم مُمْتعة وسِهْلة بذات الوَقْت. حابِب خبْرُك وخبِّر المُسْتمعين إنّو رِياضةْ التّزلُّج بلِبْنان منّا بسّ تُعْتبر هوِاية أوْ رِياضة مْنِعْملا مِن فتْرة لفتْرة، هيّ تجْرِبة كامْلة. يَعْني اليوْم عنّا مِتِل ما مْنِسمِّيا ثقافةْ الـaprès ski. يَعْني بسّ واحد يْخلِّص التّزلُّج، كْتير حِلْوة لأنّو بْتِسْتِرْخي بالمنازل الجّبلية بالشّالِيّات الدّافِقة، بْتِتْمتّع بالأكْل اللِّبْناني التّقْليدي وما فينا نِنْسى بعِد الغدا كاسةْ الـchocolat chaux.

**Omar:** That's right! One of the great things about our ski resorts in Lebanon is that we have some of the best trainers, who are usually locals from the mountain areas. They grew up with this sport, and they have a lot of experience. They pass on their knowledge in a fun and friendly way, making the learning process enjoyable and easy. I want to tell you and the listeners that skiing in Lebanon isn't just a hobby or a sport we do occasionally—it's a full experience. Today, we have what we call "après-ski" culture. After you finish skiing, you can relax in cozy mountain chalets, enjoy traditional Lebanese food, and you can't forget a cup of hot chocolate after lunch.

شَرْبِل: عَنْجَدّ يَعْني شَهَّيْتْنا على الـhot chocolate يا عُمَر! عَنْجَدّ ما في أَحْلى مِن هيْك تْقَضّي نْهارِك بَعِد يوْم إذا بَدّك طَويل عم تَعْمِل ski بالمُنْحَدِرات. ما في أَحْلى مِن إنّو تْقْعُد حَدّ هالـcheminee وبْشي هيْك شاليه جَبَلي وتِسْتَمْتِع بالميِّزات وتِتْحَدَّث مع هالأصْحاب تْقَضّي وَقْتِك مَعُن يَعْني، وهيْدي الطَّريقة الأنْسَب وتْكون عَنْجَدّ مِثالية لَتَعْمِل... تْخَلِّص نْهارِك.

Charbel: Honestly, you've really made us crave hot chocolate, Omar! There's truly nothing better than spending your day after a long day skiing on these slopes. There's nothing better than sitting by the fireplace in a cozy mountain chalet, enjoying the atmosphere, chatting with friends, and spending time with them. This is the best and truly ideal way to end your day.

عُمَر: وعلى فِكْرة شَرْبِل، عادةً بالبُلْدان الأوروبيّة بيْسوقوا مَسافات بْتاخِدُن ساعات طَويلة لَيوصَلوا على المُنْتَجَعات. نِحْنا بِلِبْنان مَعْروف عَنّا إنّو هالمُنْتَجَعات التَّزَلُّج قَريبة على العاصِمة بَيْروت وقَريبة على السّاحِل. فا عَنْجَدّ للأشْخاص اللي حابّين يْزوروا لِبْنان عِنْدُن فُرْصة إنّو يِطْلَعوا الصُّبْح يِتْزَلّجوا ويِرْجَعوا على بَيْروت لَيِتْعَشّوا على حَدّ البَحِر. وأنا جَرَّبْتا وبْتْخَلّيك تَعْرِف أهميّة هَيْدا التَّنَوُّع بالنَّشاطات اللي فيك تَعْمِلا بيوْم واحِد، ومِش عَ طول هَيْدا الشّي مَوْجود بْغيْر بِلْدان.

Omar: And by the way, Charbel, in European countries, people often have to drive for hours to reach the ski resorts. But in Lebanon, our ski resorts are close to the capital, Beirut, and near the coast. So, for those who want to visit Lebanon, they can ski in the morning and then return to Beirut for dinner by the sea. I've tried it, and it really shows the importance of the variety of activities you can do in one day—something you can't always find in other countries.

شَرْبِل: ميّة بالميّة عُمَر. وحَتّى إذا تْأَخَّر المَوْسِم إذا كان مَوْسِم الـski وكان في تَلْج كْتير فيك حَتّى إنّو مِش بَسّ تِتْعَشّى عَ البَحِر، تِتْسَبّح! بيْضَلّ التَّلْج لأيّار بِتْكون عالَم عم تَعْمِل ski بِتْلاقي عالَم عم تَعْمِل... تِتْسَبّح على البَحِر. ليْك جِغْرافية لِبْنان إذا بَدّك المَضْغوطة هيْك بْتِسْمَح لهيْك قُصَص وهيْك تَجارِب غَريدة وفَريدة ما في مِنّا بْغيْر بَلَد مِتِل ما عم تْقول.

Charbel: One hundred percent, Omar. And even if the ski season is delayed or if there's a lot of snow, you can not only have dinner by the sea, but you can also go swimming! The snow stays until May, and you'll find people skiing while others are swimming in the sea. Lebanon's compact geography allows for such unique and rare experiences that you won't find in other countries, as you said.

**عُمر:** صحيح! فا أنا نصيحْتي للْمُسْتَمِعين كِلّ حدا عم بِخطِّط يْزور لِبْنان بِفصْل الشِّتي ما يِنْسى يْجيب معو مْعدّات التّزلُّج. وحتّى إذا ما عِنْدو مْعدّات تزلُّج في محلّات كْتير بِتْأجِّر وبِتْبيع وهِيّ كمان بْتُعْرُض خدماتا للْأَشْخاص اللي جايين مِن برّا. وبِنْصحُن أكيد ما يْفقّوا التجْرِبِة زْيارِةِ المُنْتجعات التّزلُّج بِلِبْنان لأِنّو رح يْعيشوا experience غير شِكِل.

Omar: That's true! So my advice to our listeners—anyone planning to visit Lebanon in winter—don't forget to bring your ski gear. And even if you don't have ski gear, there are plenty of places that rent and sell equipment, and they also offer services for those coming from abroad. I definitely recommend not missing out on the experience of visiting Lebanon's ski resorts because it's a unique experience.

**شَربِل:** مِيِّة بالْمِيِّة! عُمر thank you عَ المُشاركِة الحِلْوِة وthank you لهالْمَوْضوع اللي عنْجدّ interesting. ميرْسي اللي عم يِسْمعْنا وانْشالله نْكون حمّسْناهُن يِجوا يَعِمْلوا ski عِنّا بِلِبْنان. يَلّا رح نِلْتِقي مرّة تانْيِة بِمَوْضوع جْديد وخِبْرية جْديدِة مِن حَياتْنا بِلِبْنان لَوَقْتا نْتِبْهوا عَ حالكُن وسْتِمْتِعوا بِالْمُغامرة.

Charbel: Absolutely! Omar, thank you for the great conversation and the interesting topic. Thanks to everyone listening, and hopefully, we've inspired you to come ski with us in Lebanon. We'll meet again with another topic and more stories from our life in Lebanon. Until then, take care and enjoy the adventure!

## Comprehension Questions

١. لَيْش بَعْض النّاس بيفكّروا إنّو التّزلُّج مِش مُمْكِن يْكون بِلِبْنان؟

٢. شو هِيِّ الوُجْهِة الأساسية والمْهِمّة للتّزلُّج بِلِبْنان؟

٣. كيف الطّقِس بْفارَيا بيأثّر على تجْرُبِة التّزلُّج؟

٤. وِيْن مَوْجود مُنْتجع التّزلُّج بِالأرِز، وشو اللي بيمَيْزو؟

٥. كيف بيساهِم المُدرِّبين المحلِّيِّين بِتجرُبِة التّزلُّج بِلِبْنان؟

٦. شو يَعْني "après ski" بِلِبْنان وكيف النّاس بْيِسْتمتْعوا فيا؟

٧. لَيْش مُنْتجعات التّزلُّج بِلِبْنان مْميّزة بِالنِّسْبة للبُلْدان الأوروبيّة؟

٨. بِأيّ مَوْسِم مُمْكِن النّاس يِجْمعوا بيْن التّزلُّج والسّْباحة بنفْس اليوْم بِلِبْنان؟

1. Why do some people think that skiing is not possible in Lebanon?
2. What is the main and important skiing destination in Lebanon?
3. How does the weather in Faraya affect the skiing experience?
4. Where is the ski resort in the Cedars, and what makes it special?
5. How do local instructors contribute to the skiing experience in Lebanon?
6. What does "après ski" mean in Lebanon, and how do people enjoy it?
7. Why are ski resorts in Lebanon unique compared to European countries?
8. In what season can people combine skiing and swimming on the same day in Lebanon?

## Discussion Questions

١. كيف بِتْشوف تَأْثير المناخ بِبلدك على أنْواع الرِّياضة اللي مُمْكِن تْمارسا؟

٢. في بِلدك مُنْتجعات تزلُّج مشهورة؟ خبِّرْنا عن تجْرِبْتك فيا.

٣. شو رأيَك بِفْكرةْ الجَّمْع بين التّزلُّج والسِّباحة بِنفْس اليوْم؟ بِرأيَك، هَيْدا الشِّي مُمْكِن يْصير بِبلدك؟

٤. كيف بْتِعْتِقِد بيأثِّر تَوَفُّر النّشاطات الشّتَوية على السِّياحة بِبلدك؟

٥. شو هِيِّ الرِّياضات الشّتَوية المُفضّلة عِنْدك؟ وليْش؟

٦. شي مرّة جرّبِت التّزلُّج؟ إذا أيْه، خبِّرْنا عن تجْرِبْتك. إذا لأ، عَ بالك تْجرِّب؟

٧. كيف بِتْشوف دوْر المْدرِّبين المحلّيِّين بِتِعْليم الرِّياضات بِبلدك؟ كيف مُمْكِن يْحسّنوا تجْرِبةْ التّعلُّم؟

٨. شو هِيِّ النّشاطات اللي بِتْحِبّ تعْمِلا بعِد مُمارسةْ الرِّياضة؟ كيف بْتِسْترْخي بعِد يوْم مِلْيان بِالنّشاط؟

1. How do you see the impact of your country's climate on the types of sports that can be practiced?
2. Are there famous ski resorts in your country? Tell us about your experience with them.
3. What do you think of the idea of combining skiing and swimming on the same day? Do you think this is possible in your country?
4. How do you think the availability of winter activities affects tourism in your country?
5. What are your favorite winter sports, and why?
6. Have you ever tried skiing? If yes, share your experience. If not, would you like to try it?
7. How do you see the role of local instructors in teaching sports in your country? How can they improve the learning experience?
8. What activities do you like to do after practicing sports? How do you relax after a busy day?

# صِناعةُ الفِخّارِ التّقْليدية بِلِبْنان
## Traditional Pottery Making in Lebanon

## In this episode...

Charbel and Farah explore the traditional craft of pottery making in Lebanon, a skill that has been passed down through generations and remains an important part of the country's heritage. They discuss how pottery has been integral to daily life in Lebanon for thousands of years, with regions like Beit Shabab, Rachaiya, and Tripoli being renowned for their unique styles and techniques. Charbel and Farah share personal stories about owning handcrafted pottery and emphasize the importance of supporting artisans to preserve this cultural tradition for future generations. Tune in to learn more about the artistry and history behind Lebanese pottery!

## Vocabulary

| | |
|---|---|
| household items | أَدَوات مَنْزِلية |
| essential | أساسي |
| drying | تِجْفيف |
| shaping the clay | تِشْكيل الطّين |
| craft | حِرْفِة (حِرف) |
| craftsman | حِرفي |
| decoration | زينِة |
| clay | طين |
| pottery | فَخّار |
| kiln (oven for firing pottery) | فُرْن (أَفْران) |
| coffee cup | فِنْجان (فْناجين) |
| antique pieces | قِطع أثرية |
| durable | متين |
| famous | مشْهور |
| texture | مِلْمس |
| tangible | مِلْموس |
| colorful | مْلوّن |
| result | نتيجِة |
| workshop | وَرْشِة |
| function | وَظيفِة |

## Transcript

**شَرْبِل:** هاي، كيفْكُن اليوْم؟ تمام؟ اليوْم رح نِحْكي عن حِرْفِة تِقْليدية كانت إذا بدُكُن جِزءِ أساسي مِن تُراث لِبْنان لعدّةِ سْنين: صِناعةِ الفِخّار. معْكُن شرْبِل ومع رْفيقْتي فرح كيفِك فرح؟

**Charbel:** Hi, how are you all today? Good? Today we're going to talk about a traditional craft that has been an essential part of Lebanon's heritage for many years: pottery making. I'm Charbel, and with me today is my friend Farah. How are you, Farah?

**فرح:** أهْلا شرْبِل! أنا مْنيحة. كْتير مْحمّسي نِحْكي عن عالم الفِخّار التِّقْليدي بلِبْنان. هالْمَوْضوع غني ومُثير لِلْإهْتمام.

**Farah:** Hi, Charbel! I'm good. I'm really excited to talk about the world of traditional pottery in Lebanon. It's such a rich and fascinating topic.

**شرْبِل:** أكيد. صِناعةِ الفِخّار بلِبْنان بْتِرْجع لآلاف السْنين. كانِت جِزءِ أساسي مِن ثقافتْنا وحَياتْنا اليَوْمية. هُوِّ مِش بسّ صِناعةِ قِطع فِخّار حِلْوة، هُوِّ كمان تْحافِظ ع هالتُّراث وتِنِقْلو مِن جيل لجيل.

**Charbel:** Absolutely. Pottery making in Lebanon goes back thousands of years. It has been an essential part of our culture and daily life. It's not just about making beautiful pottery pieces but also about preserving this heritage and passing it down from generation to generation.

**فرح:** صحّ. الفِخّار اللِّبْناني معْروف بِتصاميمو الفَريدِة وجَوْدةِ صِناعْتو العالْية. التِّقْنيّات اللي بْيِسْتعِمْلُوا لِصِناعةِ هالْفِخّار نْتقلِت عبْر الأجْيال، وكِلّ مِنْطقة بلِبْنان عِنْدا أُسْلوبا وطُرُقا الْمُميّزة.

**Farah:** Right. Lebanese pottery is known for its unique designs and high-quality craftsmanship. The techniques used in making this pottery have been passed down through generations, and every region in Lebanon has its own distinctive style and methods.

**شرْبِل:** واحْدِة مِن أشْهر مراكِز الفِخّار لِبْنان هِيِّ ضَيْعةِ بيْت شباب. هالضّيْعة عِنْدا تاريخ طَويل بِصِناعةِ الفِخّار والحِرافيّين هوْنيك مشهورين إذا بدّك بمِهاراتُن وكْتير

creative مُبْدِعين بْيِصْنعوا مجْموعة كْبيرة مِن قِطع الفخّار وحتّى أدَوات منْزِلية للْمطْبخ وقِطع للزّينة.

**Charbel:** One of the most famous pottery centers in Lebanon is the village of Beit Shabab. This village has a long history of pottery making, and the artisans there are renowned for their skills and creativity. They create a wide range of pottery pieces, including household items for the kitchen and decorative pieces.

**فرح:** مِيّة بالْمِيّة، بيْت شباب معْروفة بِفخّارا. الطّين اللي بْيِسْتعمْلو بِفخّارُن مُسْتخْرج محلّيّاً، وهالشّي بْيَعْطي القِطع ملْمس ولوْن مْميّز. عملية صناعةْ الفخّار بِبيْت شباب بْتِشْمل عِدّةْ خْطوات، مِنّا تشْكيل الطّين، بعْدينْ بْيِرْجعوا يْجفّفوا، وبعْدينْ بْيِحرْقوا بالْأفْران. النّتيجة النّهائية بتْكون فِخّار كْتير حِلو ومتين، وعملي وفنّي بْنفْس الوَقت.

**Farah:** Absolutely. Beit Shabab is famous for its pottery. The clay they use is locally sourced, which gives the pieces a unique texture and color. The pottery-making process in Beit Shabab involves several steps, from shaping the clay to drying it and finally firing it in kilns. The final result is very beautiful and sturdy pottery, both practical and artistic at the same time.

**شرْبِل:** و في كمان عِدّةْ محلّات غيْر بيْت شباب. في محلّ كْتير مْميّز بِصناعةْ الفخّار بِلبْنان هِيّ ضَيْعةْ راشيّا. اللي بْيَعمْلوا فِخّار براشيّا معْروفين إذا بدّك بالتّقْنيّات التّقْليدية وتصاميمُن هيْك شْوَيّ مْعقّدة. بْيِسْتعمْلوا رُموز بْيِسْتوْحوا مِن الطّبيعة والتّرُاث اللّبْناني وهَيْدا الشّي بيخلّي كلّ قِطْعة فريدة ومْميّزة عن غَيْرا.

**Charbel:** There are also other places besides Beit Shabab. A very notable spot for pottery in Lebanon is the village of Rachaiya. The potters in Rachaiya are known for their traditional techniques and slightly more intricate designs. They use symbols inspired by nature and Lebanese heritage, making each piece unique and special.

**فرح:** كمان شرْبِل وما تِنْسى فِخّار طْرابُلْس. المدينة عِنْدا تاريخ غني بِصناعةْ الفخّار، واللي بْيَعمْلوا فِخّار بِطْرابُلْس مشْهورين بِتْصاميمُن المْلوّنة والمْفصّلة. أسْواق الفخّار بِطْرابُلْس كْتير حِلْوة، وعنْجدّ لازِم كِلّ واحد مِهْتمّ بِهَيْدي الحِرفية التّقْليدية اللّبْنانية يْزورا.

**Farah:** And don't forget Tripoli pottery. The city has a rich history of pottery making, and the potters in Tripoli are famous for their colorful and detailed designs. The pottery markets in Tripoli are beautiful, and anyone interested in this traditional Lebanese craft should definitely visit them.

**شَرْبِل:** عِنْدي بِبَيْتي بَعْض القُطَع الفخّار اللي شتريَتا مِن هَيْدي المناطِق. كُلّ قِطْعة هيْك بِتْذكِّرْني بِقِصّة وبْتَعْطيني هيْك لمْسة مِن التُراث اللُبْناني لديكُور البيْت. إنْتي عِنْدِك شي قِطْعة... قِطْعةْ فخّار بالبيْت يا فرح؟

Charbel: I have some pottery pieces at home that I bought from these regions. Each piece reminds me of a story and adds a touch of Lebanese heritage to my home décor. Do you have any pottery pieces at home, Farah?

**فرح:** أكيد عِنْدي! عِنْدي فاز كْتير حِلْوة مِن بيْت شباب وطقْم فْناجين قهْوة تقْليدية مِن راشيّا. بْحِبّ كيف هالقُطَع هيْك بْتِحْكي عن حالا، بيكون في مزيج بينْ الوَظيفة والفنّ.

Farah: Of course, I do! I have a beautiful vase from Beit Shabab and a traditional coffee cup set from Rachaiya. I love how these pieces speak for themselves, blending functionality with art.

**شَرْبِل:** عنْجدّ بسّ نِحْكي عن صِناعةْ الفخّار بلِبْنان ما مِنْكون عم نِحْكي بسّ عن الصِّناعة كـitems أوّ كفخّار، عم نِحْكي عن القِصص والتّقاليد اللي وَراها. كُلّ قِطْعةْ فِخّار هِيّ شْهادة على مهارة وإخْلاص مِن الصّانِع تبعا.

Charbel: Honestly, when we talk about pottery making in Lebanon, we're not just talking about crafting items or pottery pieces. We're talking about the stories and traditions behind it. Each pottery piece is a testament to the skill and dedication of its maker.

**فرح:** مِن المُهِمّ نِدْعم هالحِرفيّين لنْحافِظ على هالصِّناعة. إنّو نِشْتري الفِخّار التّقْليدي لنْساعِد بالحِفاظ عَ هالتُراث ونتْأكّد إنّو الأجْيال الجاية تِقْدر تِسْتمْتِع وتِتْعلّم مِنّو.

Farah: It's important to support these artisans to preserve this craft. By buying traditional pottery, we help maintain this heritage and ensure that future generations can enjoy and learn from it.

**شَرْبِل:** هَيْدا الشّي اللي عم تْقولي فرح كْتير مظْبوط وكْتير أساسي. لازِم هالصّناعة كْتير نِدْعما! وهِيّ فنّ بْحاجة لصبْرٍ ودِقّة وحتّى إذا بدِّك هيْك فِهْم عميق للْمَوادّ

والتّقْنِيّات لَيْرِكْبوا هالـitem اللي عم بْيَعْمِلوا. هيِّ حِرْفِة بِتْمثِّل تاريخ وثقافِة لُبْنان بِطريقة كْتير مِلْموسِة.

**Charbel:** What you're saying, Farah, is absolutely right and essential. We need to support this craft! It's an art that requires patience, precision, and a deep understanding of the materials and techniques to create the item they're making. This craft represents Lebanon's history and culture in a very tangible way.

**فرح:** صحّ، وزْيارِةْ وَرْشات الفخّار والأسْواق بِلُبْنان هيِّ طريقة رائْعة لنِتْعلّم أكْتر عن هالْحِرْفِة. كْتير هالشّي مُهِمّ إنّو نْشوف هالْحِرفيِّين عم بْيِشْتِغْلوا ونِتْفهّم الجِهِد اللي بْتِطِلّبو كِلّ قِطْعة.

**Farah:** True, and visiting pottery workshops and markets in Lebanon is a great way to learn more about this craft. It's so important to see the artisans working and to understand the effort that goes into each piece.

**شرْبِل:** صحّ، يَعْني إذا صار عِنْدْكُن أيّ فُرْصة، بْليز بِنْصَحْكُن تْزوروا هالْمحلّات هيِّ experience رح تعْطيكُن تِقْدير أكْتر لهالصّناعة وتْخلّيكُن تْحِبُّوا أكْتر.

**Charbel:** Exactly, so if you ever get the chance, I highly recommend visiting these places. It's an experience that will give you a greater appreciation for this craft and make you love it even more.

**فرح:** أكيد شرْبِل، ميرْسي كْتير، وشُكْراً لكِلّ المُسْتِمِعين اللي تابعونا اليوْم.

**Farah:** Absolutely. Thank you so much, Charbel, and thanks to all our listeners who joined us today.

**شرْبِل:** thank you إلِك فرح. وانْشالله تْكونوا نْبسطوا وتْعلّمْتوا شْوَيّ هيْك عن هالصّناعة الحِلْوة والتّقْليدية بِلُبْنان. يَلّا مْنِلْتِقي بِموَضوع جْديد وخبرِيّات جْديدِة من لِبْنان لَوَقْتا ضلّوا بْخيْر.

**Charbel:** Thank you, Farah. I hope you all enjoyed and learned a little about this beautiful traditional craft in Lebanon. We'll meet again with a new topic and new stories from Lebanon. Until then, stay well.

## Comprehension Questions

1. شو هُوِّ مَوْضوع الحلْقة اللي حِكْيوا عنّو شرْبِل وفرح؟

2. ليْش تُعْتبر صناعةْ الفخّار جزِء أساسي مِن تُراث لِبْنان؟

3. شو بيميِّز الفخّار اللِّبْناني؟

4. ويْن واحْدِة مِن أشْهر مراكِز الفخّار بلِبْنان؟

5. كيف بيتِمّ صناعةْ الفخّار بِبيْت شباب؟

6. شو بيميِّز فخّار راشيّا؟

7. شو هيِّ أهمية فخّار طْرابْلُس؟

8. كيف بْيوصُف شرْبِل شُعورو لقِطع الفِخّار اللي عِنْدو بالْبيْت؟

1. What is the topic of the episode that Charbel and Farah talked about?
2. Why is pottery considered an essential part of Lebanon's heritage?
3. What distinguishes Lebanese pottery?
4. Where is one of the most famous pottery centers in Lebanon?
5. How is pottery made in Beit Shabab?
6. What distinguishes Rachaiya pottery?
7. What is the importance of Tripoli pottery?
8. How does Charbel describe his feeling towards the pottery pieces he has at home?

## Discussion Questions

1. عِنْدك قُطع فِخّار بِبَيْتك؟ إذا نعم ، خبِّرْنا قُصِّتا؟

2. كيف بِتْشوف دوْر الحِرف اليَدَوية التَّقْليدية بِحَياتْنا اليوْم؟

3. شو هِيِّ بعْض الحِرف التِّقْليدية مِن مِنْطقْتك؟

4. كيف بْتِدْعم الحِرف اليَدَوية التَّقْليدية بِبلدك؟

5. شو رأْيَك بِأهميةْ الحِفاظ على التُراث الثَّقافي والفنّي؟

6. هل جرّبِت صِناعةْ الفِخّار مِن قبِل؟ إذا نعم ، خبِّرْنا عن تجْرِبْتك.

7. كيف بِتْشوف الفرق بينْ الفِخّار التَّقْليدي والفِخّار الحديث؟

8. شو هِيِّ النّصايح اللي بْتعْطيا لشخِص مِهتمِّ بِتعلُّم صِناعةْ الفِخّار؟

1. Do you have any pottery pieces at home? If yes, what is their story?
2. How do you see the role of traditional handicrafts in our lives today?
3. What are some traditional handicrafts from your area?
4. How do you support traditional handicrafts in your country?
5. What do you think about the importance of preserving cultural and artistic heritage?
6. Have you ever tried making pottery before? If yes, tell us about your experience.
7. How do you see the difference between traditional pottery and modern pottery?
8. What advice would you give to someone interested in learning pottery?

# التّجمُّعات العائِلية
## Family Gatherings

## In this episode...

Charbel and Omar reminisce about family gatherings, a cherished part of Lebanese culture. They discuss the laughter, awkward moments, and funny memories that come from these large get-togethers, especially during holidays and special occasions. From being asked about marriage by an eager relative to funny slip-ups during speeches, they share stories that highlight the warmth and humor found in family gatherings. Whether it's sharing meals or telling stories, these moments create lasting memories that bring families closer together. Join them as they celebrate the importance of family and the joy of togetherness.

## Vocabulary

| | |
|---|---|
| cousin (specifically one's father's sister's son) | إبِن خالةِ |
| garden | بِسْتان (بساتين) |
| between you and me | بَيْني وبَيْنك |
| gathering | تجمُّع |
| speech | خُطاب |
| engagement | خُطْبة |
| engagement | خُطوبة |
| bonds, connections | رَوابِط |
| to escape; to get away [with something] | زمط (يِزْمُط) |
| to [do] by chance | ساقب (يْساقِب) |
| to ask for someone's hand in marriage | طلب (يُطْلُب) إيد |
| emotional | عاطِفي |
| single man, bachelor | عِزّابي |
| uncle (paternal) | عمّ (عْموم) |
| an opportunity presented itself | فُرْصة سنحِت |
| to break the tension | كسر (يِكْسُر) جوّ التَّوَتُّر |
| together | مع بعْض |
| crowded, busy | معْجوق |
| enjoyable | مُمْتِع |
| occasion, event | مُناسبةِ |

## Transcript

**شرْبِل:** هاي، كيفْكُن؟ تمام؟ اليوْم رح نِحْكي عن شي كمان هيْك قريب للْقلب نِحْنا اللّبْنانية وغالباً ما بيكون هيْك مُمْتع: التّجمُّعات العائِلية وأكْتر هيْك اللّحْظات اللي بِتْضحِّك ومِنْتذكّرا. أنا شرْبِل ومعي رْفيقي عُمر اليوْم حَيْشاركْنا بالْحديث. كيفك عُمر؟

Charbel: Hi, how are you all? All good? Today, we're going to talk about something that's really close to our hearts as Lebanese, and often very fun: family gatherings and the funniest moments we remember. I'm Charbel, and with me today is my friend Omar, who's going to join in the conversation. How are you, Omar?

**عُمر:** أهْلا شرْبِل، أنا مْنيح، thank you! مْحمّس هيْك شارك... شارْكك إلك وشارِك المُسْتمِعين بِقْصص كْتير بِتْضحِّك وsomtimes هيْك مُحْرِجة عن التّجمُّعات العائِلية أوْ جمْعات العائِلية بلِبْنان.

Omar: Hello, Charbel. I'm good, thank you! I'm excited to share... share with you and the listeners many funny and sometimes embarrassing stories about family gatherings in Lebanon.

**شرْبِل:** أكيد، ليْك عُمر، نِحْنا ثقافتْنا بلِبْنان هِيِّ كْتير مْهمّة بالنِّسْبة لإلا التّجمُّعات العائِلية أوْ تْقْعُد مع العَيْلة، خاصّةً بالْمُناسبات الكِبيرة. كْتير مِنْحِبّ نِجْتِمِع مع عَيْلِتْنا الكِبيرة بالْمُناسبات مِتِل New Year، Christmas، ونْقضّي وَقت مع بعْض. وبهالتّجمُّعات أكيد إنْتَ بْتعْرِف، ما بيْخْلى الأمِر من لحْظات هيْك بِتْضحِّك، بْتحْرِج، وبِتْصير ذِكْرى مهْضومة نْخبِّرا لبعْديْن.

Charbel: Definitely, look Omar, in our Lebanese culture, family gatherings are very important to us, especially during big occasions. We love getting together with our extended family during events like New Year and Christmas, and spending time together. And in these gatherings, as you know, there are always funny, awkward moments that happen, turning into memorable stories we'll laugh about and share later on.

**عُمر:** صحيح، وهيْك الشّي المُميّز بالْجمْعات اللّبْنانية إنّو بيكونوا كلّ العَيْلة extended family يَعْني عمّاتك، عْمومْتك، خْوالك وخالاتك وْولادْن. بيْبْقى البيْت معْجوق كِلّو سَوا وكِلّو عم بيحضّر لوَقِت الغدا لنِتْشارك بالأكِل. بسّ على سيرةٍ هيْك

الأَوْقات المُحْرِجة، بْخبْرَك مرّة كنّا مجْتِمْعين كِلّ العَيْلة، يَعْني عم نِحْكي شي ٤٠ شخِص وعم نِتْناوَل الغدا. وبِتْقرّر عمْتي تِسْألني: "أمْتين بدْنا نِفْرح مِنّك." فا... وشكْلو كان كِلّ هالْعالم المَوْجودين ناطْرين الجَواب. فا كِلّ العالم سكتِت، كِلُّن صاروا عم بيطلّعوا فيّي وأنا تْفاجأْت كْتير بالسُّؤال وبَيْني وبَيْنك ما كان عِنْدي جَواب واضِح. الحَمْدِلله إبِن خالتي الصِّغير يَلّي كان عُمْرو يِمْكِن شي ١٠ سْنين قِلُّن: "يا جماعة شو بيكُن؟ ناطِر العروس المْناسْبة!" فا وَقْتا هيْك كسر جوّ التَّوتُّر وخلّصني مِن هالْجَواب شْوَيّ الصَّعِب.

**Omar:** Exactly, and what's special about Lebanese gatherings is that the whole extended family comes together, like your aunts, uncles, cousins, and everyone. The house gets packed, and everyone's busy preparing for lunch so we can share a meal. Speaking of those awkward moments, I'll tell you about a time when the whole family was gathered—about 40 people, and we were having lunch. My aunt decided to ask me, "So, when are we going to celebrate with you [i.e., when are you getting married]?" It seemed like everyone there was waiting for my answer. Suddenly, the whole room went quiet, and everyone was looking at me. I was really surprised by the question, and, between you and me, I didn't have a clear answer. Thankfully, my little cousin, who was around ten years old, said, "Everyone, what's wrong with you? He's waiting for the right bride!" That broke the tension and saved me from giving that somewhat difficult answer.

**شرْبِل:** عنْجدّ عُمر زمطِت! بسّ عنْجدّ عُمر أيْمتى بدّنا نِفْرح مِنّك؟ ليْك كْتير بيصير قُصص بِتْضحّك؟ هيْدا مَوْقف عنْجدّ كْلاسيكي إذا بدّك بين كِلّ العيّل يِبْقى مثلاً واحد عِزابي بيصيروا ناطْرينو عَ الدّقّرة أيْمتى، بدّو يِتْجوّز أيْمتى! هيْدا كمان شي مِن التُّراث عنّا. خبْرَك خبْرِية بِتْضحّك. مرّة كان في خُطْبة إبِن عمّي وتْحمّس عمّي كْتير وقرّر يْقوم يِلْقي هيْك خُطاب يِحْكي ويِجود بإبْنو. فا بلّش هيْك صار كْتير عاطِفي وبلّش يِحْكي عن إيّام الحِلْوة وكيف لازِم نْقدّر العَيْلة وما نِنْسى العَيْلة. بعْدين بالْغلط ما بعْرف شو كان عم يْخبّر خبْرِية عن إبْنو وساقب ذكر صاحِبْتو القديمة لإبِن عمّي. فا بدل ما يْقول الخطيبْتو جاب سيرِة إسْم صاحِبْتو القديمة. فجْأة الأوْضة صارِت ساكْتة ووجّ إبِن عمّي صار لَوْنو مِش معْروف وما بعْرف كيف مرّة عمّي غيّرِت المَوْضوع وزمط.

**Charbel:** Honestly, Omar, you really dodged that one! But seriously, Omar, when are we going to celebrate with you? Look, a lot of funny things happen in these situations, right? That's such a classic moment in every family—when someone's still single, everyone's just waiting, like, "When is he getting married?" That's also part of our heritage. Let me tell you a funny story. One time, at my cousin's engagement, my uncle got really excited and decided to give a little speech to praise his son. So, he started getting really emotional, talking about the good old days, how we should appreciate family, and never forget its importance. Then, by mistake, while telling a story about his son, he accidentally mentioned my cousin's ex-girlfriend instead of his fiancée. Suddenly, the room went silent, and my cousin's face turned a color no one could describe! Somehow, my aunt managed to change the subject, and he dodged that awkward moment.

**عُمر:** أيْه والله! أنا يَعْني هيْك هوْل أَعْطيك تجْرِبة شْوَيّ شخْصِيّة كمان بمُناسبات مِتِل الخُطوبِة والأَعْراس عَيْلِة العريس بتْروح كِلّا عِنْد عَيْلِة العروس لَيْطِلْبوا إيدا للْعروس فا مِن أَهْلا. فا أنا بْتِذكّر وَقْتا رِحِت مع أهْلي عِنْد أَهِل مرْتي لنُطْلُب إيدا شْوَيّ كان هيْك أَوّل شي غريب الوَضِع، إنّو الأشْخاص ما كْتير بْيَعِرْفوا بعْض وما في أحاديث يِحْكوا وهيْك وبيّي كان كْتير عِتْلان همّ كيف بدّو يْبِلِّش الحديث. فا صار ناطِر أَوّل فُرْصة سنحِتْلو وَقِت كِلّ العالم سكتِت، بيقِلُّن لأَهْل مرْتي: "اليوْم نِحْنا حابّين نُقْطُف هالوَرْدِة مِن بِسْتانْكُن لنِزْرعا بِبِسْتانّا!" أنا بسّ سْمِعِت هَيْدا الشّي حسّيْت إنّو أَوّل شي ما فْهِمِت عن شو عم يِحْكي. فا حمْدِلله يَعْني هِنّي ضِحْكوا ونِحْنا ضِحِكْنا ومِشي الحال. بسّ هَيْدي هيْك على فِكْرِة اللّحْظات المُحْرِجِة.

Omar: Oh yeah, for sure! Let me share a personal experience as well. During occasions like engagements and weddings, the groom's family usually goes to the bride's family to formally ask for her hand in marriage. So, I remember when I went with my family to my wife's family to ask for her hand; it was a bit awkward at first. You know, the people don't really know each other well, and there aren't many conversations going on, and my dad was really anxious about how to start the conversation. So, he was waiting for the first opportunity, and when everyone went quiet, he said to my wife's family, "Today, we'd like to pick this flower from your garden and plant it in ours!" When I heard that, at first, I didn't quite understand what he was saying. Thankfully, they laughed, we laughed, and everything went smoothly. But yeah, that was definitely one of those embarrassing moments!

**شَرْبِل:** يَعْني بِتْخايَل المَشْهَد وبِتْخايَلِك إنْتَ قاعِد هُوْنِيك ومِش فِهْمان شو عم بيصير! لَيْك هَيْدي اللّحْظات عنْجِدّ بِتْخلّي هالتّجمُّعات مُميّزة وثَقافتْنا نِحْنا بِلبْنان هالتّجمُّعات مِش بسّ عن الأكِل والشّرِب هيِّ مُشاركةِ القُصص، الضّحِك مع بعْض.

Charbel: I can totally picture the scene and imagine you sitting there, not understanding what's going on! Honestly, these moments are what make family gatherings so special. In our Lebanese culture, these gatherings aren't just about food and drink; they're about sharing stories and laughing together.

**عُمر:** لَيْك مع إنّو يَعْني بِالْعالم كِلّو بلّشِت تِنْفِقِد شْوَيّ هَيْدي الرّوابِط العائِلية. نِحْنا بِلبْنان لحدّيت هلّأ بعدْنا مْحافْظين عْلَيا وعم تِتْناقل مِن جيل لجيل. هَيْدا شي عِنْدو جمالو وعِنْدو سيّاتو، بسّ أكيد الحسنات بْتِطْغى عْلَيْه. وانْشالله يِسْتمِرّ وانْشالله نْشوف عَ طول جمْعات العائِلية الحِلْوة المِلْيانة فرح واللي بْتِعْمِل بْتِصْنع ذِكْرَيات لِلْمُسْتقْبل.

Omar: You know, while family bonds are starting to fade a bit around the world, in Lebanon, we've managed to preserve them, passing them down from generation to generation. This has its beauty and its downsides, but the positives definitely outweigh them. Hopefully, it continues, and hopefully, we will always see beautiful family gatherings full of joy, which create memories for the future.

**شَرْبِل:** عنْجِدّ وانْشالله مِنْقدّما لَوْلادْنا. عُمر thank you لإلك عَ هالِخْبار الحِلْوة اللي بِتْضحِّك، عنْجِدّ بيضلّوا بذاكرْتْنا. ميرْسي لِلْمُسْتمعين وانْشالله نْكون بسطْناهُن وهيْك ذكّرْناهُن بالْعَيْلة وبالقِيَم. مْنِتْلاقا بِمَوْضوع جْديد مرّة تانْية مِن حَياتْنا بِلبْنان لَوَقْتا نْتِبْهوا عَ حالكُن نْتِبْهوا عَ عيِلكُن ميرْسي لإلك عُمر.

Charbel: Really, and hopefully, we can pass this on to our kids. Omar, thank you for sharing these funny stories. They'll truly stay in our memories. Thanks to the listeners, and hopefully, we brought some joy to them and reminded them of family and values. We'll meet again with a new topic from our life in Lebanon. Until then, take care of yourselves and your families. Thanks again, Omar.

**عُمر:** ميرْسي شرْبِل وانْشالله بِتْضلّوا بْخير جميعاً وعلى فِكْرة هيْك الجمْعات العائِلية برْكي وانْشالله بِالْمِسْتقْبل القَريب نِقْدر نعْمِل جمْعة مع المُسْتمعين لأنّو هِنّي صِرْنا عَيْلِة واحْدِة كْبيرِة كمان.

**Omar:** Thanks, Charbel, and I hope you all stay well. By the way, maybe in the near future, we can have a family gathering with our listeners too, since they've become part of our big family as well!

## Comprehension Questions

١.  شو أهميةْ التّجمُّعات العائِلية بالثّقافةِ اللّبْنانية حسب شرْبِل وعُمر؟

٢.  كيف وَصف عُمر المَوْقف المُحْرِج اللي صار معو بالتّجمُّع العائِلي؟

٣.  شو هيِّ اللّحْظة المُحْرِجة اللي شاركا شرْبِل عن خُطْبةِ اِبْن عمّو؟

٤.  كيف حسّ عُمر لمّا سِمِع بيّو عُمر يعبِّر عن العروس قِدّام أهْلا؟ وكيف تْصرّف بالمَوْقف؟

٥.  ليْش عْتبر شرْبِل هاللّحْظات المُحْرِجة ويَلّي بِتْضحّك مْهِمّة بالتّجمُّعات العائِلية؟

٦.  كيف بيشوف عُمر تأْثير الرَّوابِط العائِلية على المُجْتمّع اللّبْناني، و قَوْلك تِتْغيّر مع الزّمن؟

٧.  شو هُوِّ رأي عُمر بِتأْثير هالرَّوابط على الأجْيال القادْمة؟

٨.  كيف ختم شرْبِل الحلْقة، وشو الأمل اللي عِنْدو للْعِيل اللّبْنانية؟

1.  What is the importance of family gatherings in Lebanese culture according to Charbel and Omar?
2.  How did Omar describe the embarrassing moment that happened to him during a family gathering?
3.  What was the embarrassing moment Charbel shared about his cousin's engagement?
4.  How did Omar feel when he heard his father expressing himself about the bride in front of her family? How did he handle the situation?
5.  Why does Charbel consider these embarrassing and funny moments important in family gatherings?
6.  How does Omar see the influence of family ties on Lebanese society, and in your opinion, does it change over time?
7.  What is Omar's opinion on the impact of these bonds on future generations?
8.  How did Charbel conclude the episode, and what is his hope for Lebanese families?

## Discussion Questions

١. كيف بِتْشوف التَّجمُّعات العائِلية بِبلدك؟ عِنْدك شي ذِكْرَيات مُحْرِجة أَوْ بِتْضحِّك بتجمُّعات العَيْلة؟

٢. شو هيِّ الأسْئِلة اللي عادةً بْتزعِجك بالتّجمُّعات العائِلية؟ كيف بْتِتْعامل معا؟

٣. كيف بِتْشوف أهميةْ الحِفاظ على الرَّوابِط العائِلية بِهَيْدا العصِر؟ معْقول هالرَّوابِط عم تِتْغيَّر مع الوَقِت؟

٤. بِتْلاحِظ شي إنّو في فرِق بين تجمُّعات العَيْلة الكِبيرة والصِّغيرة؟ أيّ واحْدِة بِتْفضِّل وليْش؟

٥. كيف مُمْكِن نِنْقُل قِيَم وروابِط العَيْلة للأجْيال الجْديدِة؟ شو التحدِّيّات اللي معْقول نْواجِها؟

٦. كيف بِتْعبِّر العيَّل بِبلدك عن الحُبّ والإحْتِرام بيْن أفْرادا؟ عِنْدكُن شي تقاليد مْعيَّنة؟

٧. كيف مُمْكِن نِتْعامل مع اللّحظات المُحْرِجة أَوْ المُضْحِكِة بالتّجمُّعات العائِلية بطريقة إيجابية؟

٨. عِنْدك تقاليد عائِلية خاصّةً بْتِتْكرّر بِكِلّ تجمُّع عائِلي؟ شو هيِّ؟

1. How do you see family gatherings in your country? Do you have any embarrassing or funny memories from family gatherings?

2. What are the questions that usually bother you at family gatherings? How do you deal with them?

3. How do you see the importance of maintaining family bonds in today's world? Are these bonds changing over time?

4. Do you notice a difference between large and small family gatherings? Which one do you prefer and why?

5. How can we pass on family values and bonds to the new generations? What challenges do you face?

6. How do families in your country express love and respect among their members? Do you have any specific traditions?

7. How can we handle embarrassing or funny moments at family gatherings in a positive way?

8. Do you have any special family traditions that are repeated at every family gathering? What are they?

# كسْر الصُّوَر النمطية: واقِع الحَياةُ بِلبْنان

## Breaking Stereotypes: The Reality of Life in Lebanon

### In this episode...

Charbel and Farah discuss the common stereotypes about Lebanon and the broader Arab world, breaking down misconceptions to reveal the reality of life in Lebanon. They highlight the country's unique blend of Eastern and Western influences, its cultural diversity, and the vibrant, multifaceted nature of Lebanese society. From the dynamic fashion scene and nightlife in Beirut to the progressive educational system and the evolving role of women, Lebanon defies many of the typical expectations. Join them as they explore how Lebanon is a land of contrasts, rich traditions, and modern outlooks, challenging the stereotypes often associated with the region.

## Vocabulary

| | |
|---|---|
| media | إعْلام |
| the Middle East | الشّرْق الأوْسط |
| coexistence | تعايُش |
| diversity | تنوُّع |
| personal freedoms | حُرِّيّات شخْصية |
| background | خلْفية |
| although | رغْم إنّو |
| behaviors | سُلوكِيّات |
| stereotype | صورة نمطية (صُوَر نمطية) |
| customs, traditions | عادات |
| open mind | عقِل مفْتوح |
| channel | قناةْ (قنَوات) |
| conservative | مُحافِظ |
| complex | مُعقّد |
| concept, notion | مفْهوم (مفاهيم) |
| urban areas | مناطِق حضارية |
| open-minded | مِنْفِتح |
| curriculum, approach | منْهج (مناهج) |
| fabric, tapestry (used metaphorically for rich diversity) | نسيج |
| reality | واقع |

## Transcript

**شَرْبِل:** مَرْحبا! اليوْم رح نِحْكي عن مَوْضوع كْتير بِيْتْكرّر لمّا نِحْكي عن الشّرْق الأَوْسط: الصُّوَر النمطية عن العرب والواقع بِلِبْنان. أنا شرْبِل ومعي رْفيقْتي فرح. كيفِك فرح؟

**Charbel:** Hello! Today, we're going to talk about a topic that comes up a lot when we talk about the Middle East—the stereotypes about Arabs and the reality in Lebanon. I'm Charbel, and with me is my friend Farah. How are you, Farah?

**فرح:** أَهْلا شرْبِل! أنا مْنيحة، الحمْدِلله. هَيْدا مَوْضوع مْهِمّ كْتير. في كْتير مفاهيم خاطْئة عن كيف الحَياةْ بِتْكون بالدُّوَل العربية، ولِبْنان مِثال مُمْتاز عن كيف ثقافِتْنا مِتْنوِّعة ومْعقّدة.

**Farah:** Hi, Charbel! I'm good, thank you. This is a very important topic. There are many misconceptions about what life is like in Arab countries, and Lebanon is a great example of how our culture is diverse and complex.

**شِرْبِل:** أكيد. كْتير مِن النّاس عِنْدُن صُوَر نمطية أَوْ فِكْرة عن العرب إنّو كلُّن نفْس الثّقافِة ومْحافْظين جِدّاً، مِتِل ما بيشوفوا مثلاً بالدُّوَل مِتِل السّعودية أَوْ اليَمن. بسّ لِبْنان بيقدِّم صورة غيْر كُلِّياً كْتير مِخْتِلْفة. هُوّ بلد بِتْلِتْقي في الشّرْق مع الغرْب، وهَيْدا الشّي بِيْنْعِكِس بِثقافِتْنا، نمط حَياتْنا، وحتّى بِلِبِسْنا.

**Charbel:** Definitely. Many people have stereotypes or a single idea about Arabs, thinking they all share the same culture and are very conservative, similar to what they see in countries like Saudi Arabia or Yemen. But Lebanon presents a completely different picture. It's a country where the East meets the West, and this is reflected in our culture, our lifestyle, and even in the way we dress.

**فرح:** مِيّة بالْمِيّة. لِبْنان معْروف بِتنوُّعو. عِنّا خليط مِن الأَدْيان، هِنّي المسيحية، الإسْلام، الدُّروز. هالتّنوُّع مِنْعِكِس بالْعادات والسُّلوكِيّات الإجْتماعية. بِتْلاقي ناس كْتير مْحافْظين وبِتْلاقي كمان ناس كْتير مِنْفِتْحين.

**Farah:** Absolutely. Lebanon is known for its diversity. We have a mix of religions, including Christianity, Islam, and Druze. And this diversity is reflected in our customs and social behaviors. You'll find people who are very conservative, and you'll also find people who are very open-minded.

**شَرْبِل:** وواحِد مِن أَوْضَح جَوانِب هالتّنَوُّع هُوَّ كيف النّاس بْيِلِبْسوا! صَراحة لِبْنان بِتْشوفي مجْموعة كْبيرِة مِن أنْماط الأزْياء. بِالْمُدُن مِتِل بَيْروت عادي بِتْشوفي النّاس لابْسين آخِر مُوْضة مِتِل أورُوبّا مثلاً. وبِنَفْس الوَقِت بالْمَناطِق المُحافْظة شْوَيّ بِتْلاقي النّاس هيْك لابْسين بِشِكِل تِقْليدي أكْتِر يَعْني.

Charbel: One of the most obvious aspects of this diversity is how people dress! Honestly, in Lebanon, you see a wide range of fashion styles. In cities like Beirut, for example, it's common to see people dressed in the latest fashion trends, similar to what you'd see in Europe. And at the same time, in more conservative areas, people might dress more traditionally.

**فرح:** صَحيح، وهالشّي بْيِنْعِكِس كمان بِنَمَط حَياتْنا. بَيْروت مثلاً، عِنْدا حَياةْ لَيْلية ما بْتوقِف معَس bars، nightclubs، مطاعِم بيضَلّوا فاتْحين للصُّبْح. هيِّ مدينِة النّاس بْيِسْتِمْتْعوا فيا بِالْميوزِك، بالْفَنّ، بالإجْتِماعات بالتّجَمُّعات مع الأصْحاب. يَعْني هيِّ مدينِة عِنْجِدّ فيا خَليط كْتير كْبير.

Farah: That's true, and this is also reflected in our lifestyle. Beirut, for example, has a vibrant nightlife with nightclubs, bars, and restaurants that stay open until dawn. It's a city where people enjoy music, art, social gatherings, and spending time with friends. It's truly a place with a big mix of everything.

**شَرْبِل:** مَظْبوط عم تِحْكي! وهيْك لمّا نِحْكي عن القِصَص الإجْتِماعية بِنْطاق الواسِع، بعْض العَيْلات القِيَم التّقْليدية كْتير مْهِمّة عِنْدا. بْيِتْمسّكوا بْمُمارسات مْحافْظة أكْتِر. وبِعَيّلات تانْية، خاصّة بِالْمناطِق الحضارية يَعْني أوْ بِالْمُدُن، بِتْلاقي هيْك مَواقِف أكْتِر... كْتير هيْك لِيبْرالية إذا بدّك فينا نْقول، هيْك تِجاهْ قَضايا مِتِل أدْوار الجِنْسيْن العَلاقات، الحُرِّيّات الشّخْصية.

Charbel: You're absolutely right! And when we talk about social issues on a broader scale, in some families, traditional values are really important to them. They hold on more to conservative practices. In other families, especially in urban areas or cities, you'll find more liberal attitudes, if you will, toward issues like gender roles, relationships, and personal freedoms.

**فرح:** وما نِنْسى كمان يا شَرْبِل التّعْليم بِلِبْنان، بْيِظْهر فيه الجانِب التّاني مِن لِبْنان. جامْعاتْنا، مثلاً الجامْعة الأميرْكية بِبَيْروت الْـ AUB معْروفِة بْمِنْهَجا التّقَدُّمي ونِظْرِتا

المِنْفِتْحة. الطُّلّاب مِن مُخْتلف الجِنْسِيّات مِن مُخْتلف الـbackgrounds بْيِجْتِمْعوا، بْيِتْبادلوا الأَفْكار بْيِتْناقشوا بِمْواضيع كْتير مِخْتِلْفة.

**Farah:** And we can't forget about education in Lebanon, which shows another side of Lebanon. Our universities, like the American University of Beirut (AUB), are known for their progressive approach and open-minded environment. Students from different nationalities and backgrounds come together, exchange ideas, and discuss a wide range of topics.

**شِرْبِل:** هَيْدا مظْبوط! المشْهد الإعْلامي بِلِبْنان كمان فينا نْقول مفْتوح كْتير! عِنّا مجْموعة مِتْنوّعة مِن القْنوات الإخْبارية إذا بدّك فينا نْقلّا، بما فِيا المِسْتَقْلِّين ويلّي بْيِنْتِقْدوا الحُكْومة. هَيْدا الشّي بْيِسْمح بِتبادُلْ ومُناقشةِ مجْموعة واسْعة مِن الأراء والأَفْكار بِشكِلْ علني.

**Charbel:** That's right! The media landscape in Lebanon is also quite open. We have a diverse range of news channels, including independent ones that criticize the government. This allows for the exchange and discussion of a wide array of opinions and ideas publicly.

**فرح:** وما لازِم نِنْسى دوْر المرْأة بالمُجْتمّع اللُّبْناني. رغْم إنّو في مناطِق بْتواجهْ فِيا النِّساء تحدِّيّات بِشكِلْ عامّ، النِّساء اللُّبْنانِيات نشيطات جِدّاً بِالْحَياةْ العامّة هِنّي أطِبّاء، مُحامِيّين، سِياسِيّين... بِكْتير نَواحي هِنّي بْيِكْسْروا الصّورة النمطية عن النِّساء بِالْعالم العربي.

**Farah:** And we shouldn't forget the role of women in Lebanese society. Although there are areas where women face challenges, in general, Lebanese women are very active in public life. They are doctors, lawyers, politicians... In many ways, they break the stereotype of women in the Arab world.

**شِرْبِل:** أكيد المُجْتمّع اللُّبْناني هيْك dynamic ودايْماً بْيِتْطوّر. ورغْم إحْتِرامْنا لتقاليدْنا وتُراثْنا الثّقافي أكيد. نِحْنا كمان مِنْفِتحين على التّغْيير وعَ طول نْجدّد. هَيْدا التّوازُن هُوَّ اللي بيخلّي لِبْنان فريد مِن نَوْعو.

**Charbel:** Definitely, the Lebanese society is dynamic and always evolving. While we respect our traditions and cultural heritage, we are also open to change and always renewing ourselves. This balance is what makes Lebanon unique.

**فرح:** بِالظَّبْط! وكْتير مْهِمّ إنّو الأجانِب يِفْهموا إنّو لِبْنان ما فينا نْصَنْفو بْسُهولة. نِحْنا بلد التّناقُضات والتّعايُش، يَعْني الحَياةْ عِنّا كْتير مِخْتِلْفة وبِتشَكِّل عِنْجَدّ نسيج غني.

**Farah:** Exactly! And it's very important for foreigners to understand that Lebanon can't be easily categorized. We are a country of contradictions and coexistence, meaning our life here is very different and forms a truly rich tapestry.

**شرْبِل:** ولِكِلّ حدا عم يْفكِّر يْزور أَوْ حتّى يِنْتِقِل لِلِبْنان، خلّي عقْلك مفْتوح وجهِّز حالك لتجْرُبِة كْتير حِلْوة. بلد بْيِكْسُر كْتير مِن الصُّوَر النمطية المعْروفة بالْعالم العربي.

**Charbel:** For anyone thinking of visiting or even moving to Lebanon, keep an open mind and get ready for an amazing experience. It's a country that breaks many of the stereotypes commonly associated with the Arab world.

**فرح:** صحّ والتّفاعُل مع العالم هوْن رح تْلاقيْن وَدودين ومِرْحين وبيحِبّوا يْشارْكوا ثقافتْن وقِصَصُن معك. وأهمّ شي التّرْحيب تبعُن. لِبْنان عِنْدو كْتير لَيْقَدْموا، وهُوّ محلّ فيك تْشوف في مزيج مِن القديم والجْديد.

**Farah:** Exactly, and when you interact with people here, you'll find them friendly, cheerful, and eager to share their culture and stories with you. The most important thing is their warm hospitality. Lebanon has so much to offer, and it's a place where you can see a blend of the old and the new.

**شرْبِل:** فرح عِنْجَدّ ميرْسي كْتير لِلْمُشاركِة شي كْتير حِلو. وميرْسي لِلْمُسْتمِعين. انْشالله تْكونوا سْتفدْتوا بْناقِشْنا وهيْك كسرْنا شوَيّ الصّورة المفْهومِة عن لِبْنان وفرجيْنا إنّو هَيْدا لِبْنان بْيِخْتِلِف شوَيّ عن اللي عم تْفكِّروا فيه.

**Charbel:** Farah, really, thank you so much for participating—it was really great. And thanks to the listeners. Hopefully, you found our discussion helpful, and we managed to break a bit of the stereotypes about Lebanon and show that Lebanon is a little different from what you might be thinking.

**فرح:** شُكْراً إلك شرْبِل وشُكْراً لكِلّ اللي تابعونا.

**Farah:** Thank you, Charbel, and thanks to everyone who followed us.

## Comprehension Questions

١. كيف وَصفِت فرح المفاهيم الخاطئة عن الحَياةْ بالدُّوَل العربية بِشكِل عام ولِبْنان بِشكِل خاصّ؟

٢. كيف بْيوصِف شرْبِل التّنوُّع الثّقافي والدّيني بِلِبْنان؟

٣. شو هِيِّ الأمْثِلة اللي قدّمُوَا شرْبِل وفرح لتَوْضيح الفرق بيْن أنْماط الحَياةْ واللِّباس بِلِبْنان؟

٤. كيف بْيوصْفوا الحَياةْ اللّيْلية بِبَيْروت؟

٥. شو هِيِّ الفُروقات الإجْتِماعية اللي ذكرا شرْبِل بيْن المناطِق المُحافِظة والمُدُنْ؟

٦. كيف بْيوَضْحوا دوْر الجامْعات بِلِبْنان بِتِقْديم بيئة تعْليمية مِنْفِتْحة وتقدُّمية؟

٧. شو هِيِّ الأدْوار اللي بْتِلْعبا المرة بالمُجْتمّع اللُّبْناني بِحسب فرح؟

٨. كيف بْيوصُف شرْبِل و فرح الصّورة الواقِعية عن لِبْنان بِالنِّسْبِة للْأجانِب؟

1. How did Farah describe the misconceptions about life in Arab countries in general and Lebanon in particular?
2. How does Charbel describe the cultural and religious diversity in Lebanon?
3. What examples did Charbel and Farah give to illustrate the differences in lifestyle and dress in Lebanon?
4. How do they describe the nightlife in Beirut?
5. What social differences did Charbel mention between conservative areas and cities?
6. How do they explain the role of universities in Lebanon in providing an open and progressive educational environment?
7. What roles do women play in Lebanese society according to Farah?
8. How do Charbel and Farah describe the real image of Lebanon for foreigners?

## Discussion Questions

١. شو هِيِّ الصُّوَر النَّمطية اللي بِتْشوفا مَوْجودِة عن بلدك، وكيف بِتْحِسّ إنّا مِخْتِلْفة عن الواقِع؟

٢. كيف بِتْشوف التَّنوُّع الثَّقافي والدّيني بِبلدك؟ هُوِّ مصدر قوّة أَوْ تحدّي؟

٣. شو هِيِّ الفُروقات بينْ الحَياةْ بِالْمناطِق المُحافْظة والحَياةْ بِالْمُدُن بِبلدك؟

٤. كيف بيوَضِّح دوْر الجامْعات بِلدك بِتِقْديم بيئة تعْليمية مِنْفِتْحة؟

٥. كيف بِتْشوف دوْر الإعْلام بِبلدك بِتِشْكيل الوَعي الثَّقافي والإجْتِماعي؟

٦. شو هِيِّ التحدّيّات اللي بِتْواجِها المرة بِبلدك؟

٧. كيف بِتْوازِن بينْ إحْتِرامِ التَّقاليد والإنْفِتاح على التَّغْيير بِبلدك؟

٨. شو هِيِّ النّصيحة اللي بِتْقدِّما للأجانِب اللي بيفكّروا يْزوروا بلدك أَوْ يِنْتِقْلوا للْعيْش فيه؟

1. What are the stereotypes you see about your country, and how do you feel they differ from reality?
2. How do you view cultural and religious diversity in your country? Is it a source of strength or a challenge?
3. What are the differences between life in conservative areas and life in cities in your country?
4. How does the role of universities in your country provide an open educational environment?
5. How do you see the role of the media in shaping cultural and social awareness in your country?
6. What challenges do women face in your country?
7. How do you balance respecting traditions and being open to change in your country?
8. What advice would you give to foreigners thinking about visiting or moving to your country?

# lingualism

*Visit our website for information on current and upcoming titles and free language learning resources.*

# www.lingualism.com

www.ingramcontent.com/pod-product-compliance
Lightning Source LLC
Chambersburg PA
CBHW081656120626
46550CB00010B/2918